Migrant Crossings

MIGRANT CROSSINGS

Witnessing Human Trafficking in the U.S.

Annie Isabel Fukushima

Stanford University Press
Stanford, California

Stanford University Press
Stanford, California

Library of Congress Cataloging-in-Publication Data

Names: Fukushima, Annie Isabel, author.
Title: Migrant crossings : witnessing human trafficking in the U.S. / Annie Isabel Fukushima.
Description: Stanford, California : Stanford University Press, 2019. | Includes bibliographical references and index.
Identifiers: LCCN 2018051457 (print) | LCCN 2018060893 (ebook) | ISBN 9781503609075 (cloth ; alk. paper) | ISBN 9781503609495 (pbk. ; alk. paper) | ISBN 9781503609501 (ebook)
Subjects: LCSH: Human trafficking—United States. | Human trafficking victims— United States. | Immigrants—Abuse of—United States. | Foreign workers, Asian— Abuse of—United States. | Foreign workers, Latin American—Abuse of—United States. | Emigration and immigration law—United States.
Classification: LCC HQ281 (ebook) | LCC HQ281 .F85 2019 (print) | DDC 306.3/620973—dc23
LC record available at https://lccn.loc.gov/2018051457

Cover design: David Drummond

Text design: Kevin Barrett Kane

Typeset by Westchester Publishing Services in 10/14 Minion

CONTENTS

PREFACE

ONE OF THE FIRST CASES I worked on was a sexual slavery case of a domestic migrant worker in California. At the time, I was a volunteer at a nonprofit, volunteering to be a "first responder" to human trafficking. At any hour or moment, if the staff needed support with an emergency case, they would turn to the list of volunteers. Through these endeavors, I met the young Filipina domestic worker who had been abused into sexual servitude. We did not talk about her experience—we talked about home, how she loved to sing with her friends, and other aspects of life. Years later, I would support her as an advocate, watching this person struggle for legibility as a migrant in the United States—someone in need of work and supporting their family. It would not be the last human-trafficking narrative I would witness intimately. Since this first case, I have worked in organizations at all levels on a wide range of cases, from informal economies—sexual economies, domestic work, and criminalized activities—to formalized industries in which survivors labor, such as agriculture and hotel and domestic work, and from cases of children to those involving seniors. Working in coalition with community advocates, attorneys, social workers, educators, government entities, nongovernmental folks, and survivors, I found myself participating in the process of witnessing a range of human trafficking cases. As I witnessed the terms of legibility surrounding citizenship, legality, and victimhood, I found trafficking was defined by multiple, contradictory witnesses: social services professionals, advocacy workers, law enforcement officers, those working in the legal system, and survivors. As a race and gender studies scholar, I myself navigated these contradictions, contradictions that sparked the commitments of this book to appeal to new modalities of witnessing. As an intellectual, educator, and activist, I invite the reader to decide for themselves what kind of witness they want to be.

Migrant Crossings

INTRODUCTION

IN 2017 I was called upon by a local organization in California to examine cases of youth who had been trafficked into the United States. The goal was to examine the cases for human trafficking and provide expert reports to supplement their cases for U.S. Citizenship and Immigration Services (USCIS) and asylum officers. Some of the youths' cases went back as far as 2014, and involved children from south of the U.S. border—migrating across the U.S.-Mexican border from countries like Mexico, El Salvador, and Guatemala—being treated as criminals and therefore deportable. Debates surrounding expedited removals circulated, in spite of story upon story of persecution, violence, and human trafficking. The youth cases spoke to dominant ideologies and misplaced anxiety surrounding the stereotype of the "hordes" of migrants entering the United States, in spite of trends showing that migration from countries like Mexico was at a net zero.[1] As migrant children and their families attempted to enter the United States through the border, policymakers were quick to criminalize the migrants, alleging visa fraud for the trafficking visa.[2] Anti-traffickers and policymakers debated the (mis)perceptions of the visibility of migrant children, exposing the gaps in U.S. immigration policy and practice. The United Nations High Commissioner for Refugees found that, based on four hundred interviews, 48 percent of children crossing the U.S.-Mexican border experienced violence or threats by organized crime groups and 22 percent experienced violence in the home or by their caretakers.[3] In spite of the perception of "illegal" migration, victim witnesses—survivors of border violence, from El Salvador, Guatemala, Honduras, and Mexico—told a more complex story.[4] While headlines focused on migrant children who were released to traffickers, others, like Saul from Honduras, illuminated experiences of being trafficked as they made their way to the United States.[5] Saul's story is found in a statement released by the Freedom Network USA in August 2014—a response to the discourse surrounding undocumented children. Saul's story is as follows:

> Saul grew up in a gang-infested neighborhood in Honduras. For several years, the local gang tried to forcibly recruit Saul. They beat him, threw battery acid on him, and threatened to kill him. One day, when Saul was walking with a female friend, the gang attacked them. Gang members beat Saul and raped his friend. Saul knew that if he did not join the gang, they would kill him. Saul begged his mother, who was in the United States, to send for him, since there was nowhere safe for him in Honduras. When Saul was 15 years old, Saul's mother finally was able to arrange for a man to bring Saul to the United States. However, before reaching the border, Saul was captured and trafficked in Mexico by armed men. His traffickers took him to a hotel room where he was kept for a couple of weeks. Saul's traffickers then forced him to carry a backpack with drugs across the border. Threatened with his life, Saul had no choice but to smuggle the backpack across the border for his traffickers. Saul was finally able to escape his traffickers when they were apprehended by CBP in Texas. Terrified, Saul reported what had happened to him to CBP and the FBI. Saul was detained at a detention center in Brownsville and later a shelter until he could be reunited with his mother in Los Angeles. Once in Los Angeles, CAST helped Saul get the services he needed to overcome the trauma of his experience. With CAST's help, Saul was able to see a therapist to address his nightmares. CAST also helped Saul apply for, and receive, a T visa. Today, Saul is entering the 12th grade, where he is a student leader with dreams of becoming a child-psychologist. Even though he is now flourishing, Saul still fears returning to Honduras, where gang members recently murdered his cousin.[6]

Stories like Saul's provide the everyday person with a sense of intimacy and insight into trafficking experiences, where anti-traffickers consider migrants to be trafficked people; therefore, such migrants may receive immigration relief in the form of a T-Visa. As Saul is identified as someone who is in need of immigration relief, he is also a reminder of those whose entry is denied due to the larger national discourse surrounding legality and migration.[7] In an effort to name migrant crossings through frames of victimhood and vulnerability, anti-trafficking practitioners reinforce heteronormative notions of exploitation by which boys are portrayed as labor exploited and girls as sexually exploited. While sexual violence on the border is a reality, Saul's labor story reinforces paternalistic ideologies and practices defining the anti-trafficking movement. Stories of danger and protection are central to human rights appeals—Saul, a victim from the Global South, contrasts with his rescuers from the United States, in the Global North. Organizations utilize these human rights modes—at congressional hearings, in the news, on their websites, in lobbying efforts, through fundraisers, and in the everyday—as a means to create a picture that *This is human trafficking* or *This is abuse*. While Saul offers a complex example of what it means to cross into visibility as a trafficking subject, his story, like the multiple case studies that appear in *Migrant Crossings,* offers lessons on the power to include/exclude through notions of legality, victimhood, and citizenship.

In *Migrant Crossings,* I therefore answer multiple questions: How do migrants like Saul cross into visibility in ways that enable their inclusion? Is this inclusion dependent on being seen as "victim"? Who is seen as "illegal," "criminal," and even deportable? What is the consequence of witnessing transnational migration through normative views? More specifically, how does a migrant cross into visibility as a trafficking subject? What are the subjectivities migrants are bound to that shape their visibility as trafficked persons? What sort of witnessing is required for the witness to see beyond the dualities that construct trafficking subjectivities? By answering these questions about migration, gender, and race, this book contributes to a range of fields of study, including women's studies/feminist studies, critical race and ethnic studies, sexuality studies, labor studies, and sociology. My goal in the book is not to recover more trafficking stories. Instead, I invite the reader to embark on a practice of witnessing that bridges theory and practice—an ethnic studies praxis. I hope to facilitate a theory and practice of witnessing how migrants cross into visibility legally, through frames of citizenship, and through narratives of victimhood. In *Migrant Crossings* I take the reader through an interdisciplinary framing of the role of the law and the legal system, the notion of perfect victimhood and iconic victims, and how trafficking subjects are resurrected for contemporary movements as illustrated in visuals, discourse, court records, and policy.[8] All of these conditions collectively reinforce human trafficking as determined by notions of victimhood, legality, and citizenship. However, to understand human trafficking beyond carceral feminist appeals, and beyond a criminal justice approach that views incarcerating traffickers as the ultimate and ideal solution for addressing gender-based violence, I center anti-racist, decolonial, and transnational feminist theories.

This project is timely—immigration is a twenty-first century issue. Saul's narrative circulated during a time when organizations appealed to the public and called on policymakers to see the victimhood in the transnational migrant experience during the Obama administration. By 2014, the Obama administration was known not only for having deported a record number of people but also for having implemented the Deferred Action for Childhood Arrivals (DACA) program. According to this program, first implemented in 2012, individuals who had come to the United States before they were sixteen years old, and had continuously resided, could request that action against them be deferred for two years.[9] However, the program was challenged in 2017 under the Trump administration. As illustrated in Chapter 2, multiple legal events have shaped the current moment surrounding immigration, labor, and sexual economies. A persistent narrative in the twenty-first century is how migrants experience both welcome and rejection. This is illuminated in recent policy events in the United States. On March 6, 2017, the Trump administration signed Executive Order 13759: Protecting the Nation from Foreign Terrorist Entry into the United States, increasing border security, limiting asylum, and increasing enforcement. As illuminated in New York, homeland security agents—from Immigration and Customs Enforcement (ICE)—have shown up to the human trafficking courts.[10] The argument made by U.S. law enforcement officials regarding their unannounced appearances was to detain immigrants who are criminalized and to recruit victim witnesses. Migrants are relegated to a precarious status of uncertainty that is tied to perceptions of their being a threat to U.S. citizenry in general. As explored by Judith Butler, the conditions of precarity encompasses "when a population appears as a direct threat to my life, they do not appear as 'lives,' but as the threat to life."[11] The treatment of immigrants in the twenty-first century is bound to narratives of migrants themselves as an economic, social, and political threat. No migratory group is untouched by twenty-first-century U.S. discourse and practice, which perpetuate the myth that migrants are dangerous. Under the Trump administration the signing of executive orders[12] and the discourse on immigration have had material consequences: asylum seekers applying for immigration relief have encountered increased restrictions; the securitization of borders requires undocumented migrants to cross them in even more dangerous terrain; and the number of individuals in detention continues to rise (although, enforcement is more unpredictable during the Trump administration).[13] Multiple witnesses—migrants and others, such as attorneys and social service providers—attest to the challenging climate migrants face in seeking jobs and finding a new place to call home. In 2018, the Coalition Against Slavery and Trafficking (CAST), Freedom Network USA, and the Polaris Project conducted a preliminary survey of 147 individuals representing social service providers, advocates, and attorneys. The consequence of not grappling with immigration and human trafficking is clear: survivors are reluctant to report being victims of crime due to fears of deportation, and traffickers depend on anti-immigration sentiment to compel survivors to stay in abusive conditions and to control migrants (see Figure 1). *Migrant Crossings* therefore contributes to a larger debate about what it means to witness migration in these migratory times—and what such crossings mean for subjects who experience violence during or after their crossing, a violence that some would call human trafficking.

Human trafficking is a familiar topic in the twenty-first century, a story that the public is called to witness in the media, in filmic representations, and in cultural representations such as art, floral and museum installations, paintings, photography, performance, and public exhibits.[14] The witnesses to human trafficking are multiple—law enforcement officers, social workers, medical professionals, advocates, community members, attorneys, educators, and even the everyday Good Samaritan. Such individuals are not simply spectators of violence; witnesses are called to action. The actions of the witness reproduce dominant ideologies about "perfect victimhood," citizenship, and legality, ideologies that become codified and reified in the courtroom, by social services, and in everyday interactions with trafficking subjects. Anti-trafficker mobilizations creating visibility of human trafficking are more than their individual actors— they are a movement.

In *Migrant Crossings,* I am committed to unveiling the contradictions shaping the lives of migrants who experience violence. Take, for example, Rigoberto Valle. In 2009, Valle's case exposed the contradictions in California law. Valle's trafficking allegations did not lead to his being witnessed as a sympathetic victim in the legal system, in spite of his testimonial that the "coyotes who brought him to San Francisco had demanded $500 for his passage from Phoenix and ordered him—at the point of a gun and then a knife—to earn it by dealing crack. The sum was on top of the $1,500 his family had paid the smugglers to get across the border."[15] Valle's defense attorney argued that Valle was a "victim." After being smuggled into the United States, he had had the option to sell drugs or "be killed." Before selling drugs in San Francisco, Valle had been locked up for three days, at which point he "was quite literally in fear for his life."[16] However, in spite of the

"In a labor trafficking/domestic violence case, the victim decided to drop civil claims on family court and in respect to unpaid wages because of trafficker's continued public disparagement of her as an illegal immigrant and repeated attempts to have her deported by contacting ICE."
– Social Service Provider in SC

"We are working on a few labor trafficking cases in which the trafficker represented themselves as attorneys or DHS officials in order to gain information about the victims and then threatened them with deportation if they did not work, etc."
– Holistic Service Provider in SC

SERVICE PROVIDERS REPORT THAT THESE CONCERNS MAY ALSO HAVE AN IMPACT ON SOME SURVIVORS' WILLINGNESS TO ASSERT THEIR LEGAL RIGHTS IN CIVIL, CRIMINAL AND IMMIGRATION COURT.

"The immigration threats from the current administration further empower traffickers to use immigration status as a threat to keep a victim under control."
– Victim Service Provider in CA

"People have expressed fear about reporting all types of abuse, rape, and trafficking. They have also expressed fear of reporting to police, but to pretty much any agency, fearing deportation, detention, or other sanctions."
– Holistic Service Provider in MN

"Trafficking survivors have had experiences and/or heard of ICE showing up at court houses."
– Legal Service Provider in CA

FIGURE 1. "Quotes."
Coalition to Abolish Slavery & Trafficking, Freedom Network USA, and the Polaris Project. 2018. *2017 Social Service, Advocate and Legal Service Survey Regarding Immigrant Survivors of Human Trafficking.*

allegations of victimhood, the assistant district attorney from the San Francisco District Attorney's Office, Richard Hechler, argued in his closing statement, "He may or may not have been trafficked. That's not the issue. The issue is, did he commit a crime?"[17] Unlike Saul, Valle's victimhood could not supersede his criminality. Cases like Valle's and Saul's are part of the repertoire of stories that circulate about human trafficking, whereby some cases are seen as human trafficking, and others are relegated to the status of quasi-human trafficking or invisible forms of human trafficking. The consequence for migrants like Valle is incarceration and deportation. But what is human trafficking?

HUMAN TRAFFICKING

In 2000, human trafficking was legislated both at the U.S. federal level, through the Trafficking Victims Protection Act (TVPA), and in international law, when the United Nations adopted the 2000 Convention Against Transnational Organized Crime to include the Protocol to Prevent, Suppress and Punish Trafficking in Persons, Especially Women and Children. The legal definition of human trafficking illuminates how diverse trafficking is. In summary, human trafficking occurs when a person is forced, defrauded, or coerced for their labor or into sexual economies. In spite of its expansive definition, human trafficking is often perceived as being synonymous with sexual economies and sex trafficking, where for some, sexual economies and prostitution are equated with slavery.[18] A complex phenomenon, trafficking is also defined by transnational migration, labor flows, and forced labor.[19] Whether it is sexual violence or labor exploitation, it cannot be separated from political economies,[20] where trafficking is a global phenomenon.[21] As such, human trafficking is perceived of in various ways: as a crime,[22] as a human rights issue,[23] or as rights spectacle,[24] and legally defined.[25] Nongovernmental organizations (NGOs) have been essential to defining human trafficking and its responses to violence.[26] The prominent rise of the NGO/nonprofit sector in anti-trafficking efforts has led scholars to become critical of the problematic reproduction of a rescue narrative that often misrepresents identities and subjects. The movement to address contemporary human rights violations has led to the creation of governmental organizations that name human trafficking as a social problem requiring services[27] and organized responses through task forces.[28] Chapter 2 offers a complex picture of the legal genealogies that converge around immigration, labor, and sexual economies, and that have created a precedent for national and international legislation on human trafficking.

While other forms of categorization have been theorized as social constructs (i.e., race and gender), through critical race theory and feminist framings, human trafficking too is defined by sociopolitical contexts. In its specificity through the law, human trafficking as a legal definition creates (in)visibilities surrounding who and what counts as trafficked. For example, the Global Slavery Index estimated that in 2016, 45.8 million were trafficked worldwide, based on variables related to political rights, safety, financial and health protections, protections of the "vulnerable," and conflict.[29] Trafficking and migration are bound up in multiple, complex discourses and practices that impact whether a transnational migrant laborer is seen as a threat to life or as a vulnerable subject in need of protection. That over three million migrants were deported between 2008 and 2016 illustrates the dominant misperception in the United States that migrants are a threat to social life.[30] The devaluation of migrant laborers, and their deportability, leads organizations and migrants themselves to make appeals for victimhood—where it is their vulnerability that leads to their legibility as humans. The image of the trafficking victim is perceived of as formulaic, appearing in the form of anti-trafficking tools. These tools take the form of an indicator card promoted by the Department of Homeland Security (DHS) in the Blue Campaign[31] and the Health Care Provider Assessment Card,[32] in which specific questions are asked to indicate whether an experience is human trafficking. As abolitionists and radical feminists call for all forms of sexual economies to be understood as trafficking, their counterparts in the sex worker movement call for trafficking to be excluded and recontextualized as a labor rights issue. And moves toward the middle unintentionally reify neoliberal logics.[33] Current mechanisms for defining human trafficking advance narratives about exploitation that do not merely reflect human conditions and conduct, but also shape them.[34] Renato Rosaldo's phrase "double vision" may be applied to how one experiences hearing/reading human trafficking narratives. In the experience of hearing or reading a narrative, the listener/reader oscillates between his or her own experience and that of the protagonist within a narrative, where the protagonist is the subject of human trafficking. The relationship the witness has to anti-trafficking, anti-violence, and immigrant narratives is not a passive one. This is sustained by what Sealing Cheng calls a site of production—activists who interact with women in laboring and sex economies produce knowledge about them and also create the absence of knowledge about such subjects.[35] Therefore, anti-traffickers facilitate the production of knowledge about human trafficking victimhood and criminality.

As a means to critically engage with human trafficking and its subjects, I draw on a rich diversity of scholars who have helped to define, and redefine, trafficking by grappling with it as a complex phenomenon. Human trafficking has transnational implications (Louise Shelley) that are responded to as a human rights issue (see Allison Brysk and Austin Choi-Fitzpatrick, and Pardis Mahdavi). In particular, I am inspired by Wendy Hesford's theoretical and applied use of discourse analysis about trafficking as shaping human rights appeals. Human trafficking has discursive (see the work of Felicity Amaya Schaeffer and Julietta Hua) and legal power (see Jennifer M. Chacón, Janie Chuang, Amy Farrell, Anne T. Gallagher, Kathleen Kim, and Jayashri Srikantiah). A few studies discuss how human trafficking produces racialized subjects and is produced by racializing projects (Hua and Kamala Kempadoo). Julietta Hua, however, illustrates how trafficking subjects and notions of national belonging are racialized and gendered. And the sociological and social implications of migration, notions of violence, and labor are illuminated in the work of Nicole Constable, Julia O'Connell Davidson, and Rhacel Salazar Parreñas. Tryon P. Woods's work illuminates the anti-blackness in the hegemonic human rights appeals, building on the rich, growing field of Asian-Latinx relational analysis furthered in the works of Fojas and Guevarra (2012), López-Garza and Diaz (2001), Chang (2017), Lowe (2015), Siu (2005), and López (2013), among other scholars who have bridged the relationship between Asia and the Americas. The unique intervention of *Migrant Crossings* is that it relationally centers the racialization of Asians and Latinx in the Americas. Therefore, this book builds upon a dynamic research on criminalization, migration, and transnational feminisms, by putting forth a decolonial form of wintessing: an unsettled witnessing. To offer up a complex framing of migration and trafficking, the following central terms are foregrounded: the criminalization of migrant laborers, tethered subjects and transnational feminisms, and unsettled witnessing.

THE CRIMINALIZATION OF MIGRANT LABORERS

Diasporic subjects, transnational actors, and mobile individuals have many names, including "migrant." Migrants are travelers, roamers, vagrants. They are defined by the walls of a border in the geographical imagination and also beholden to its enforcement, which is dispersed through chaotic geographies. Migrants may or may not be bound to a home. Their movement is central to how they are viewed in the public, by institutions, and in the everyday. They may be settler migrants or mobile indigenous persons. Migrants are defined by how they cross into visibility, hide, or are relegated to the shadows as the invisible. Therefore, to discuss migrant crossings is to discuss the journey one takes as a crosser of multiple borders that encompass borders of the nation-state, borders of categorical constructions, borders of the body, and borders that are ideological (i.e., that surround citizenship and legality). The witness who participates in public discourse, in institutional and socio-legal practices, and in everyday acts of how one sees border crossing, not only enables a crossing but may also reify as a colluder the denials of some to cross into visibility—or in legal contexts, into legibility. Throughout *Migrant Crossings,* migrant laborers and diasporas are used interchangeably. Building on the dynamic scholarship of immigration theorists such as Catherine Ceniza Choy, David Scott Fitzgerald, Evelyn Nakano Glenn, Erika Lee, Eithne Luibhéid, Douglas Massey, Cecilia Menjivar, Mae Ngai, Alejandro Portes, Mary Romero, Wendy D. Roth, and Tom K. Wong—among others—I conceptualize migrants as figures and collectives of complex sociopolitical and legal processes. Migrants are participants in transnational processes, and their experiences are shaped by multiple, overlapping, and discrete oppressions.[36] The transnational migrant subject is deeply shaped by notions of criminality, criminalizing processes, and the criminal justice system. Migrants produce and are produced by the racial and gender schemas of sending and destination countries, which define them as "criminal," "illegal," and the antithesis to the nation-state's project of citizen subjects. As delineated through the example of Rigoberto Valle in this introduction, migrant laborers are impacted by processes of criminalization. The United States has a long history of criminalizing migrant laborers. One may trace the criminalizing of migrant laborers to the Page Act of 1875, as well as to other U.S. carceral responses to immigration, for example the Asiatic Barred Zone Act (1917), Operation Wetback (1954), Operation Hold the Line (1993), and Arizona's SB 1070 (2010), which legalized the racial profiling of migrants, among other more recent state policies such as SB 4 in Texas, which allows law enforcement to racially profile any person for their papers.

In spite of the growing body of scholarly literature that illuminates that there is a disjuncture between the rates of migrant criminality and public perception, and that migrants are less likely to participate in criminalized activities, migrants—in particular those who are bound to a notion of victimhood—are also shaped by discourses and practices surrounding criminality.[37] The perception and the practices that sustain the imaginary of migrant criminality are bound to the following: (1) colonial nation-state practices of including/ excluding citizen subjects; (2) colonial nation-state ideologies of inclusion that materialize legally and socially to reinforce dichotomies of state ideologies surrounding "desirable" versus "undesirable" migrants;[38] (3) the militarization of border security to reinforce settler colonial boundaries;[39] and (4) the demand for transnational migrant laborers to fulfill labor demands on a temporary status or on a status that is unsustainable in the long-term. Therefore, the naming of diasporic subjects is part of a mechanism of governing populations through notions of legality and citizenship, where "ideal" victims are eligible for citizenship or a path to citizenship. Since the implementation of the TVPA in 2000, legal relief has been afforded to migrants considered trafficked through the T Nonimmigrant Status (T-Visa), which allows a person to remain in the United States for up to four years, to protect them and also to allow them to aid in investigating or prosecuting their traffickers as a witness.[40] Although the T-Visa is an important form of immigration relief for migrants, only 7,067 migrants have received such a visa since 2008. The cap for issuing T-Visas is 5,000 visas a year. This means that over a ten-year period, the United States has not even issued visas for a two-year period.[41] The bar for qualifying for immigration relief as a victim of human trafficking is high—so much so, that many applicants are denied. And ineligible subjects are subject to criminalization and deportation. The role of the state in perpetuating the violence and exploitation of migrants is invisible.

In spite of the impositions on diasporic migrants through militarized and carceral responses, feminists responding to human trafficking have turned to the justice system. As illustrated in the United States' Trafficking in Persons (TIP) report and the United States Department of Justice, convictions in the United States for human trafficking are on the rise.[42] This is reflected in global trends. The appeals in the feminist responses in the anti-trafficking movement to convict, incarcerate, and detain reflect what Elizabeth Bernstein develops as a carceral feminism. Carceral feminism envisions social justice as "criminal justice," where the "punitive systems of control . . . are embraced" by anti-traffickers.[43] As such, human trafficking is treated as a crime against a person, and human smuggling, a crime against the border. The limits of carceral (feminist) approaches have been developed by feminist and anti-racist scholars such as Elizabeth Bernstein, Angela Davis, Beth Richie, Eric A. Stanley, and Nat Smith. In this book, I contribute to the discussions surrounding migration and criminalization by offering a transnational feminist conceptualization of what I call a "tethered subjectivity" to examine the discursive, socio-legal practices and visual implications of constructing migrants through the duality of dangerous criminal/helpless victim.

TETHERED SUBJECTIVITY AND A TRANSNATIONAL FEMINIST FRAMEWORK

Although migration has been analyzed through a range of paradigms (e.g., selectivity, classical assimilation, segmented assimilation, and dissimilation[44]), this book draws on transnationalism, in particular, on a transnational feminist framework. Transnationalism rejects rigidly defined points of comparison, recognizing that migrants are shaped by a diffuse transnational field.[45] A theory of transnational feminisms is a theoretical and political project that pays attention to border crossing[46] and draws on the works of transnational feminist thinkers and practitioners M. Jacqui Alexander, Tina Campt and Deborah A. Thomas, Inderpal Grewal, and Chandra Talpade Mohanty. Diasporas are shaped by global flows that are racialized and gendered. These flows cut across borders. And border crossings are shaped by multiplicity. At times, these crossings are subversive; at times, they are constrained by the nation-state in the form of deportation, anti-immigration laws and practices, and criminalization. Trafficked migrants are Diasporans who are connected to their homeland through legal proceedings, media representations, and socio-economic exchanges that take the shape of remittances, letters, and other forms of staying connected with a "home." The transnational subject who crosses the borders of the "nation-state" in many trafficking narratives is often equated with the feminized migrant. Therefore, to contend with the gendered dynamics of transnational processes and violence, a majority of the cases examined in *Migrant Crossings* focus on women trafficking women, albeit not exclusively.

The terms of visibility for transnational trafficked subjects is how they are bound to dualities that Other and reinforce colonial modernities.[47] This duality that witnesses are bound to is what I have referred to elsewhere as a tethered subjectivity. Here, I refer to witnessing as encompassing the self-witness, the account of events,[48] the witnessing of the process of witnessing,[49] and the witness as human and nonhuman (i.e., the law).[50] A tethered subjectivity is the product of neoliberal governance and security. Therefore, new forms of witnessing are required to see and be called to actions that do not reify the dualities migrant laborers and trafficking subjects are bound to. To see subjects beyond a duality requires new forms of witnessing—an unsettled witnessing.

UNSETTLED WITNESSING AS DECOLONIAL

Witnessing is a central part of the human rights appeals to respond to human trafficking and migration. Witnessing is not merely passive; witnesses construct, participate in, and create the normative visions of what it means to experience contemporary violence and human rights violations in the twenty-first century. To speak to witnessing is to grapple with narrative, storytelling, listening, testimonio, and subjectivity.[51] Normative forms of witnessing reinscribe what it means to be legible as a victim of trafficking. This is not to minimize or reduce those who believe their experience is trafficking, nor is it to relegate it to myth. Rather, it is to provide a framework for analyzing why and how some migrants are able to cross into legibility, whereas others are always relegated to the invisible. As illustrated through Lyotard's concept of the differend, victims are those whose victimization is invisible.[52] Therefore, *Migrant Crossings* is an appeal for a bearing witness that disputes the norms and normative processes of witnessing, as a means to conceptualize how dualities shape migratory trafficking subjects—as a myth, as something that does not exist, or contrastingly as hypervisible as anywhere, anyone, and any place—and how witnesses participate in reifying colonial dualities that construct experience.

Current modalities of witnessing are bound to affective and visual responses that render suffering as a norm, whereby freedom/un-freedom are bound to notions of national belonging. These affective responses to human rights visions further what Wendy Hesford has theorized as a spectacle that furthers a politics of pity in anti-trafficking discourse.[53] The anti-trafficking movement and categorical constructions of victimhood are deeply embedded in Euro-American feminisms and Eurocentric logics. To work within a discourse that participates in oppressive ideologies, I find Chela Sandoval's concept of "differential consciousness" central to my own theoretical framework. Differential consciousness is the recognition and working upon of "other modes of consciousness in opposition to transfigure their meanings: they convert into repositories within which subjugated citizens either occupy or throw off subjectivity, a process that simultaneously enacts yet decolonizes their various relations to their real conditions of existence. . . . The differential form of oppositional consciousness thus is composed of narrative worked self-consciously."[54] I therefore centralize a differential consciousness as a means to self-consciously narrate *Migrant Crossings*. Human trafficking is exploitation that, on the one hand, is a human rights violation by individuals and groups of people, and on the other, is produced through systems and structures that render difference normal—what Walter D. Mignolo refers to as "colonial difference."[55] The colonial difference of those who are trafficked is described in the demand for racialized and gendered labor in service sectors, sexual economies, and low-wage to free-labor industries. But it also means that one must see difference beyond what María Lugones has critiqued as "arrogant perception." In drawing on decolonial forms of witnessing, I invite the reader to invoke a practice of witnessing that I have referred to as unsettled. An unsettled witnessing is a commitment to witnessing without being settled with what is constituted as legible—whether in the legal system, in policy, in the media, or in everyday social relations. This type of witnessing is inspired by Lugones's notion of "world traveling."[56] One cannot know the other if one does not enact new ways of seeing that disrupt arrogant perception. Therefore, enacting a decolonial form of witnessing necessitates a type of witnessing that is informed by the uncomfortable, contending with the contradictions, reconciling difference, and traveling into each other's worlds in ways that push against voyeurism and colonization.

In bearing witness to the multiple locations in which human trafficking is constituted, I reconcile how human trafficking, both trafficking and its response, jumps scales[57] from local to national, which is reinforced by a myriad of institutions.[58] Human trafficking is defined by individuals and collectives who are called to witness.

To witness migrant crossings is to inhabit Gloria Anzaldúa's Coatlicue state. The Coatlicue state is an invocation of the Aztec goddess Coatlicue, where it is a state of creation in which one is able to push against oppression and where a new identity emerges at the borderland. As stated by Anzaldúa, the Coatlicue state represents a "duality in life, a synthesis of duality, and a third perspective, something more than mere duality or a synthesis of duality"[59]—that is, a state that grapples with duality as synthesized and a state where the witness moves beyond the duality to embrace plurality and multiplicity. Inspired by Anzaldúa, inhabiting the role of the witness, what would it mean for the reader to inhabit this third space, a place of alterity? This is made possible through new modalities of witnessing. Being an unsettled witness enables one to inhabit the boundary, to embrace alterity, the third space that is needed to witness beyond normative frames and also to see this boundary as a site of flux. It is therefore a move toward being unsettled.

I implore the reader to enact what I have called an unsettled witnessing. An unsettled witnessing is a commitment to witnessing without being settled with what one is seeing. Unlike spectators, witnesses are called to action. The necessary actions to unsettled witnessing include raising questions about normative aspects of events and examining the politics of representation around victimhood/criminality, citizenship, and legality, as infused with the discourse of nationhood, race, and gender. Such witnessing enables the witness to see a migrant for their complex personhood, beyond the narratives that construct them as Other, as a victim/criminal, and as a subject to be pitied. As anti-traffickers are called to witness human trafficking, *Migrant Crossings* appeals to the reader to consider categorical definitions of trafficking as tethered to dualities of victimhood, legality, and citizenship. That is, I ask the reader to see the Saul's and Valle's stories for their complexity, to raise questions about the normative aspects in their stories surrounding abuse, gender, race, national origins, and sexuality, and to reconcile the tension that this book embarks on, and is in the midst of—that I too, am a participant in processes that further a politics of representation about human trafficking. Therefore, I refer to witnessing as encompassing the self-witness, the account of events,[60] the witnessing the process of witnessing,[61] and the witness as human and nonhuman (i.e., the law).[62]

Even as slavery is relegated to the past, human trafficking discourse and practice are haunted by U.S. policy and its implementation through anti-immigration policies that normalize settler colonial logics by way of appeals for citizenship, racism in the law and its enforcement, and the construction of legality and illegality. What this means, as migrants are denied citizenship, which exacerbates their vulnerabilities, is that anti-traffickers, community organizers, and witnesses appeal for their legitimization by the state. However, such appeals, although effective in the short term and within the confines of the law, limit one from seeing how indigenous communities are erased or marginalized, or both. They also fail to address the nature of global neoliberal markets. Also notable is the haunting of slavery in its contemporary manifestation as human trafficking. Testimonials from multiple witnesses—witnesses as survivors, as generationally impacted, and as witnesses to other people's experiences—are significant for movement building and for defining a discourse of freedom. It is through survivors of human trafficking narrating their trauma that a "knowing" of events is created.[63] And in knowing these events, the normative scripts of human trafficking sustain dualities surrounding migrant subjectivities. Through *Migrant Crossings* I examine the sociopolitical and cultural landscape, where migrants are tethered to dualities: victim/criminal, legal/illegal, citizen/noncitizen, and even human/subhuman, or, as phrased by Lisa Marie Cacho, "dead to others." Therefore, in *Migrant Crossings* I call for a new form of witnessing: an unsettled witnessing—that is, a kind of witnessing that commits to seeing the multiple and the complex, that pays attentions to contradictions, and that raises questions about a story's normative aspects.

A METHODOLOGY OF DECOLONIAL WITNESSING OF MIGRANT CROSSINGS

The methodology offered here is one that centers subjugated knowledge. Although Dan Berger defines subjugated knowledge as "forms of knowing that are either co-opted or ignored, interpellated 'in a functionalist coherence or formal systemization' or 'naïve knowledges' that are outright 'disqualified as inadequate,'"[64] through *Migrant Crossings* I offer an important analysis of multiple sites of display, and the material consequences of witnessing through normative frames. In this way, this book furthers what Patti Lather terms "research as praxis"[65]—that is, the emancipatory possibilities made available through research on migrant subjects who are defined by human rights and categorical constructions of violence. Anti-trafficking visions are narrated through human trafficking stories in social relations of the everyday, in the media of newspapers, in filmic representation, and discursively through cases that emerge in the legal realm. By offering a new modality of seeing, this book envisions itself as making possible the witnessing of subjugated perspectives and experiences. This project is an emancipatory and decolonial one, of the theory and applied practice of witnessing.

Due to the limited data on human trafficking and traffickers, there is no quantifiable information on how many trafficking cases are coethnic. However, in surveying the nearly five hundred cases collected in the University of Michigan Law Database on Human Trafficking, the data shows that communities of color are more likely to be criminalized. It is no surprise that many of the traffickers convicted are from the same communities as those who are trafficked. This does not mean that communities of color are more likely to traffic their own. Rather, in the prevalence of conviction, they are more likely to be criminalized for it, and racializing and colonial projects impact migratory and communities of color as well. Not only do I examine homosocial violence, the cases analyzed focus on transnational ties from Asia to the Americas and through the Americas, making this a transnational feminist project. There is a need to bridge an analysis of experiences relationally—Asian and Latinx.

The methodology I employ is an ethnic studies and gender studies one. In other words, it is transdisciplinary and transnational. A transdisciplinary method here incorporates socio-legal analysis of the discourses and practices produced in the language and visuality of the media, law, nongovernmental/ governmental organizations, law enforcement officers, social services agents, and human trafficking movement activists, and knowledge that exceeds the bounds of academe that can be found in websites, campaigns, reports, email communications, and press releases. A transnational feminist methodology is a transdisciplinary one. Therefore, I interrogate the structural forces that manifest in the social acts occurring in laws and policies,[66] media production,[67] and institutional practices. Each chapter not only examines specific case studies but also situates those case studies in a larger social, political, and institutional context. Such categorizations enable the production of narratives. A transnational feminist project also takes seriously the local. Therefore, the localized contexts of the cases explored in *Migrant Crossings* are essential for conceptualizing their transnational nature. Therefore, a transnational feminist examination of human trafficking is needed. Third-world feminisms,[68] and the diasporic movements that began in the 1960s and have continued to the present,[69] continue to influence transnational feminisms.[70]

As a scholar activist, my research is deeply informed by praxis. This book began as a dissertation, where my own participation in the anti-trafficking movement informed the theories, frameworks, and writing. Over the past twelve years I have worked at all levels of organizations: as a volunteer, as a case manager for trafficking survivors, as a programs coordinator for anti-trafficking and anti-violence initiatives, as a technical assistant provider to Office for Victims of Crime-funded organizations, as an expert witness on human trafficking cases, as a consultant for organizations, as an expert on immigration cases for USCIS, and in various leadership roles at a number of organizations, ranging from executive director to member of the board of directors. Through my collaborations with community organizations (which continue), a theory manifested itself—a theory on witnessing violence. In *Migrant Crossings*, I interrogate the mechanisms and modalities of witnessing, and even the role of the witness. It is an interrogation of my own role as a witness.

A majority of the cases examined are cases of homosocial or coethnic violence, or both, extracted from a database of 455 cases I organized and fleshed out. Most cases discussed in *Migrant Crossings* are captured in that database, which was made publicly available as the University of Michigan Law Database on Human Trafficking. However, this database has since become unavailable, after a majority of the cases migrated to the United Nations Office on Drugs and Crime (UNODC) Human Trafficking Knowledge Portal.[71] I have since then continued to track additional cases in a private database of over 500 human trafficking cases that have occurred in the United States since 2000. Rather than quantify what human trafficking means from a nominal data set that only reproduces norms, in this book I take a qualitative approach to analyzing human trafficking through familiar methods of case-study analysis. This is essential for creating a more nuanced understanding of gender-based violence and racism. Therefore, I examine human trafficking as a violence that is imbricated in racial and gender violence. And the economies discussed are a diversity of informal and formal economies such as sexual economies, massage parlor work, and domestic work. In many ways, trafficked people are like the marginal workers described by Ruben Garcia, workers who fall in the fault lines of legal work without protection.[72] Inadequate protections make the massage parlor worker, the domestic worker, and the low-wage industry worker more vulnerable, and these workers are then coerced or defrauded by their employers to labor in conditions they did not agree to or in an industry entirely different to the one they expected to be working in. However, unlike marginal workers, workers in informal economies are always defined by their unprotected and delegitimized status. Through an epistemological approach, I theorize how it is that a trafficked person exists as a sociopolitical and juridically defined category. The goal is not to locate an anti-trafficking ontology but rather to elucidate how notions of violence are produced through sociopolitical, cultural, and juridical processes.

ON HOW TO READ *MIGRANT CROSSINGS*

Migrant Crossings is an invitation—an invitation for the reader to see this as a project of witnessing the stories that are archived in U.S. law, in the media, and in organizations that work to end human trafficking. It is a project of storytelling. Storytelling is a powerful method in social justice fields to assert the rights of people around the world.[73] The story that is told here is the story of the discursive and political modes and modalities that facilitate, prevent, and recreate migrant crossings as (in)visible trafficking subjects.

The book is organized to encourage multiple modalities of witnessing migration and violence. Chapter 1, "An American Haunting," invites the reader to embark on a praxis of an unsettled witnessing. It offers the exemplar of the "ghost case," or the blessing scam, a scam that fell into the realm of quasi-human trafficking, where Chinese migrants alleged that they had been forced to commit a scam. Through the ghost case, a praxis, the practice of theory of unsettled witnessing is offered as a means to untether how subjects are produced in the anti-trafficking movement surrounding legal, citizenship, and victimhood. Chapter 2, "Legal Control of Migrant Crossings," offers the reader a legal tracing of the multiple legal moments that have shaped anti-trafficking norms of witnessing surrounding immigration, labor, and sexualities. Such legal tracings lead to the current normative narratives in U.S. publics surrounding victimhood. Therefore, Chapter 3, "'Perfect Victims' and Labor Migration," illuminates the complexity of perfect victimhood through two cases of trafficked Filipinas—a Filipina trafficked into domestic servitude (Cindy) and a Filipina trafficked into domestic servitude and sexual slavery (Tess). However, perfect victimhood not only discursively circulates, but also is performed in the courtroom. Therefore, Chapter 4, "Witnessing Legal Narratives, Court Performances, and Translations," navigates an exemplar of Peruvian servitude through the case of *United States v. Dann*. Through the role of crying, the (mis)translations, and the court performances, this chapter highlights how multiple witnesses—from the jury, to the media, to the witnesses who took the stand—participate in a collective witnessing of violence and migration. As a means to theorize a modality of witnessing beyond individual cases, Chapter 5, "(Living)Dead Subjects," illuminates the movement implications of witnessing that continues to Other migratory and trafficking subjects and turn them into the (living)dead. Through the figure of the comfort woman, the reader witnesses how subjects are recovered time and again. To conclude, *Migrant Crossings* moves the reader to consider the role of the state and the technologies that continue to reify forms of witnessing that create insecurities through a rhetoric of anti-terrorism. Asia and Latin America—like Africa, the Arab countries, and southwest Asia—continue to be shaped by a rhetoric and practice of welcome and rejection that is deeply tied to the colonial state.

As the reader embarks on reading *Migrant Crossings*, the goal is not to create a voyeuristic opportunity. Although the case studies are from real legal cases, from real people's lives, in *Migrant Crossings* I offer a way to contend with the distance and the multiplicities of Othering that are reified through and within human rights movements. Some people may fear the unknown—because, in anti-violence theory and practice, there is a need to essentialize who is a victim to facilitate legibility of what it means to survive violence. It may even bring up ghosts that haunt readers, institutional responses, and communities—these ghosts haunt the present, are a person, a memory, and/or systemic violence. As described by Gloria Anzaldúa, "humans fear the supernatural, both the undivine . . . and the divine."[74] *Migrant Crossings* invokes a woman-of-color praxis where the uncomfortable and the seemingly dangerous are seen as productive. Therefore, *Migrant Crossings* is an invitation to the reader to grapple with the unconscious, the Other as the unknown, and the spooks, suspending normative impulses surrounding sexuality and race, and questioning the human as bound to the nonhuman/superhuman. It is through this mechanism of witnessing, an unsettled witnessing, that an ethical witnessing may be enacted and decolonial visions rendered possible in appeals to redress twenty-first-century human rights violations. Therefore, while one is compelled to contend with what it means to witness violence, I invite the reader to engage in a critique of institutional knowledge (from academic to legal) that reproduces dominant narratives and the parameters of witnessing. This does not mean victimization does not occur. Rather, normative visions have disallowed some migrants from being seen; and like Rigoberto, they can never become Saul.

1 AN AMERICAN HAUNTING

Witnessing Human Trafficking and Ghostly Exclusions

IN 2012 I ENCOUNTERED A CASE that had various names.[1] News headlines and media outlets referred to it as the "blessing fraud," the "street scam," the "ghost scam,"[2] and the "weird Asian ghost scam."[3] I will refer to it as the "ghost case."[4] The newspapers covering the case ranged from national news outlets such as National Public Radio (NPR) to local daily newspapers such as the *San Jose Mercury News*, and even alternative news outlets such as the *San Francisco Weekly* and the *Village Voice*. The scam varied, but in general it is described as follows: a senior Chinese American woman is approached by three to four other Chinese (immigrants), who tell her that she is plagued by "evil spirits" and that a family member is in danger. To save this family member, she must have her money and valuables blessed.[5] A "doctor" in the group places the items into a bag and blesses it. After the blessing, the bag is returned to the woman. She is told not to look in the bag until she returns home or some time has passed. Once she opens the bag, she discovers that her items have been stolen and that the bag is filled with items that are not her jewels or money. In San Francisco, the district attorney estimates money and property to the value of $1.5 million have been stolen in this way.[6] The district attorney has pursued felony charges against these Chinese immigrants, stating, "These suspects understand the vulnerabilities of these particular communities and are abusing or they're certainly taking advantage of that."[7] In contrast, defense attorneys have attempted to position their clients as vulnerable subjects— vulnerable to transnational traffickers—arguing that the immigrants are trafficked to facilitate a scam, a form of labor trafficking into informal economies. The ghost case is a "criminal case"—the criminal charges included extortion and grand theft, which are felony crimes.[8] The Chinese migrants in this case were not charged with trafficking charges. Instead, they used trafficking as their defense, testifying that trafficking was a part of their victimization, where the crimes committed were out of necessity. While some victims of human trafficking are certified by Health & Human Services, the migrants of the Chinese ghost case were relegated to the alleged. Alleged victims of human trafficking are individuals whose victimization is not recognized by the justice or immigration systems—they only fall into the realm of making allegation of human trafficking. As ghosts were deployed to facilitate the scam, other ghosts haunted the case. The ghosts in the "ghost case" encompass the twenty-first-century haunting regarding the vulnerability of some immigrants as trafficking subjects. This vulnerability contrasts those whose vulnerability is denied in the face of criminal charges and criminalization. Ghosts are unsettling; they spook the living, are the supernatural and beyond reason. Therefore, I analyze the multiple social figures of ghosts produced through exclusions and colonial modernities that shape transnational migration, vulnerability, and human trafficking.

The ghost case leads me to ask: as multiple ghosts are deployed in the ghost case—from the ghosts in the scam to the ghostly matter of the human trafficking case that never was—what kind of social life do the ghosts in the ghost case enable? What do ghosts reveal about crossing the threshold of visibility as a vulnerable subject? What does vulnerability look like for the transnational migrant in the face of criminal charges? What are the ghosts that haunt antiviolence narratives in the United States as some immigrants cross into visibility as trafficked subjects and others remain invisible or hypervisible as criminals? Drawing on transnational feminist theories about vulnerability and human trafficking, what sort of witnessing may be invoked and practiced to enable an ethical witnessing?

To answer these questions necessitates a transnational feminist and interdisciplinary method. Transnational feminisms interrogate border crossings—geographical, political, social, and national.[9] A theory and practice of transnational feminisms is made possible through an intercontextual approach to analyzing hauntings. Wendy Hesford defines intercontextuality as the foregrounding of both the textual and contextual dimensions of representational practices.[10] The texts and contexts examined are multiple: I trace the genealogy of U.S. immigration policies impacting Asian migration as the backdrop of legal cases like that of the ghost case. Therefore, I also juxtapose the ghost case with other trafficking cases, in particular, other transnational migration cases where immigrants were trafficked from China to the United States, by drawing on court records and legal opinions. The archive of how transnational subjects are witnessed extends beyond the law—the material consequence of who is seen as a vulnerable transnational subject is reified in Department of Justice press releases and media representations. To make sense of that which is not living, but which haunts the living, I turn to sociologist Avery Gordon. Gordon illustrates how "investigating [ghosts] can lead to that dense site where history and subjectivity make social life."[11] Examining ghosts in the ghost case disrupts dichotomies surrounding victimhood, criminality, legality, and citizenship, shaping transnational processes and subjectivities. This approach to haunting enables a new form of witnessing—what I call unsettled witnessing.

An unsettled witnessing is a commitment to witnessing without being settled with what one is seeing. Unlike spectators, witnesses are called to action. The necessary actions to unsettled witnessing include raising questions about normative aspects of events and examining the politics of representation surrounding victimhood/criminality, citizenship, and legality, as infused with the discourse of nationhood, race, and gender. Such witnessing enables the witness to see a migrant for their complex personhood, beyond the narratives that construct them as other, victim/criminal, and a subject to be pitied. Gordon defines complex personhood as encompassing a variety of meanings, where all people remember and forget; are shaped by contradictions; recognize and misrecognize themselves and others; suffer graciously and selfishly too; those called "Other" are never that; those who haunt dominant institutions and systems of value are haunted as well; and their life is straightforward and filled with meaning.[12] An unsettled witnessing is an invocation of a practice that contends with ghosts and hauntings in social life, a type of witnessing that embraces seeing the complex personhood subjects embody and that centers that which the eye cannot perceive—it is a politics and practice of foregrounding the invisible, unknowable, and that which haunts the living.

To unsettle witnessing I begin with an analysis of the hauntings of exclusions by discussing eventfulness. Chinese exclusionary policies such as the Page Act and its predecessor, the Coolie Trade Prohibition Act, collectively frame the discourse of exclusions as tethered to notions of freedom and slavery. The discourse surrounding exclusion, freedom, and slavery shapes contemporary perceptions of China as a threat. Next, I contend with the ghosts in the ghost case by examining how ghosts were deployed in the scam. These ghosts shed light on normative assumptions in human rights appeals surrounding capitalism and modernity, cloaked by what is lost (capital) and what is legible (Western modernity). I compare the ghost case to another labor trafficking case (*United States v. Fang Ping Ding, Wei Wei Liang, a.k.a. Xia Hui Liang and We We Shen*, 2010[13]) because this case, unlike the ghost case, is legitimated as a human trafficking one. This comparison enables an understanding of the kinds of subjectivities that are necessitated to be legible as a trafficking subject. To conclude, I end with a move toward what the ghost case can teach us through unsettling witnessing of the kinds of horrors that are grieved, and whose lives are foreclosed from grievability. I argue that an unsettled witnessing contends with the multiple ghosts that haunt human rights discourses and practices.

HUMAN TRAFFICKING, TRANSNATIONAL FEMINISM, AND (AN UNSETTLED) WITNESSING OF VULNERABILITY

There are various laws one may draw on to interpret whether or not the ghost case constituted the kinds of vulnerability that are understood to be "human trafficking," including the California Trafficking Victims Protection Act (2005), the Trafficking Victims Protection Act (2000) and its reauthorizations, and the Protocol to Prevent, Suppress and Punish Trafficking in Persons, Especially Women and Children, supplementing the United Nations Convention Against Transnational Organized Crime (2000). Therefore, immigrants who experience violence are shaped by assumptions about freedom and being unfree from a life or experience of violence. Judith Butler illustrates how vulnerability is "fundamentally dependent on existing norms of recognition."[14] Human trafficking victims are assumed to share a particular kind of vulnerability—the "loss of freedom."[15] A trafficked immigrant's subjectivity is shaped by their assumed shared vulnerability with other trafficking victims, reinforcing a type of precarity described by Julietta Hua and Katsuri Ray as the "differential dispersal of deserving subjectivity—hierarchized humanizations instituted and reified through the law . . . the law works to draw and redraw the boundaries of the human."[16] The material conditions of human trafficking make it a part of social life.[17] Immigrants who access immigration relief in the form of a T-Visa or U-Visa further what Felicity Amaya Schaeffer calls a pliable citizenship: "The ways [diasporans] remaking of their bodies and affective trajectories augment their local value but also reinforce how states authorize moral migration and national inclusion."[18] The body becomes a site of pliable remaking that enables some diasporic subjects to become legible as citizen subjects.

Nation-states regulate how subjects are witnessed; this regulation furthers normative understandings of citizenship and its antithesis of deportability, inadmissibility, and illegibility. Immigrants are an example of a transnational subject who crosses the border of the "nation-state." A transnational feminist analysis disrupts the "regulatory practices" of the nation-state.[19] Transnational migrants are the embodiment of border crossers, for how they cross not only the nation-state but also the boundaries of dualities that shape their subjectivity. As migrants cross borders, how they are witnessed "functions as an economy of regulation."[20] The immigrants in the ghost case are reflective of a particular anxiety that perseveres about transnational migration. Immigrants are positioned as inhabiting a threshold between criminality and victimhood (especially those involved in the legal system), even before sentencing. As immigrants cross into visibility in the U.S. legal system, their legibility is made possible by how they are seen as not only victims/criminals but also citizens and legal people. The ability for immigrants navigating criminal systems to cross into legible terms that do not lead to imprisonment or deportation, as seen in the ghost case, is dependent on how they are able to utilize intermediaries to translate their experience into new meanings. The intermediaries include attorneys, judges, juries, the news media, advocates, expert witnesses, social services, health-care providers, law enforcement officers, and so forth. Therefore, immigrants are and have always been precarious and exist under conditions of risk and insecurity.[21] To cross into visibility is dependent on narratives about migration and violence and the role of the witness who sees an experience as encompassing popular notions of un-freedom and trafficking. Therefore, to shift the paradigm of how immigrants are defined by dualities is to call for a new way of seeing—this is the role of the witness.

Witnessing encompasses the self-witness, the accounting of what is witnessing beyond being "lost" in the event, and the witnessing of the process of witnessing.[22] Examining the construction of legal narratives in literature, Cathy Caruth contends that there are two forms of witnessing occurring: the human, and the witness that cannot be recognized as human, the law.[23] The law is only legible to those it functions to benefit—people. As such, witnessing is part of an economy of affect where the human rights appeals of suffering foster certain forms of recognition, engagement, and action. Witnesses are multiple actors who are a part of institutions, including attorneys, law enforcement agents, and social workers. The witness also encompasses the participants in an anti-trafficking and/or human rights movement—consumers of media who are moved to action, the lobbied electorate, jurors in a courtroom, and students or community members who, after viewing a film, reading a newspaper, or hearing a speaker, are called to participate in the movement. Therefore, witnessing is embodied, but it also manifests in discursive sites where knowledge and history are documented and produced. If witnessing encompasses the multiple, what sort of witnessing must be enacted to move witnesses and sites of witnessing beyond "popular regime(s) of truth"[24] that produce "national sentimentality"?[25] An unsettled witnessing is a mode of witnessing that does not problematically reproduce "carceral feminisms" as the new twenty-first-century norm or reproduce dominant knowledge formations, politics of pity, and heteronormative values that privilege crime control and neoliberalism.[26] An unsettled witnessing is a transnational feminist practice that disrupts dualities and contends with ghosts.

The witnessing of the representation of anti-trafficking images in the media reproduces what I have referred to elsewhere as "anti-violence iconographies."[27] In this chapter, the "ghosts" were central to how the case was received. Iconography means "image writing." Content and form are central to what circulates. As such, iconographies encompass singular images as well as signs that come to represent a "whole host of historical occurrences and processes."[28] As I have illuminated elsewhere, the historical and cultural context of anti-trafficking iconography emerges from the politics of anti-traffickers.[29] Therefore, the language and practices of rescuing and restoring victims of human trafficking are accompanied by images that shape the legibility of trafficking subjects. While some scholars refer to anti-trafficking images as "abolition iconographies," I find it useful to broaden the politics deployed through iconographies.[30] Whereas "abolition" privileges individuals and collectives who are committed to ending all forms of slavery, not all individual actors or collectives are committed to the abolition of slavery in all its forms. Sex workers who call for the legalization and legitimization of sex as work[31] differ from a radical feminist approach that sees sexual slavery as an expression of sexual violence against women. However, both utilize familiar motifs of the cage to comment on twenty-first-century sexuality and trafficking, albeit informed and shaped by polarized commitments surrounding sexual economies. Therefore, anti-violence iconographies encompass the image writing and practices where institutions, individuals, and collectives deploy images to address an array of concerns that encompass popular understandings of violence (i.e., domestic violence, human trafficking, sexual assault, and violence against women).

Anti-violence iconographies cut across borders, where the imagery, discourse, and practices in the United States circulate in "media-scapes."[32] Anti-violence iconographies are intentionally produced in media, political campaign materials, the legal system, and social networks. The images reinforce popular and legal understandings about violence, leaving the viewer with specific impressions about human trafficking.

The materiality of the hauntings in transnational migration and violence cannot be separated from a U.S. treatment of Asian immigrants and Asian Americans.[33] In particular, the perception of China as a threat cannot be separated from the treatment of Chinese immigrants in the U.S. criminal system. And like a poltergeist, the manifestations of such ghosts materialize in ways that at times cannot be ignored. The ghosts that continue to haunt anti-trafficking discourse are the ghosts surrounding exclusions. The past and present are linked, where racializing discourse in the law shapes notions of citizenship. What follows is an examination of how notions of illegality, inadmissibility, and deportability shape the Chinese and Asian American immigrant experience, where exclusions are tied to settler colonialism.

THE HAUNTINGS OF EXCLUSION: INADMISSIBLE FOR (RE)ENTRY, DEPORTABLE SUBJECTS

> Haunting . . . is the relentless remembering and reminding that will not be appeased by settler society's assurances of innocence and reconciliation. . . . For ghosts, the haunting is the resolving, it is not what needs to be resolved.
>
> —Eve Tuck and C. Ree 2013[34]

I first learned of the ghost case in 2013, when I was asked to be the human trafficking expert witness for the case.[35] The defendants were from China and had immigrated to the United States for work. ICE initially opened an investigation based on trafficking allegations. Regardless of the trafficking allegations, local police enforcement and the district attorney's offices pursued the case on criminal charges against the Chinese immigrants. The defense used testimonies—my testimony and the charged immigrants' testimonies—to paint a picture of necessity. The crimes committed were out of necessity, because the consequences of not participating in criminalized activities were far worse. The ghost case is familiar in major cities like Boston, Vancouver,[36] Chicago, Honolulu,[37] Las Vegas, Los Angeles, New York,[38] and San Francisco, where prosecutions or allegations have occurred. At the close of the case in April 2013, four of the defendants were convicted on charges of grand theft and attempted grand theft, and there was a hung jury on charges of extortion and attempted extortion (of which, the extortion charges were then dropped). The case itself is a ghostly matter haunting anti-trafficking discourse, as it will never be archived as a trafficking case in public memory via the media or the law. In the context of the ghost case, settler colonialism manifested through law enforcement responses to crimes against Chinese Americans. Drawing on Jodi Byrd, the settler colonial takes the form of a liberal, multicultural settler who "attempts to flex the exceptions and exclusions that first constituted the United States to now provisionally include those people othered and abjected from the nation-state's origins, it instead creates a cacophony of moral claims that help to deflect progressive and transformative activism from dismantling the ongoing conditions of colonialism that continue to make the United States a desired state formation within which to be included."[39] The criminalized Chinese migrants serve as a mechanism to reassert colonial conditions when they are contrasted against the good Chinese Americans and Chinese migrants who are legible as "victims" of trafficking. If the archive (in this case, a legal one) prevents us from making the links between settler colonialism and slavery,[40] we must turn to the ghosts haunting narratives about migration that continue to be sustained.

The ghost case became eventful as a criminal case, but not as a trafficking one: a quasi-event as human trafficking. A quasi-event of human trafficking encompasses events that could not be verified as happening or not happening. This is legitimized through the law when two seemingly opposing conditions—the ability to participate in criminalized acts and also experience victimization—are not diametrically opposed events, but are treated as such. In the ghost case, the migrant's criminalized actions of grand theft and extortion were prioritized over a human trafficking.[41] In an unpublished report of the case, it was surmised that the "jury had all the information it needed about human trafficking, combined with its own collective common sense, to determine whether the defendants' circumstances . . . supported a necessity defense."[42] The necessity clause was invoked, where the defense argued that the immigrants had committed the crimes because they were victims of human trafficking. However, the immigrants' victimhood as trafficked could not be separated from a legacy of immigration and a general perception of China as a threat. The clauses of inadmissibility and deportability must be situated in a genealogy of

legal events, including prostitution and labor laws. These legal events continue
to haunt present-day perceptions about victimhood/criminality, legality, and
citizenship. The passage of anti-immigration laws solidified who is imagined
as a desirable citizen subject.[43] Contemporary human trafficking cases, even
quasi-cases like the ghost case, are haunted by the figure of the Chinese immigrant as framing the legal standard for exclusionary principles.

The Page Act (1875) and the Coolie Trade Prohibition Act (1862) paved the
way for present-day exclusions, dualisms, and colonial modernities surrounding freedom for Asian immigrants.[44] Lisa Lowe illuminates how settler colonial
systems, systems that manage free/unfree laborers through a contract system
and multiple mechanisms of control, do so also through citizenship. For the
unfree laborer denied citizenship, they are a transitional figure between slavery and free laborers.[45] None of the ghost case defendants were sex trafficked,
but their role in informal economies, their deportability, and their perceived
and legalized criminality are reminiscent of the treatment of prostituted Chinese
women at the turn of the twentieth century. Take, for example, the Page Act of
1875, which is frequently discussed as the first federalized immigration law.[46]
Popular images circulated about Chinese women and girls as prostituted,
sex slaves, and opium addicts subject to beatings and death.[47] Women migrating for sexual economies were homogenized as unlawful and inadmissible for entry, and were likened to criminals. As European women in sexual
economies were described as trafficked through descriptors such as *persuaded,
induced, enticed,* or *coerced,*[48] Chinese women's treatment was compounded
by their unlawful and deportable status. Deportability and exclusions went
hand in hand with freedom, labor, and slavery. The Coolie Trade Prohibition
Act reinforced social and cultural dualisms: slavery/freedom, black/white,
domestic/foreign, alien/citizen, and modern/premodern.[49] Even as the United
States debated and eventually outlawed slavery domestically, slavery remained
central to the implementation of the coolie trade in its territories.[50] Coolie
trade laborers were entrenched in the debates about slavery and violence in the
United States, where laborers embodied the "hopes, fears, and contradictions
surrounding emancipation."[51] These laborers represented two contrasting
images: a departure from chattel slavery and the maintenance of slavery's worst
features.[52] As a collectivized figure, they were a "fantasy of 'free' yet racialized and
indentured labor . . . a figure for this division of labor, a new racial mode of
managing and dividing labor groups through the liberal promise of *freedom*
that would commence with the end of slavery."[53] The figures of the coolie and

the prostituted Chinese woman are examples of the general sentiment to deport Asian immigrants arriving to Angel Island Station in San Francisco.[54] Following Chinese exclusions, a series of anti-immigration acts excluding Asian immigration through quotas ensued, such as the Emergency Quota Law 1921,[55] the Immigration Act 1924, and the Immigration and Nationality Act 1965.[56]

Seemingly disconnected from the present, the legacies of exclusions as a racializing discourse continue to mark the body of the Chinese migrant in the U.S. criminal court system. In spite of the Chinese migrants' testifying to their victimization, the district attorney convicted the defendants in the ghost case on felony charges, meaning the immigrants will serve time, eventually be deported, and under the Illegal Immigration Reform and Immigrant Responsibility Act (IIRAIRA) 1996 are inadmissible for reentry.[57] Their criminality foreclosed any possibility of seeing them as desirable citizens, or even as complex subjects whose vulnerability was tied to their criminality. Concepts of deportability and "illegal" migration are intrinsic to polarized constitutions of transnational migrants. As conveyed by Nicholas de Genova, the definitiveness of deportability is due to the legal production of migrant "'illegality' and militarized policy of nation-state borders."[58] Deportation regimes produce and maintain migrant "illegality"; the effects are material.[59] U.S. policies shaping the transnational migrant's experience have included anti-immigration,[60] anti-miscegenation,[61] labor agreements and practices,[62] laws preventing ownership of property,[63] and limitation and even denial of access to public services.[64] Immigrants who are unable to fulfill popular, social, and legal requirements of what is a "good" subject are ineligible for citizenship. Excluded immigrants, like the immigrants of the ghost case, are deemed undesirable, therefore illegible and unintelligible as citizen subjects, vulnerable to being criminalized, Othered, deported, and eventually deemed inadmissible. For the Chinese immigrants, their criminality and deportability are defined not only by their legal status but also by racializing discourse. It is well documented that a norm in U.S. jurisprudence (1854–1954) is the perception of Chinese witnesses as suspect.[65] Although the Civil Rights Act 1964 outlawed discrimination based on race, the racializing logics shaping everyday social perceptions of particular bodies in and outside of the legal system, and the legacies of the suspect Chinese witness, raise questions about contemporary experiences for immigrants in and outside the legal system. However, few studies examine the Asian immigrant experience.[66]

The perception of China, and de facto Chinese, as threatening cannot be relegated to the past. The "discovery" of Golden Venture and smuggling rings in the 1990s brought back into popular cultural imaginary Asian immigrants not only as threatening politically and economically[67] but also as circumventing U.S. legal institutions and systems. Chinese immigrate for diverse reasons: for economic factors, because of social networks that spur cumulative causation, or to seek asylum.[68] China is regularly portrayed in the media as a threat to the United States and to the global economic and colonial order (e.g., as a health threat—because of swine flu—as an economic threat, as a political threat, and as a security threat).[69] China's presence in the global economy has sustained the United States' presence in Asia and the Pacific through a triad of interventions: military, political, and economic. Migrants propelled into the international arena are at the center of translocal debates. The buildup of bases in Jeju, South Korea, Guam, Japan, Okinawa, and Hawai'i cannot be separated from what China represents politically and economically to the United States. The Asia pivot appears in everyday interactions and perceptions of migrant Asians, even making its way into the courtroom.

Situating the multiple histories shaping transnational migrants like the immigrants who faced criminal charges is a maneuver to unsettle witnessing. The perception of China—both contemporary and historical—as a threat, as inadmissible, and as undesirable impacts how Chinese immigrants are witnessed in a courtroom. As called for by Avery Gordon, "to write stories concerning exclusions and invisibilities is to write ghost stories."[70] Next, I examine these ghosts and what they represent surrounding colonial modernities and the state.

CONTENDING WITH GHOSTS: COLONIAL MODERNITIES AND THE STATE

By engaging with the haunting as the sociality of living with ghosts—the tangible, tactile, ephemeral, and imaginary—what is made visible is how ghosts in an anti-trafficking narrative are marginalized as the Other, an affect of colonial modernity.[71] On a November morning in 2012, Wu, one of the criminalized migrants, approached Wong, a victim of the scam. After approaching, Tan, another of the criminalized immigrants, was introduced to Wong:

[Tan] claimed [Wong's] ancestors had pushed her to see them because Wong's youngest son would die in three days, possibly in a car accident. [Tan] said a ghost wanted to marry this son and when Wong turned 55, she would meet a ghost and her husband would become ill. Wong, who had spent much of her life in a small town in China where people were superstitious about ghosts, believed the prediction completely and was very afraid. Tan told Wong she should retrieve all her money and possessions, wrap them up, and bring them back for a ceremony to prevent the predicted misfortunes from befalling her family. Wong agreed to do so, but once she was alone she recalled reading newspaper reports about similar scams and decided to call the police.[72]

Other versions of the scam included one of the scammers stating that they had "yin-yang eyes," where they could see ghosts.[73] The appeasement of an unsettled ghost is not unusual in China. In China and Chinese American communities, some families practice marrying ghosts as a tradition that appeases the affects of an angry ghost, usually a person whose death was untimely, shameful (i.e., by execution or suicide), a person without heirs who then haunts the living with illness or damage to property.[74] A ghost will approach their family to have their marriage arranged. Sometimes the ghost will visit their family in dreams, guiding the living toward a living suitor (or bride).[75] A living man married to a ghost can remarry (or have multiple marriages). In contrast to a culture of contending with and engaging with the dead, in a U.S. westernized context, ghost marriages are relegated to the fantastical of popular culture (e.g., in the Tim Burton movies *Beetlejuice* and *Corpse Bride*).

Citizens were called to participate in the witnessing and reproduction of the perception of ghosts as "backward," in effect reproducing dominant ideologies of the West as modern, in contrast to Asian ideologies as Other. The normative collective witnessing of the ghost case reinforces how assimilated modern subjects engage with ghosts—it is to relegate them as the weird, the bizarre, and even the "crazy."[76] The portrayal of the scam as weird was not limited to mainstream U.S. news sources such as the *San Francisco Weekly*. Asian American producers of discourse such as the blog *Angry Asian Man* repeatedly referred to the ghost case as crazy:[77] "Incidents involved scammers approaching an Asian woman in her 60s and spinning a crazy story about stepping in blood and warding off evil spirits. Not kidding."[78] Revisiting the story, *Angry Asian Man* reminds the reader of the "crazy story," concluding that the good news was that the scammers were caught. The belief in ghosts was relegated to the fantastical and backward, and one who believed, was perceived to be out of their mind. Those who believed (believed enough to give up their life savings)

FIGURE 2. Graphic from the San Francisco district attorney's campaign to counter the blessing scam.
Office of the District Attorney, San Francisco. Mina Kim, "To Ward Off Ghosts, Chinese Seniors Give up Life Savings to Scammers," *The California Report*, June 21–23, 2013, http://audio .californiareport.org/archive/R201306211630/d.

were also reduced to shame and embarrassment,[79] furthering the uncanny perception of the scam.

Ghosts also represent loss, and the loss privileged in the media coverage of the ghost case was material and capitalist based. What mattered in the case was the perception of how the Chinese immigrants were a threat to local San Francisco citizens and their finances. The narrative of institutional cooperation and neoliberal ideologies of the role of the government as defenders of rights[80] was at the forefront: "S.F. Officials Reach Out to Banks to Help Staunch Chinese Blessing Scam"[81] and "San Francisco Warning Elderly About 'Blessing' Scam."[82] The legible victim in this way is envisioned as restoring the state as a benevolent rescuer. Chinese Americans were called to cooperate with law enforcement, as illustrated in the campaign materials of tote bags and posters (see Figure 2). The risk to global capitalism and the need to control the risk Chinese immigrants pose through order and the state is our post-9-11 inheritance. In a "world risk society," the necessity of the state (and statehood) in neoliberal times is apparent.[83] Subjects who cooperated with law enforcement were rewarded, and even redeemed in the media, as seen in the deployment of the scammed person, Wong, who is described in *San Francisco Weekly* headlines as the "Would be Victim [Who] Outsmarts Suspects in Weird Asian Ghost Scam."[84] The effacements in the media portrayals of the ghost case are multiple, including the larger narrative of China as threat, the move toward participating in carceral logics, and indigenous displacement due to settler colonialism that requires community complicity.

WITNESSING EVENTFULNESS

To frame colonial modernities as shaping vulnerability, human rights, and trafficking subjectivities, I turn to an eventful human trafficking case, *United States v. Ding et al.* (henceforth referred to as *the Dings*),[85] in which Chinese American Fang Ping Ding was convicted for trafficking a Chinese national, "Amy."[86] In 2007 sixty-two-year-old Ding recruited Amy to enter into a five-year contract as a domestic worker/servant to commence in April 2008. Amy migrated from Shanghai, China, to Fremont, California, on a visitor's visa (B1/B2 visa). At the time, Amy was a forty-nine-year-old native from rural Anhui province with a high-school education and previous experience in domestic work. Two years prior to migrating to the United States, she worked for three different families as a "domestic servant" in Shanghai. Amy migrated with experience of working in a culture of servitude for Chinese families, only to enter one that eventually propelled her into the public eye of the media and the law as "human trafficked." The images surrounding China as "failing" to protect domestic workers put forth an image of a "traveling culture of servitude,"[87] from China to the United States. Amy's employment with the Dings in the United States is described as abusive, coercive, and unpaid labor that violated standard working conditions. Amy worked seven days a week from seven or eight in the morning until past midnight (one in the morning the next day) for a year, "cooking, cleaning and caring" for her employers, Shen and Liang's two children, with "abuse" through restrictions of what she could eat and physical abuse. Amy was also compelled by Ding to "write notes confessing that she stole from Ding's family." This abusive strategy appeared to be a way to force Amy to be fearful of law enforcement, having written documentation that she "stole." This was compounded by Ding's confiscating Amy's documents, which was followed by threats to falsely report Amy to law enforcement, instructing the "victim not to leave the house."[88] In April 2009, Amy "fled" the Ding home and reported her experience to the "authorities,"[89] solidifying her trust in the nation-state as an arbiter and protector of freedom. What mattered in the court performances was an image of Amy as a desirable immigrant—victim, educated, and "modern"—a good victim is an assimilable subject. In 2010, Fang Ping Ding was convicted for forced labor;[90] Wei Wei Liang and Bo Shen, for harboring an illegal alien for private financial gain.[91]

The abuse faced by Amy and the immigrants in the ghost case cannot be denied. However, their difference is in how the media and the courts portrayed them as being able to assimilate into modern capitalist economies. Unlike the ghost case, Fang Ping Ding trafficked Amy through an industry that is legally recognized in the United States, albeit with limited protections—domestic work. The demand for domestic workers is increasing within China as well as abroad, where companies recruit Chinese workers to go abroad.[92] Perceptions in the United States of China's laws are that domestic workers are viewed as unprotected laborers.[93] In contrast to Amy, the ghost case immigrants facilitated a scam, an informal economy. Additionally, Amy came from a Westernized Shanghai and was educated. And, in contrast to Amy, who was hired by employers, the ghost case immigrants carried with them debt and relations with transnational organized criminals. The terms of legibility surrounding vulnerability hinged on shared values with the dominant society. Upon fleeing her traffickers, Amy turned immediately to the state, in contrast to the ghost case immigrants, who only turned after they were caught by law enforcement when facilitating criminalized activities (theft). Therefore, problematically reinforced in both cases is how the only legible, vulnerable human trafficking subject is one who participates in modern global capitalist economies and also places their trust in the state—this subject is, regardless of intention, a neoliberal subject.

CLOSING: AN UNSETTLED WITNESSING OF THE HORROR OF UNGRIEVABLE LIVES

Certain kinds of horrors continue to hold center stage in the scenes of witnessing. Take, for example, Kil Soo Lee, who trafficked two hundred immigrants from Vietnam, China, and American Samoa into Daewoosa garment factories in American Samoa (1999–2000). In 2001 the case was prosecuted in the U.S. courts in Hawai'i. Kil Soo Lee and his co-conspirators imprisoned, starved, threatened, extorted, and physically abused their employees.[94] A number of stories circulated beyond the legal networks, in the media. One woman related how her eye had been gouged with a pipe after she demanded her wages. Another worker testified about the beatings workers experienced: "It was [like] watching a film where the people are being brutally beaten to the point of like massacre. . . . [T]here was a lot of blood on the line and on the floor of the factory and on the fabrics."[95] The imagery of the bloodied workers, factory, and garments highlights the multiple wounds that are enacted beyond the beating of the workers—consumers buy the garments that are the product of exploitive labor. American Samoa's unincorporated territory status with the United States led to justifications of the case being prosecuted in Hawai'i. How transnational laborers figure in such processes and the geopolitics of jurisdictions are invisible. Not all horrors are perceptible to the eye. As Lee was fashioned as committing acts of horror, the Chinese immigrants in the ghost case and the horrors they faced were invisible. One of the Chinese immigrants narrated being beaten along with his son due to the debts he owed the triads: he "was kidnapped by three triad members at gunpoint,"[96] who beat him and forced him to sign a promissory note. To pay his debt he went to the United States. The horror of his criminality—his scamming the senior citizens—disallowed seeing his multiple vulnerabilities.

To grieve is to know what one has lost.[97] What makes for a grievable life is one that is socially constituted; therefore, to contend with the social figure of the ghosts in the ghost case is an endeavor to unsettled witnessing of violence, human trafficking, and U.S. courts. Relegated to the weird, the ghost case will be remembered as a scam and disavowed as a human trafficking case, as it will never be archived as a human trafficking case, except as a quasi-case in this chapter. Normative belief systems were upheld in the ghost case, including misperceptions of China as backward, in contrast to the United States as rational. The complicity, and need for complicity, within the Asian American community are also central to reinforcing the narratives about victimhood, citizenship, and legality that circulated via media networks.[98] The ghosts in the ghost case are multiple, and some ghosts are even apparitions within this chapter; therefore, the dispossessions that haunt the present are multiple. However, as described by Avery Gordon, "Ghostly matters are part of social life. If we want to study social life well . . . we must learn how to identify hauntings and reckon with ghosts, must learn how to make contact with what is without doubt often painful, difficult and unsettling."[99]

The ghost case is an example of how an assemblage of narratives about violence are produced through semiotic chains and power relations, archived in public memory of the media and the law, and reproduced across time and space. And the material consequence is through the body of the migrant who is figured as a trafficked victim or criminal migrant. One cannot reconcile one ghost at a time with the ghostly matters that stretch across time and space, nor with all ghosts at once. For the ghostly matters that haunt the Americas—colonial modernities sustained through the dualities of citizenship, legality, and victimhood, and the centralization of the nation-state as the response to vulnerability—cannot be witnessed through a place of security, stability, and normative logics. A lesson from the precariat is that an ethical witnessing in neoliberal times is one that invokes being unsettled.

2 LEGAL CONTROL OF MIGRANT CROSSINGS
Citizenship, Labor, and Racialized Sexualities

> *If we truly wish to know knowledge, to know what it is, to*
> *apprehend it at its root, in its manufacture, we must look not to*
> *philosophers but to politicians—we need to understand what the*
> *relations of struggle and power are.*
>
> —Michel Foucault, Power

IN 2012, CALIFORNIA SOUGHT TO PASS Proposition 35 (Prop 35), the Ban on Human Trafficking and Sex Slavery. Proponents of the bill contended it would increase prison terms for traffickers, require sex traffickers to register as sex offenders, fine traffickers to "help" victims, mandate training, and require sex offenders to disclose their internet accounts. Nearly $4 million was raised in support of Prop 35, where arguments included: "In California, vulnerable women and children are held against their will and forced into prostitution for the financial gain of human traffickers. Many victims are girls as young as 12. Human trafficking is one of the fastest-growing criminal enterprises in the world, and it's happening right here on California's streets and online where young girls are bought and sold."[1] On the surface, for those who are for an approach that punishes traffickers, it seems ideal. It is a simple solution: prosecute traffickers. However, opponents—including those working directly on human trafficking such as Cindy Liou, an attorney, and Perla Flores, a program manager, and a nonprofit—critiqued the limitations of prosecution as prevention.[2] Experts such as legal scholar Kathleen Kim, social service provider Lois Lee, and scholars such as Ami Carpenter and myself, offered perspectives highlighting the limits: money gained from forfeiture would go to the state and not directly to the survivors; prosecution is a difficult end goal if survivors of trafficking see their traffickers as their "boyfriends" or lovers; and, for a range of reasons, most survivors do not immediately admit they are victims. Other arguments supported the critique, conveying the policy's limitation would not address why migrants are afraid to come forth as witnesses, where "the measure seems to take for granted imposing longer sentences and bigger fines" as being persuasive enough for survivors to testify. The collective argument was summarized in *Time Magazine*—it simply would not improve conditions for survivors of human trafficking.[3] Mobilizing from a "human trafficking is complex," and the complexity of the critiques of Prop 35 contrasted with the simplicity of the solution offered to voters in voting yes—yes to increase penalties, yes to have the traffickers pay for trafficking, and yes to registering sex traffickers as sex offenders. Additionally, not all human trafficking is in sexual economies—will corporate companies, individuals, and organized groups be registered as sex offenders for trafficking people for their labor on construction sites, farms, in homes as domestic workers, in hotels, in janitorial services, among other industries and contexts, where trafficking did not encompass any sexual exploitation? It is clear from exemplars like Prop 35 that the law shapes anti-trafficking responses and its subjects—where these carceral responses are impacted by notions of labor, migration, and racialized sexuality. The law dictates how human trafficking is understood and who is categorized as trafficked, trafficker, and anti-trafficker. The socio-legal implications of state, federal, and international law are that the law reproduces an imagining of the trafficking subject as Other, whose Otherness is entangled in a rhetoric of freedom, labor migration, and sexual economies. Tracing U.S. labor history with a history of sexual economies, migration, and human trafficking illuminates how racialized invisibility perseveres for transnational migrant laborers, where trafficking is not exceptional, but rather is a contemporary term that describes transnational racialized labor migration. Therefore, this chapter offers a legal tracing of how the history of criminalizing migrants is deeply bound to notions of victimhood, citizenship, and legality. These notions are bound to dualities of victimhood/criminality, citizenship/noncitizenship, and legality/illegality due to systems of labor, migration, and racialized sexuality.

As illuminated by Felicity Amaya Schaeffer, the appeals in anti-trafficking responses—the panics, the narratives of fear, and the responses to the eradication of human trafficking as a crime—go hand in hand with a collective support for "an increase in state power and in the state's budget (in militarizing the border, building more prison detention centers, and deporting more immigrants), in order to apprehend and return subjects at the border."[4] Recognizing the empirical connections made by scholars such as Schaeffer, Parreñas, and Hua, among others, regarding immigration, violence, labor, and racialized sexualities, this chapter provides an important legal genealogy of citizenship, immigration law, and labor laws. Building upon the rich intellectual theorizing on labor, migration, and violence, the contribution here is to illuminate how witnessing migrant experiences with violence is shaped by formal and informal economies (i.e., sexual economies) and laws surrounding sexuality and migration that collectively sustain the contemporary metanarrative about "modern-day slavery." Where looking for "vulnerable victims," one finds that such vulnerability has been historically reinforced by the state through U.S. laws. And through historicizing the manifestation of contemporary human trafficking, one finds that the struggle is not just about who and what constitutes trafficking; it is also a struggle bound to freedom, modernity, labor, citizenship, race, gender, and sexuality.

Human trafficking is undoubtedly a criminal justice issue.[5] Beyond it being a priority, human trafficking is a legal definition. When one turns to the U.S. federal definition of human trafficking, put forth through the Trafficking Victims Protection Act (TVPA) and supplemented by state laws, to trace this law is to not only see it as a law in itself. The legislation of trafficking laws has the power to create (in)visibility in experiences. Those who fit legal definitions are eligible for benefits, support, and even, for some, the prosecution of their trafficker. However, those who fall outside of these legal definitions—or who see moving beyond a life of experiencing trafficking as beyond prosecution and legal recognition—are oftentimes invisible. This is the power of the law.

As delineated by Max Weber, the law is a central site of analysis due to its ability to legitimate and transform social organization and activities—constituting and mobilizing economic, political, and cultural actors, norms, values, interests, and power.[6] Migrant subjects who are defined by human trafficking are bound to be witnessed through the law—as victims of a crime, seeking immigration relief in the form of the T-Visa, or even pursuing a civil case to seek restitution for wages and other monetary compensation for their exploitation. Central to human trafficking is legibility through legal structures. The legal contexts of the law and its discursive power cannot be separated from its social implications and sociological impacts. Migratory subjects cross borders and are deeply shaped by immigration law, notions of criminality, labor laws, and practices. These notions circulate as discourse that is understood as existing in two distinct ways. The first is as a "regular set of linguistic facts;" the other is as "an order set of polemical and strategic facts."[7] Therefore, an understanding of human trafficking discourse as impacting social life and practices is made possible through examining the law.[8] By analyzing the socio-legal context of human trafficking, one may understand why human trafficking has come to matter nearly one hundred fifty years after slavery was abolished in the United States. The interpretations, practices, and systems about human trafficking, the trafficked, the trafficker, and the anti-trafficker give meaning to a group of people. This chapter traces the socio-legal construction of the "Other" in anti-trafficking law and practice as intertwined with notions of freedom, labor, and sexuality. This tracing enables a deeper engagement with the multiple histories that shape the historic present regarding violence. To begin, I discuss the contested description of human trafficking as "modern-day slavery."

TRAFFICKING AS "MODERN-DAY SLAVERY" AND ITS DISCONTENTS

Human trafficking, unique legal definition of the twenty-first century, is oftentimes referred to as "modern-day slavery." The image of human trafficking as synonymous with modern-day slavery circulates discursively. "Modern-day slavery" as a concept and way to name trafficking problematically furthers the circulation of slavery as ahistorical and decontextualized. Twenty-first-century anti-trafficking discourse depends on an image that connects human trafficking to antebellum slavery yet distinguishes itself from it. Slavery is when a person lives in servile[9] conditions and continues to be defined by legal structures around the world.[10] Others define slavery as legal ownership of another person—therefore this person no longer has a personhood. Slavery is understood as a power relation. Some scholars refer to the legal definition of slavery as when a person has legal ownership over another.[11] Orlando Patterson delineates slavery as being relegated by how one enters into a relation of domination: capture in warfare, kidnapping, tribute and tax payment, debt, punishment for crimes, abandonment and sale, self-enslavement, and through birth.[12] Slavery "is the permanent violent domination of alienated and generally dishonored persons."[13] Additionally, slavery is historically contextual (especially when one refers to particular moments, such as antebellum slavery or the transatlantic slave trade), is perpetuated by systems (i.e., race, class, and/or gender), and is solidified by institutional processes. When used to describe human trafficking, slavery is a systemic violence that is enforced by institutional processes that are historically located.

Human trafficking is also euphemistically referred to as "modern-day slavery." The Homeland Security Initiative states that "human trafficking is modern day slavery."[14] The U.S. Department of State refers to "modern slavery" as an umbrella term for human trafficking.[15] One need to merely perform an online search for the phrase "modern-day slavery" to find that it is commonly used to describe a range of phenomena, including slavery and human trafficking. There is political stake in using "modern-day slavery" to describe a range of experiences, including trafficking and slavery. Luis C. de Baca, the former U.S. Ambassador for Human Trafficking, explains that slavery is used to refer to human trafficking because "we cannot create terms that are too bland, [because they] ameliorate the conditions victims experience."[16] However, beyond the spectacle, human trafficking may in some instances be slavery. For some, the language of slavery brings forth the potency of what victims of human trafficking experience, suggesting that "human trafficking" is too weak a phrase. *To traffic* conjures up movement when related to drugs and congestion. The reference to slavery, after the abolition of slavery, necessitates a distinguishing of this new type of slavery to antebellum slavery. "Modern-day" suggests that there is not only something familiar about this slavery but also something new. Newness is a political realization that assumes modern is "better."[17] "Modern-day slavery" perpetuates particular images of human trafficking as the same as antebellum slavery, yet new, and as being extensive and massive.

Antebellum slavery was a part of a U.S. modernity during the Enlightenment. During that era, the abolition of slavery became a way by which the "West" distinguished itself from "the rest."[18] However, slavery had already been a part of the project of modernity in Western societies/the Global North. It is not yet known whether contemporary communities understand slavery as less severe than antebellum slavery (therefore better), or whether modern movements perceive themselves as "combatting modern-day slavery" better than earlier abolitionist movements. However, the interchangeability of modern slavery as a new kind of slavery with the term *trafficking*, furthers a common belief that human trafficking is "slavery like."

The flattening of slavery and human trafficking into singular categories reinforces a mythology that slavery is more prevalent in the twenty-first century than it was during the antebellum period. In spite of the abolition of slavery worldwide, Kevin Bales, economist and president of the Global Slavery Index, estimated that there were as many as twenty-seven million slaves in 2004.[19] In 2017, thirteen years later, his organization, which estimates the prevalence of human trafficking by country, suggested that the number of enslaved people in the world had increased, with an estimated 40.3 million people living in slavery worldwide, at "any given moment."[20] Bales's work furthers a popular perception that there are more slaves today than all the persons taken from Africa by the transatlantic slave trade. Bales, however, distinguishes human trafficking from antebellum slavery by calling it "New Slavery."[21] This likening of slavery to trafficking is common. Similarly, David Batstone, founder of the Not for Sale campaign, links human trafficking and antebellum slavery: "Like slaves who came to America's shores two hundred years ago, today's slaves are not free to pursue their own destinies. They are coerced to perform work for the personal gain of those who subjugate them. If they try to escape the clutches of their masters, modern slaves risk personal violence or reprisals to their families."[22] The intellectual, social, and political climate has created an urgency to link human trafficking with slavery—or to liken it to slavery.

The synonymous use of slavery and trafficking erases the racist experiences that black Americans and indigenous and Native peoples experienced during the antebellum period, by suggesting that in the contemporary United States, and even around the world, there are more enslaved people today. Simply put, one cannot know if there are more or less enslaved people today than during the time prior to 1865 when slavery was legal. The global economy, colonial relations, and legal definitions of slavery make the historical moments incomparable. One cannot compare the context of Sally Hemings—an enslaved African American[23]—and Bukulo Love Oriola[24]—who was trafficked and experienced contemporary domestic violence in the United States, and is from Nigeria. Race, gender, sexuality, class, and citizenship both define Hemings and Oriola. However, their contexts differ greatly. Hemings lived in an age when legal citizenship was denied to enslaved persons; Oriola lives at a time when legal citizenship is denied to persons not born on U.S. soil and when post-racialism furthers the belief that for people with legal status as citizens and birthright citizens, which today include African Americans, things are "fine." How history, communities, and the law recognize personhood has shifted. Hemings lived at a time when inheritance was a central part of one's life—slavery was passed on generationally. Although Oriola's abuse may not be literally passed on, she lives in a time when working and living conditions are more precarious for those who do not have legal status, and such conditions have generational implications. This is compounded by racializing logics that are furthered through color-blind logics. When it is narrowed down to its specificity of the individual, and zoomed out to its macro contexts,

Hemings and Oriola simply cannot be compared, but rather relationally situated. Therefore, how does one count them as the same? The critiques of the anti-trafficking movement's usage of slavery "remembers slavery primarily as a metaphor, and a foil, to highlight the trafficking and exploitation of what it defines as the 'new slaves' of the modern world."[25] What is clear is how the anti-trafficking movement has mobilized with the image of slavery rediscovered in the twenty-first century. Although some scholars have worked to depict human trafficking as "modern-day slavery," they have not gone unchallenged. Kempadoo, Sanghera, and Pattanaik argue that slaves make up the smallest percentage of people smuggled, trafficked, or engaged in forced labor, distinguishing between human trafficking and slavery.[26] As scholars debate slavery and trafficking, trafficking's severity in the United States has been questioned, with some arguing that it is "not nearly as extensive" in the United States as it is in other countries, such as India, Nepal, Italy, western Europe, Moldova, the former Soviet Union, Albania, the Balkans, Thailand, and the Mekong subregion.[27] Whether one sees human trafficking as modern-day slavery or not, or the prevalence in numbers as massive or minimal, the reality is that survivors of human trafficking comprise observed and unobserved accounts. The consensus is that human trafficking, whether one links it with slavery or not, has constituted human trafficking as slavery (or not) as a huge problem here (or over there) as part of the discursive power of the twenty-first-century anti-trafficking movement—it is seen as a social problem.

U.S. human trafficking discourse depends on its imagery as new and massive, elsewhere and "Other." The portrayal of such a phenomenon is a political tool that enables human trafficking to shift from being an invisible subject to being one with discursive power. Although some experiences of human trafficking are slavery, describing all human trafficking experiences as slavery is a political tool. And the minimizing of the scope of human trafficking enables states to not be fully accountable for addressing human trafficking when those whose experiences of violence fall outside of subjects who are seen as rights holders, are then perceived as those who are excluded from protections. If one is unable to cross into legibility as experiencing this slave-like or enslaved experience, one is positioned as criminal, Other, deportable. The politics of trafficking is most salient in how it is constituted by the law. Contemporary trafficking laws are assumed to have a genealogy tied to slavery (and freedom). However, this linkage is myopic if it does not include a legal tracing to citizenship/immigration laws, labor laws, and laws impacting sexuality.

HUMAN TRAFFICKING LAWS

There are sociological implications to how one is constituted as trafficked, by the law, its enforcement, and its production through discourse (i.e., the media). If the law creates "structures of legitimizing for relations of power that already exist, acting in a conservative fashion to support existing systems of power and control,"[28] then it is necessary to analyze human trafficking laws, their legal ramifications, and their production in social relations. The law produces knowledge and assumptions about truths—the meaning of who constitutes trafficked/not trafficked. The knowledge production about human trafficking necessitates a bringing to the fore the scales within which it is produced: the local (state), the nation-state, and the international.

Currently there are a variety of scales in which human trafficking laws are implemented: at the local level of the state, in the nation-state at the federal, and in the international (see Figure 3). Human trafficking policies are imbricated in relations of power, and to begin to paint this picture I start with the larger context within which human trafficking policies are situated—international law.[29] Classicist views became the main staple in U.S. foreign policy throughout the 1920s.[30] Such views of international law disintegrated in the 1930s with the Great Depression and the invasions in Asia and Europe by Japan and Germany, when the old vision of international law could no longer apply; the League of Nations exposed that disjuncture between nation-state behaviors and international law.[31] Since the 1940s, a realist view of international law has developed that has ranged from the perception that international laws are meaningless to the perception that they are central to understanding state behavior.[32]

Throughout the twentieth century, human trafficking laws have been a part of the international scene. The United Nations policies were intended to suppress transnational prostitution, as seen with the International Agreement for the Suppression of the White Slave Traffic (1904). The commitment to a language of rescuing white women and girls was abandoned in 1917.[33] And the subsequent policies, Suppression of the Traffic in Women and Children (1921) and the Suppression of The Traffic in Women of Full Age (1933), illustrate the development of trafficking as a crime of movement that focused on sexual crimes. However, the pre-2000 international laws did not have a legal definition of human trafficking. It was not until the Palermo Protocol that the international bodies facilitated the legitimization of human trafficking as a legal concept.

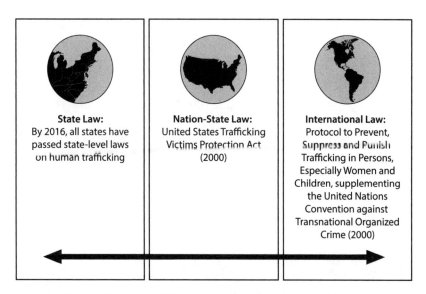

State Law:	Nation-State Law:	International Law:
By 2016, all states have passed state-level laws on human trafficking	United States Trafficking Victims Protection Act (2000)	Protocol to Prevent, Suppress and Punish Trafficking in Persons, Especially Women and Children, supplementing the United Nations Convention against Transnational Organized Crime (2000)

FIGURE 3. Scales of human-trafficking law: International law, nation-state law, and state law.
"2014 State Ratings on Human Trafficking Laws," Polaris Project, 2014, accessed August 13, 2018, http://polarisproject.org/resources/2014-state-ratings-human-trafficking-laws.

In 2000, the Palermo Protocol was implemented as a response to the absence of an international definition of human trafficking[34] with goals to prevent and combat human trafficking, to protect and assist victims of human trafficking, and to promote cooperation among states with an emphasis on women and children.[35] The Protocol to Prevent, Suppress and Punish Trafficking in Persons, Especially Women and Children, supplementing the United Nations Convention Against Transnational Organized Crime,[36] was enacted by the United Nations in Palermo, Italy, October 28, 2000, not long after the implementation of a U.S. policy on human trafficking (the Trafficking Victim's Protection Act, soon to be discussed in more detail). It defines human trafficking as follows:

(a) "Trafficking in persons" shall mean the recruitment, transportation, transfer, harbouring or receipt of persons, by means of the threat or use of force or other forms of coercion, of abduction, of fraud, of deception, of the abuse of power or of a position of vulnerability or of the giving or receiving of payments or benefits to achieve the consent of a person having control over another person, for the purpose of exploitation. Exploitation shall include, at a minimum, the exploitation of the prostitution of others or other forms of sexual exploitation, forced labour or services, slavery or practices similar to slavery, servitude or the removal of organs;

(b) The consent of a victim of trafficking in persons to the intended exploitation set forth in subparagraph (a) of this article shall be irrelevant where any of the means set forth in subparagraph (a) have been used;

(c) The recruitment, transportation, transfer, harbouring or receipt of a child for the purpose of exploitation shall be considered "trafficking in persons" even if this does not involve any of the means set forth in subparagraph (a) of this article.

The Palermo Protocol as a legal text in itself is a "living document, with a history and political relevance."[37] The influence upon the protocol was vast: NGOs and international bodies (i.e., an ad hoc committee was organized by the United Nations). At its genesis, the protocol was conceived in polarized perception of who is trafficked. The international debates are most notable in the position of Janice Raymond, from the Coalition Against Trafficking in Women, who brought to the fore an interest in exploitation and the prostitution of people; they argue that consent is a nonissue because "all victims of prostitution and trafficking fall into a protected class because of the extreme violence of their abuse."[38] In contrast, Ann Jordan, from the International Human Rights Law Group, challenged Raymond's positions; Jordan's perspectives aligned with human rights activists from a labor perspective. Jordan, and the entities she represents, stress worker issues in the global economy. Human trafficking laws are living documents that are built upon the tensions that define the anti-trafficking movement.

The Palermo Protocol definition of human trafficking is distinctive from the U.S. federal definition of human trafficking in two specific ways: the issue of consent and organ trafficking. First, the consent of "victims" in the international definition does not preclude them from being categorized as victims of human trafficking. The issue of consent is significant. In the United States, "consent" is an important issue because it is also determined by the age of the person; there is an age of consent (any person eighteen years old or older). Therefore, whether one has reached the age of consent or literally consents to their own exploitation, they may still be seen as trafficked. Second, organ

LEGAL CONTROL OF MIGRANT CROSSINGS 49

trafficking is delineated as a form of human trafficking. This broadens the recognition of human trafficking to mean not only the whole person but also parts of a person.

The Palermo Protocol came into effect the same year as the United States' TVPA, illustrating legal scholar Janie Chuang's critique of U.S. hegemony in international law (i.e., the TVPA), where U.S. law has the power to influence the global arena on human rights issues.[39] This has been most notable in the debates surrounding the U.S. anti-prostitution pledge, which mandated that U.S. grantees would not use funds to promote, support, or advocate for the legalization or practice of prostitution. U.S. anti-trafficking endeavors have been internationalized, with domestic implications.[40]

Human trafficking under the TVPA, s. 103, defines severe human trafficking[41] as:

(A) sex trafficking in which a commercial sex act is induced by force,[42] fraud,[43] or coercion,[44] or in which the person induced to perform such act has not attained 18 years of age; or

(B) the recruitment, harboring, transportation, provision, or obtaining of a person for labor or services, through the use of force, fraud, or coercion for the purpose of subjection to involuntary servitude,[45] peonage,[46] debt bondage,[47] or slavery.[48]

Central to defining human trafficking is the understanding of force,[49] fraud,[50] and/or coercion.[51] Although a person may or may not experience all three, it is a means that is oftentimes used to describe trafficking. The actions in force vary but may include beatings, rape, assault, or other forms of physical harm. Fraud is when someone tells a person lies about the industry or working conditions they will work. Coercion is the perception of threat, which is central to understanding the psychological implications of human trafficking. The U.S. term of "severe" suggests there is a non-severe human trafficking; however, this is not so. There are only two forms of trafficking: severe human trafficking (which includes labor trafficking) and/or sex trafficking. The inclusion of "severe" in the U.S. definition of human trafficking implies that U.S. law only guarantees such protections for victims of "severe forms of trafficking in persons."[52]

The TVPA was implemented to strengthen the "legal teeth" of existing sanctions on involuntary servitude, peonage, and slavery by adding the new crimes of human trafficking, sex trafficking, forced labor, and document servitude.[53]

The TVPA resolved the debates in legal cases that were unable to utilize the Thirteenth Amendment and the abolition of slavery to prosecute slavery conditions that were enforced through psychological coercion. The absence of legal standards to address psychological coercion, and the need for new laws, was illuminated in the case *United States v. Kozminski*.[54] In 1988 the Supreme Court resolved the circuit court split in Kozminski, in which the core of the debate was psychological coercion. Two farmworker, who were homeless and had a mental disability, were recruited to work on the Kozminski dairy farm in exchange for room and board. The two men endured years of abusive conditions—no running water, spoiled food, and physical and verbal abuse. They were isolated from visitors and discouraged from speaking with them. When the case went to trial, the prosecution made a case for involuntary servitude as including psychological coercion. The courts had a narrow understanding of psychological coercion, so the TVPA now offers an interpretation of involuntary servitude to include a more expansive understanding of psychological coercion. The TVPA also enables victim identification, the terms of legibility, through law enforcement investigations and prosecutions of traffickers and legal relief to international victims of human trafficking.[55] There are two major gaps in the U.S. TVPA: the absence of organ trafficking and the requirement for evidence of force, fraud, or coercion for labor trafficked individuals. Organ trafficking is not covered under the TVPA, because the National Organ Transplant Act (1984) covers such activities by making organ sales illegal. The only individuals who are not required to show force, fraud, or coercion are minors trafficked into sexual economies or into sexual slavery. The logic is that minors are unable to consent to their own exploitation. If a minor is labor trafficked, they must still prove force, fraud, or coercion.

Transnational migrants designated as having been trafficked must navigate a variety of legal systems, including family law, the criminal justice system, the immigration legal system, and civil law. Human trafficking victims who are in need of immigration relief are eligible for a T-Visa or U-Visa.[56] Not all survivors of human trafficking move in and out of a variety of legal systems, nor does an open case in one legal system such as a criminal case lead to the emotional closure survivors of exploitation need to move on from their trafficking. And for those that require immigration relief, which then in effect leads to them cooperating with law enforcement in an investigation, and the desire for restitution in a civil case, human trafficking survivors and even traffickers, may experience a variety of legal systems. The legal landscape impacts human trafficking definitions and the practices to prosecute traffickers and support survivors. The TVPA affords victims some protection through T- and U-Visas and the creation of a network of advocates and service providers.[57] What is essential for T- and U-Visa eligibility is that victims are required to comply "with any reasonable request for assistance in investigating or prosecuting trafficking (if 18 or older)."[58] As human trafficking is clearly a twenty-first-century issue, it continues to operationalize through a logic of trafficking as hidden.

SOCIO-LEGAL IMPLICATIONS: IMAGINING THE OTHER AS HIDDEN

A central image that human trafficking operates under, that is then furthered through legal and law enforcement practices, is that human trafficking is "hidden." The furtherance of the belief that human trafficking is hidden reifies practices such as law enforcement raids and legal responses, that then grapples with how one finds subjects who are hidden. To further U.S. policy and service agendas addressing human trafficking in the United States, in 2015, the Office for Trafficking in Persons was formed within the Administration for Children and Families Services at the U.S. Department of Health and Human Services (HHS). Since the first anti-trafficking funds were appropriated in 2001, HHS has aided 8,543 survivors of human trafficking.[59]

To further its outreach in 2004, HHS launched the Rescue & Restore campaign. Eventually the Rescue & Restore campaign was refashioned to be called the Look Beneath the Surface campaign in 2017. The campaign encouraged "intermediaries to look beneath the surface by recognizing clues and asking the right questions because they may be the only witnesses with the chance to reach out and help victims."[60] Campaign materials are disseminated in English, Chinese, Spanish, Indonesian, Korean, Thai, and Vietnamese. The target victim population is Asian and Latina/o, as seen with the prioritization of Asian and Spanish languages. HHS coalitions throughout the United States (a total of forty-four) receive funding through the HHS to facilitate outreach to those who might identify victims of human trafficking or interact with trafficked people.[61] The campaign materials purport an image that trafficked people are people of color or immigrants. The visual representation of human trafficking includes poster materials.[62]

Visitors to the Look Beneath the Surface campaign site are immediately greeted with a video link.[63] The video begins with a montage of individuals, and viewers are called to look beneath the surface of these individuals—a white girl assumed to be in sexual economies, a black domestic worker, and a Latino restaurant worker. The video states, "Every day human beings are forced into slavery. Hundreds of thousands of men, women and children are trafficked each year throughout the world and in the United States." Therefore, beneath the surface of these workers is a story of victimization. The video includes survivor perspectives, as well as governmental and law enforcement perspectives. The viewer meets Sarah, who was "forced to engage in stripping and prostitution." She describes the physical horrors of being trafficked—having a match lit while having gasoline poured on her, and being stomped and kicked. Sarah was trafficked across state lines, where it was "fear, not shackles" that kept her from leaving her abuse. Sarah's story is described as "typical" for "victims of human trafficking." A series of images follow Sarah's story—an Asian woman sitting with her legs curled upwards in a corner, a black woman mopping, another holding a vacuum as she stares longingly out of a window—suggesting these, too, are typical of human trafficking. The story the viewer is told is that human trafficking encompasses people being forced into commercial sex, restaurants, domestic servitude, hotels, farms, and sweatshops. The Look Beneath the Surface video campaign also introduces us to Esmeralda, whose national origins are disclosed, unlike Sarah's, which leads one to normalize Sarah as a U.S. citizen. Esmeralda is a Guatemalan woman who traversed not only nation-state boundaries but also boundaries of sex and labor, experiencing sexual slavery and domestic servitude. Cooking and cleaning during the day, at night she would be raped. Trafficking survivors are highlighted as originating from Africa, Southeast Asia, Latin America, and Eastern Europe, although data on human trafficking show that trafficking survivors come from all parts of Asia, the Americas, Europe, the Arab World, and Africa. The viewer is called to see the stories as those of "victims." Force, fraud, and coercion are central. The goal of the Rescue & Restore campaign is to increase public awareness about human trafficking, through a larger narrative that it is hidden, reaching out to "people on the front lines": faith-based communities, social service providers, health workers, and law enforcement officers. The viewer is called to "look beneath the surface" by recognizing the signs of human trafficking.

The images furthered through the Look Beneath the Surface campaign are reminiscent of Roland Barthes's understanding of photography: photographs do not call the past or restore what has been abolished by time/space, but rather "attest that what I see has indeed existed."[64] To participate in this campaign of looking beneath the surface is to find that "human trafficking *is* modern-day slavery." A surface is an uppermost layer to something that is much deeper than what can be perceived by the eye. Like a photograph, a surface creates a mirage of being three-dimensional, of having depth. To frame trafficking in relation to a surface locates "modern-day slavery" and its subjects as hidden, below, and unseen, meaning that the trafficked subject is relegated to alterity. To be seen, one's suffering is recognizable as undeserved; the politics of pity is sustained by certain assumptions about freedom.[65] The discourse of freedom manifests in the campaign materials and cannot be understood merely by looking beneath the surface or even at the face value of what is seen. Under the TVPA, the HHS was assigned as the government agency to support victims in becoming eligible to receive benefits and services in the United States. Immigration lawyers, social service providers, health-care providers, and law enforcement officers are key "identifiers" of who is a "victim"[66] of human trafficking. To imagine trafficking subjects as hidden then reinforces a response that necessitates making subjects seen. Therefore, anti-trafficking discourse and challenges have been deeply shaped by the challenges of describing the unobserved.[67] What one knows about violence occurs from micro to macro contexts, and it is the tip of the iceberg. More difficult to know are those who fall below and are considered the unknown, and therefore the unmeasurable.[68] Although viewers are called to look beneath the surface, one must also contend with what creates the surface to begin with and, if something is hidden, what else is unseen to anti-traffickers and witnesses of human trafficking. Thus, to understand human trafficking necessitates a situating of how trafficking is produced in contrast to freedom.

BEYOND A RHETORIC OF FREEDOM—TOWARD THE SOLIDIFICATION OF CITIZEN SUBJECTS

To call human trafficking "modern-day slavery" is to render the norm that it is the antithesis to freedom. The genealogies of human trafficking are often connected to antebellum slavery. Therefore, here it is necessary to examine the language of "liberation" called for in U.S. anti-trafficking efforts. David L. Eng's analysis of *Lawrence v. Texas* leads him to assert that liberty is intended for a "social group to whom rights, recognition, and privileges are granted . . . the liberty of some can certainly be in conflict with the freedom of others. Hence, we need to ask, liberty and freedom for whom, where, and under what conditions."[69] U.S. governmental and nongovernmental campaigns assert that victims of human trafficking do not have freedom. The U.S. anti-trafficking movement promotes that the person who can restore freedom to a trafficked person is not the trafficked person but rather a "liberator" or a "rescuer." It is the "you," the stakeholders,[70] who participate in U.S. anti-trafficking initiatives to liberate trafficked people. Freedom is defined by the *Oxford Dictionary* as "the power or right to act, speak, or think as one wants, . . . the state of not being imprisoned or enslaved."[71] This definition is too broad. Therefore, drawing upon a variety of scholars (historians, philosophers, and women-of-color theorists), I posit that freedom is: (1) understood to be what it is not—in this case, slavery; (2) not automatically realized with abolition or an end of slavery or slave-like conditions over time; (3) defined by individuals; and (4) solidified by the collective through nation-states (even if this practice means denying freedom to a subgroup of people). I provide an interpretation of freedom to frame how it shapes how one is constructed as trafficked or not. Notions of freedom are formed through a paired contrast with slavery.[72] For some, freedom is universalized,[73] where liberty is the "will to act," excluding those in prison or in chains. For philosophers like Hume, the opposite of freedom is imprisonment and chains. The imagery of chains and antebellum slavery in the United States is iconic due to the practices of chattel slavery.[74] However, through it all, a rhetoric of freedom is also deeply bound to notions of citizenship.

Freedom during antebellum slavery was not merely the absence of slavery, but rather a concept that was shaped by a "terrain of conflict, its substance open to different, often contradictory interpretations."[75] It is this conflict that haunts the present. Angela Davis remarks that "after eight long decades of 'emancipation,' the signs of freedom were shadows so vague and so distant that one strained to get a glimpse of them."[76] As freedom is bound to a legacy of colonization and slavery in the Americas as a story of citizenship denied, it also has a gender story. Therefore, to conceptualize how the trafficking subject is created through notions of freedom, is to also contextualize notions of servitude in the United States.

The debates surrounding servitude (and involuntary servitude) in the United States are not only racial, but also gender-based. The Thirteenth Amendment exemplifies that U.S. practices and ideologies of freedom are imbricated in individualisms and individual choices that are tied to heteropatriarchy. In particular, freedom is motivated by individual desires and mediated by cultural and historical conditions.[77] On January 31, 1865, the Thirteenth Amendment to the U.S. Constitution was implemented, officially abolishing and prohibiting slavery and involuntary servitude.[78] The language of involuntary servitude implies that slavery excludes individuals that voluntarily enter servitude. Nineteenth-century understandings of involuntary servitude were narrow, where the focus was on coerced wage labor in a market economy. The goal of including "involuntary servitude" was to prohibit "the creation of slave-like conditions through the private use of force."[79] Congressional and legal debates about involuntary servitude illuminate that servitude is gendered as a practice of marriage. Women were seen as property, as illustrated in an 1865 statement by Representative White during the discussion: "A husband has a right of property in the service of his wife; he has the right to the management of his household affairs. . . . All these rights rest upon the same basis as a man's right of property in the service of slaves."[80] Although the present-day anti-slavery movement has continually worked to address the diversity of genders enslaved or trafficked, the historical development of U.S. servitude is gendered as feminine—women and slaves as property. Euro-American women were categorized as slaves to their husbands, as property but, at the same time, as beneficiaries to racialized slave practices. The negotiation, redefinition, and engagement with freedom in the twenty-first century continues to persist in spite of the passage of the Thirteenth Amendment. This ongoing discussion of freedom reifies how abolition has not been actualized and that, in the United States, there is an ongoing tension around the inability to provide freedom to all people. The decisions about the language of the Thirteenth Amendment elucidate the historical context of the feminization of those enslaved; it is also intrinsically tied to capitalist practices. In the late twentieth and early twenty-first centuries, national and international definitions of human trafficking spoke directly to the gender-based legacies of servitude and trafficking, naming trafficking as a particular phenomenon—as gender-based violence. This is most explicitly traced to the United Nations' Fourth World Conference on Women and to the development of the Beijing Platform for Action.[81]

The inability for some people to access freedom is not only the consequence of gender-based violence; it is also due to ongoing historical racisms in U.S. ideologies and institutional practices that haunt the anti-trafficking movement. This haunting emerges in the inequalities created through racial, gender, and class difference, and the social climate of a Jim Crow society. Contemporary slavery is seen as distinctively different than chattel slavery; the chains that bind a person into slave conditions in contemporary slavery are not necessarily physical chains. There are legal differences—slavery was abolished. Albeit different than slavery, where slavery is about ownership, the haunting of slavery is articulated in the assumed connection between slavery and twenty-first-century trafficking. At the core of antebellum slavery were racism and colonization. However, there is no position of innocence. As delineated by Tryon Woods, anti-blackness not only creates the conditions of slavery but also defines the anti-trafficking movement and furthers practices and ideologies where black suffering becomes the "surrogate selves" for reflecting on freedom.[82]

Drawing upon the ongoing historical making of notions of freedom, one finds that freedom is not merely about ownership; in its origins it is defined by who is believed to have the rights to have rights. The citizenship clause of the Fourteenth Amendment was integral to U.S. abolition. The Fourteenth Amendment solidified the government as the "custodian of freedoms."[83] The role of nation-states and governments in defining freedom, as well as in facilitating freedom, is further solidified by the Thirteenth Amendment, through which "Congress shall have power to enforce this article by appropriate legislation." Freedom is forged by those who are able to access citizenship, which created a system of people unable to access rights—noncitizens. Therefore, subjects who were once hidden subjects, who become seen as trafficked, are deeply tied to notions of a freedom that is inextricably linked to citizenship.

Transnational migrants entering the United States have been socially as well as legally denied access to freedom.[84] The complex relationship of inclusions, exclusions, and national debates was articulated and understood when relationally examining two racialized groups side by side. Transnational migrants are considered to be Lisa Lowe's perpetual aliens, categorized as such to be unable to share in America.[85] Regardless of their formal citizenship, they are seen as "alien citizens," racialized as the "inassimilable" Asian and the "illegal" Mexican.[86] There is a long history of anti-immigration policies targeting the Asian region—the 1907 Gentlemen's Agreement, the 1924 Immigration Act, and the 1934 Tydings McDuffie Act. The historic prevention of Asians from entering the United States began with Chinese exclusions in 1882, and was solidified with the 1924 Immigration Act, which barred Asian immigrants from becoming naturalized citizens. The 1921 quota system set up policies that enabled only a certain number of individuals to access rights in the United States. Transnational Asian migrants were constructed through exclusions in policies such as the 1917 Asiatic Barred Zone Act. The ideological constitution of Asians as a subcategory was solidified before 1917, and scholars date the beginning of the exclusion of Asians to the Chinese Exclusionary Act of 1882. As African Americans were legally codified by their difference during antebellum slavery, so too were Asians and Latinas/os/x,[87] in a climate in which slave systems in the United States were on their last legs. Latinas/os/x were impacted by U.S. expansion and racialized nationalism. The creation of the southern border spawned anxieties toward Mexicans, even though the northern border between the United States and Canada is the world's longest border. As the United States saw Asia as a threat and a sender of "perpetual foreigners," half of Mexico had already been incorporated into the United States with the 1848 Treaty of Guadalupe, which solidified the United States' southern border. The U.S. solidification of its borders, coupled with nativism, set the tone for how migrants from the Asia-Pacific and south of the U.S. border were perceived. Not only has policy solidified who has access to citizenship, but there are also cultural dimensions of those who, in spite of their legal status, are deemed "alien citizens."[88] Although citizenship created a subclass of noncitizens, it is not citizenship and the rights it confers that have come to impact those that are categorized as trafficked, but also the relationship between freedom, labor, and transnational processes.

Freedom and slavery are contextualized by the modern capitalist economy. For Marx, slavery is an "economic category"; it gave rise to modern industry.[89] Marx describes modern slavery as a social system that came out of a capitalist society. Capital is "social power"; therefore, in a capitalist society, freedom under such conditions is "production, free trade, free selling and buying."[90] In contrast to the free individual in a capitalist system, the slave has unique qualities.[91] In order to further understand freedom (and rights) necessitates an understanding of the social (and economic) system of slavery that the modern U.S. system was built upon. Laws shift practices of who has freedom in an economy of individualism, and the marker of unhealthy capitalism is then assumed to be involuntary servitude and slavery.

In understanding freedom as bound to notions of slavery, what I have traced is its racial, gender, class, and national-origin historic tracings. However, trafficking is not just a narrative of freedom; it is also a story of labor migration. Therefore, what follows is an unpacking of how human trafficking is deeply shaped by labor migration policies that are furthered by the nation-state.

LABOR AND (UNDOCUMENTED) MIGRATION

Human trafficking as a twenty-first-century issue is deeply bound to labor migration and the laws that shape migratory subjects. Conceptualizations of migration are often problematically broken into a binary: legal versus illegal migration. Discursive and applied response to immigration takes the form of hysteria,[92] implicit bias, and stereotyping.[93] Although the face of the migrant is diverse, the mass media's portrayal of immigrants links them to criminalized activities such as smuggling initiatives at the U.S. southern border. Human trafficking and smuggling are forms of irregular migration. Smuggling is seen as short-term and in legal terms is understood as a crime against a border, whereas human trafficking is a long-term form of exploitation that is codified as a crime against a person.[94] Not all trafficked people are human smuggled, and not all human smuggling experiences lead to human trafficking. However, one must understand smuggling and trafficking as systems that intersect.

Place becomes an important site of contestation in debates about migration. For example, San Diego is an important corridor, or entry point, for human-smuggling networks.[95] The United States' southern border is policed by nearly twenty thousand agents, which can be traced to the Mexican Revolution, when the border patrol was created in 1924. U.S. media renditions of human smuggling are among the variety of illustrations of the attitudes toward immigration and smuggling in the United States. The border is a sociopolitically constructed space that is defined by those who cross it and those who police it.[96] Immigrants fall into a tenuous polarization of being welcomed into particular labor industries such as agriculture and service sectors, and also being rejected, as seen in the tightening of U.S. borders and the arrest of migrant laborers. Transnational migrants are targeted by state policies that lead to the policing of borders and the detaining of individuals who have limited access to citizenship, even though migration patterns suggest that there is a clear demand for their labor that is raced and gendered.[97]

Migration during the twentieth and twenty-first centuries is organized by transnational connectivities;[98] the global market has a permanent demand for both highly skilled professionals as well as unskilled laborers.[99] The International Office of Migration, an intergovernmental organization that is seen as the "migration agency" on global debates about social, economic, and political implications of migration in the twenty-first century, estimated in 2006 that 139,000 people migrate from Mexico to the United States each year.[100] And Asian migrants account for 5.8 percent of the total U.S. population, where 74.1 percent are foreign born.[101] Global migrants are not homogeneous, but rather are a diverse group whose migration is based on individual and macro decisions that are impacted by national/international policies and global/local dynamics; migrants differ along lines of race, class, gender, and sex. Global patterns of migration have shifted, and what is witnessed in the United States is an increase in women on the move.[102] Women have increased in numbers not only in the labor force but also in their visibility due to the "feminization of the job supply."[103] The United Nations Development Fund for Women (UNIFEM) illustrates how labor migration and the movement of people from conflict zones and crisis situations interact with structures of gender equality at "every level—national and global."[104] Global processes and transnational migration impact not only women but also men. And as migrants move from their home countries to destinations such as the United States, they leave one gender stratification system only to enter another. These experiences exacerbate what Rhacel Salazar Parreñas refers to as "dislocation." Dislocation is a "narrative of displacement"; it is a structural location inhabited by the migrant, a marginalized location, and includes the process by which migrants resist their dislocation.[105]

Transnational migrants oftentimes depend on their social networks to emigrate, in order to "reduce travel costs by providing information on safe and cheap routes or smugglers, and to reduce emotional costs."[106] By contrast, forced migration includes refugees[107] and displaced persons fleeing conditions such as human slavery, ethnic cleansing, and deportation.[108] Historic examples of forced migration include the transatlantic slave trade, whereby fifteen million Africans were trafficked to the Americas; the forced migration of Jews during the Holocaust; and the fleeing of Vietnamese refugees during the fall of Saigon. All are examples of forced migration, a system that is characterized by state action. Human trafficking is not simply about those forced to migrate or forced to flee; one may be trafficked into the United States even after entering or migrating to the United States without coercion. Historically, there are legitimized forms of labor migration that are embedded in slavery practices. In order to discuss concepts of freedom for that of migrants, their limited mobility must be understood in labor industries that naturalized stratified racial and gender labor (agricultural work and domestic work) that continued after the abolition of slavery through the figures of the bracero and the coolie.

THE VESTIGES OF SLAVERY AND SLAVE-LIKE ECONOMIES: AGRICULTURAL WORKERS AND DOMESTIC WORKERS

This section seeks to point to important events that are part of the legacy and genealogies of labor migration practices in the United States and to show how particular events have shaped the transnational migrant labor experience, creating and sustaining what we now understand as trafficking subjects: labor industries that stem from slavery in the United States—agricultural industries and domestic work. The coolie trade, the bracero program, and the treatment of domestic workers are exemplars of the role of the state in facilitating slave-like industries.

The coolie laborer is an important genealogical turning point for examining the racialization of migrant laborers in the United States. Coolie trade laborers migrated to Hawai'i, Peru, and Cuba during the 1800s.[109] Some scholars contend that the experience of those laborers included kidnapping and coercion.[110] Coolie trade laborers were entrenched in the debates about slavery and violence in the United States; these laborers embodied U.S. "hopes, fears, and contradictions surrounding emancipation."[111] They represented the contradictions in U.S. policy, where it was a departure from chattel slavery and the maintenance of slavery's worst features.[112] The example of the coolie trade laborer in the nineteenth century was reflective of the ideological challenge presented by an economy that demanded cheap labor when slavery had been abolished. Moon-ho Jung conveys how "the racialization of Asian workers as coolies vis-à-vis the Caribbean and the South—served to upset and recreate social and cultural dualisms at the heart of race (black and white), class (enslaved and free), and nation (alien and citizen, domestic and foreign) in the United States."[113] The debates about freedom and slavery impacted Asian migrants entering U.S. laboring industries, but the resolution was not one to guarantee rights; rather, it was to exclude Asians from entry, thus rendering them vulnerable to further exploitation. Such a positionality has normalized appeals for citizenship status.

Similar to their Asian counterparts, Latino migrants are shaped by labor policies that are bound to legal status. Mexican migrants experienced a legal form of migration for labor through the Bracero Program of the 1940s and 1950s, a form of quasi-slave labor that was normalized in the United States. The Bracero Program was the first systematic government-endorsed exploitation of migrant laborers.[114] This is evident when the U.S. Congress passed Public Law 78 (1951) to give the Bracero Program a permanent presence until 1964.[115] The Bracero Program is also referred to as a "bilateral immigration program" that enabled circuitous labor between Mexico and the United States. The intention was to return migrant laborers to Mexico. World War II created labor shortages in the United States; therefore between 1948 and 1951 five million braceros were transported to the United States for work.[116] With the establishment of the Partido Revolucionario Institucional (PRI) in Mexico, President Lazaro Cardenas (1934–40) nationalized Mexican oil. This measure strained

U.S.-Mexican relations, and the Bracero Program was seen as reestablishing friendship and cooperation between the two neighboring countries. Although the worker agreement prescribed that braceros were entitled to receive adequate food, they experienced food shortages and came up against a U.S. government indifferent to their treatment.[117] The racialization of braceros as better at "this type of work" due to the stereotype of their short stature was widely accepted. Even when this meant U.S. farm representatives saw workers stoop over for hours without standing straight, they did not see this as a problem or a human rights violation. Opponents of the Bracero Program criticized the exploitive and unsanitary living and work conditions for braceros, as well as their abuse and maltreatment by growers, their neglect by the United States, and racism.

Like their Asian counterparts, just as quick as the United States was to open up the border to workers, Mexicans in the United States found themselves facing a culture that perceived them as criminals (as "illegal" migrants). In 1954, Operation Wetback was put into effect and led Immigration Naturalization Services (INS) to apprehend over one million migrants: "The expansion of the *bracero* migration satisfied growers, while the militarization of the border and the massive number of apprehensions reassured voters and assuaged their nativist fears, creating the widespread perception that the border was under control."[118] Just as the border was seen as something to be controlled, so too were racialized laboring transnational migrant laborers. The bracero represents the normalization of racialized brown bodies laboring in agricultural industries. Even though they were legitimate laborers, like the coolie laborers that came before them, the braceros were denied citizenship, and therefore rights—a condition of contract labor. Although farming in itself is not defined by human trafficking, U.S. labor laws and practices illuminate a history of utilizing coerced, defrauded, and forced labor in the farming industry that may be traced to slavery. Similarly, such may be said about domestic work, which like the agricultural industries is an industry where the treatment of workers is based on the legacies of slavery.

Domestic workers in the United States may be traced to antebellum slavery. During the colonial period (sixteenth century–1776) in the United States, Euro-Americans (children, vagrants, petty criminals, and Irish were a common sight) experienced slavery as indentured servants.[119] Servitude for Euro-Americans did not lead to social death, nor was it always generational; eventually, Euro-American indentured slaves were able to gain their freedom. The poor and the homeless were commonly found in domestic service during this colonial era.[120]

European indentured workers during the early colonial period found themselves side by side with Black and Native enslaved peoples. And the institutionalization of slavery solidified the distinction between European indentured workers and Black slaves. The eventual abolition of slavery did not rid the demand for domestic service. Evelyn Nakano Glenn asserts that "marketization and industrialization fundamentally transformed the household economy by making it increasingly reliant on earnings from wage labor."[121] The prevalence of African men in domestic service shifted after slavery ended. By 1870, gender dynamics changed dramatically, with 85 percent of domestic workers being female. Although African American women were visible in the domestic worker workforce until the 1970s, with the primary image of the black American domestic worker during the early 1900s being an older women residing outside their employer's home.[122] The composition changed throughout the 1900s, with increasing numbers of Asian and Latina/o/x transnational migrants in domestic service due to their material and legal status being exploitable. Nineteenth-century European immigrant women escaped occupational ghettoization. And by the 1980s, the Euro-American employer and the woman-of-color domestic worker both became the norm.

A generational mapping of Asian domestic workers in relation to anti-immigration policies such as the Chinese exclusions in 1882 did not quell the demand for immigrant "help" in the home. Japanese men were a common feature in the Euro-American home in California.[123] The 1907 Gentlemen's Agreement led to the increase in Nisei,[124] Japanese women migrating to the United States to join their husbands, some of them as picture brides.[125] As more women migrated to the United States, a shift in gender demand for Asian domestic workers shifted the industry from a predominantly male to an increasingly female workforce. Japanese men paved the way for an industry in which the women could work. The generational impacts of Asian women in domestic work occurred after World War II, which heightened the perception of Asian Americans as a "yellow peril." Franklin Delano Roosevelt signed Executive Order 9066, which designated the west coast a military zone, leading to the internment of approximately 120,000 Japanese, of which approximately 70,000 were American citizens.[126] Asian women workers were impacted by their relocation. The numbers of Japanese women entering domestic work increased after World War II.[127] Japanese/American women who once held other positions found their work no longer available after they had been forced into relocation, leading them to also enter domestic work. Social pariahs, Nisei also found

LEGAL CONTROL OF MIGRANT CROSSINGS   63

themselves entering domestic service like the women of the first generation. Domestic work after World War II became situated in a stratified U.S. labor industry, designated as primarily work by women of color—not just any women of color, but working-class immigrant women of color in particular.

At present, domestic work is commonly characterized as being invisible, racialized, and gendered labor; from the sociological analysis by scholars such as Ann Oakley in the 1970s to Mary Romero's ethnographic research in the 1990s, invisibility has been located as a central aspect of domestic work. The Philippines and Mexico are major exporters of people, a trend that has led to these countries experiencing higher numbers of transnational citizens in laboring markets such as domestic work. Domestic worker trends are similar in all informal economies, in which hard numbers are difficult to find due to underreporting. The number of domestic workers in the United States has declined, while the number of Latinas and Filipinas working in domestic work has increased. The presence of Latinas in domestic work as an occupation ghetto may be traced to the Mexican–American War (1846–48).[128] In 1900, 29 percent of the female workforce was employed in domestic work; this number had declined to 5 percent by 1970. Since the 1970s, Latinas have continued to constitute the largest category of women entering the occupation, due to their ability to migrate to the United States; the 1965 Immigration Act enabled family members to join their families in the United States, and the economic depression in Mexico and the civil war and conflicts in Central America in the 1980s led others to migrate due to dislocations.

Transnational migrant laborers are integral to keeping economies afloat with their status as foreign migrant laborers, and they figure into global processes in an under-the-table economy that perpetuates their "nonperson" role as "aliens."[129] Their nonperson status leads workers to have rights and family needs that are invisible issues in immigration reform, along with the abuse that they are vulnerable to and for many, experience—sexual, physical, verbal, and in worst-case scenarios, involuntary servitude. The Fair Labor Standard Act (1937), which guaranteed a minimum wage standard and overtime provisions, left out domestic workers and agricultural workers, on the basis that they "lay within the realm of intrastate commerce and were subject to only state laws."[130] Domestic and agricultural workers' vulnerability is contingent on labor exploitation due to poor enforcement of labor laws, anti-immigration policies, and labor market segregation that prevents migrants from upward mobility. Additionally, sex and gender are central to the discourse surrounding freedom and labor. Therefore, to trace transnational migration and labor laws as central to creating the conditions of exploitation, it is also essential to contextualize the legal story about sex.

RACIALIZED SEXUALITIES AND SEXUAL ECONOMIES

To contend with human trafficking and its legal genealogies is to understand it as being deeply shaped by a legacy of racialized sexualities. Julietta Hua defines racialized sexualities as follows: Understandings of sexuality are relationally constructed against notions of sexual deviancy, where some racial groups are seen as deviant over and against other racial groups.[131] As some groups are produced and seen through racializing logics as victims, others are seen as criminal.

Human trafficking has historically been referred to synonymously as sex trafficking. In part, this is due to the events in twentieth-century anti-trafficking efforts that linked slavery with the transnational economies of white women in prostitution.[132] U.S. policies define the debates about sexual economies as being embedded in gendered[133] (and racialized) logics. The attention to Euro-American women as sex slaves invokes images of the "White Slave Trade" panic at the turn of the twentieth century.[134] There was a movement to rescue trafficked white women through policy implementation of the Mann Act (1910). The current perceptions—and for some scholars, misperceptions—of human trafficking link anti-trafficking campaigns to "moral crusades."[135]

This linking is problematic because the broad spectrum of organizations that have found a common context of organizing against trafficking are varied in their beliefs and practices—from conservative to radical.[136] The image of saving Euro-American women from sex traffickers is not new. As a result, there is a need to center race and gender as being historically situated in the United States; such a framing renders visible the production of categories of the trafficked and the anti-trafficker as inextricably linked to debates about choice and freedom. Scholars such as Jo Doezema and Stephanie Limoncelli have traced the legacies of white slavery, trafficking, and freedom. Here, I build on the work of Julietta Hua to offer a way to consider the multifaceted racialized sexualities[137] as not only about the constitution of whiteness and the "Other" but also about a reifying of colonial modernities, where space, zones, and the settler colonial context become subsumed under a generalized narrative of rights (freedom and choice) and violence (slavery and trafficking).

U.S. practices and policies regarding sexual economies reflect national identity as expressed in the examples of Texas and Hawai'i. The incorporation of Texas as a state led to a shift in prostitution policies; prior to incorporation, Texas represented a "zone of tolerance" for prostitution.[138] Such zoning of tolerance at the U.S. border affirms that the national identity that is behind acceptable/unacceptable sexualized economies is tied to colonial relations. Women prostituted in Texas were not seen as slaves or as victims in need of rescue. A language of slavery was not linked to these experiences at the border zone, because slavery was abolished in California and Texas (prior to the Mexican–American War, 1846–48).[139] After Texas was incorporated, prostitution there shifted from belonging to a zone of tolerance to being criminalized. The shift in prostitution policies and the normalization of sexual economies in U.S. territories is not unique to Texas; it is also described in the border limit in the Pacific with Hawai'i. Prior to the annexation of Hawai'i (1898), prostitution was illegal. A kapu (Hawaiian prohibition) on prostitution was proclaimed by the alii (nobility), forbidding women from traveling to foreign ships in order to engage in sex acts.[140] Because Hawai'i was a territory, prostitution in Hawai'i was politically, militarily, and economically endorsed.[141] By 1932, prostitution was officially controlled by the U.S. army. Women brought to Hawai'i were Euro-Americans, as described by editor for the *Hawaiian Journal of History*: "It was a white slave sort of thing."[142] Honolulu was considered a vice area, and when World War II broke out, the demand for prostitution became more visible.

As a discourse of victimhood and rescue circulated, the control of women's sexuality was most apparent in the practices of social and political exclusion, and their criminalization. During the late 1800s, Chinese women and girls were found prostituted in mining outposts, railroad camps, agricultural villages, and Chinatowns in Sacramento, Marysville, and San Francisco, California.[143] The site of dispossessed indigenous Ohlone lands served as the backdrop for U.S. expansion and growth. Victimhood and the transnational migrant experience became a way to reify acceptable settlers (Euro-Americans) in U.S. colonization. Transnational migrants such as prostituted Chinese women were described as virtual slaves and opium addicts who were subject to violence—beatings and death. It is documented that women in prostitution committed suicide to escape the abuse.[144] These circumstances led to the passage of the Page Act in 1875, which opened the door for anti-immigration policies. The Page Act set the tone for the conception of undesirable migrants as contrasted to desirable citizens. It prohibited transnational migrants from working in sexual economies. Although the United States treated Chinese prostituted individuals like criminals, its treatment of Euro-Americans was quite different. In spite of U.S.

anti-immigration policies (i.e., the Chinese Exclusionary Act of 1882), women were documented as sold in San Francisco in the early 1900s, well after Chinese exclusions.[145] Anti-immigration policies were visible in the United States as a means to prevent Chinese women from migrating and trafficking into sex industries; the legal discourse situated Chinese women brought to the United States for the purposes of prostitution as "unlawful."[146]

The legacy of the U.S. anti-slavery movement also furthered Victorian ideals of innocence and purity, exemplified in the responses that led to the passage of the 1910 Mann Act (aka the White Slave Traffic Act). The White Slave Traffic Act was initiated by a series of U.S. federal legislative responses to rescue sex trafficked European and Euro-American women that began in 1875 ("The Scope of the White Slave Traffic Act" 1917). Before it was finalized in 1910, Congress included a declaration that it should be referred to as the "White Slave Traffic Act"—explicitly defining who the Act was intended to protect. The Act shaped the discourse on sex trafficking as a racialized industry. Through legal endorsement, it made a public outcry of a particular raced and gendered form of sexual slavery—the sex trafficking of Euro-American women. The passage of the Act would further "regulate interstate and foreign commerce by prohibiting the transportation therein for immoral purposes of women and girls, and for other purposes."[147] The Act also solidified the notion of human trafficking to include crossing state boundaries. The passage of the Act was a response to the public outcry against white women being trafficked. The trafficking of women from Europe is likened to the trafficking of African slaves. The language of "white slave trade" produced a dichotomy that some women are to be saved, and others are to be jailed. It is at this historical turning point during the late 1800s and early 1900s that choice is a visible aspect of the discourse on slavery and sexual economies. In 1902, the term "white slavery" was formally used at a Paris conference.[148] Clifford Roe describes the sexual slavery of Euro-Americans as dehumanizing sixty thousand people per year: "Like cattle girls are herded for the slaughter, while men like stallions prance about in their drunken revelry. Yet, there is more, there is the market, aye the 'Market for Souls,' where human beings are sold into 'Houses of Bondage.' You will find in this great awful exhibition of vice Panders and Their White Slaves."[149] Multiple stories are told of trafficked women and girls. Their surnames are absent, but their race is clear; they are white women. Without a surname, the "Fannies" and "Mildreds," with their typical American first names, represented the nation's daughters as being Euro-American and European migrants.

"White slave" discourse drew upon Yellow Peril discourse to support saving young white women from New York Chinatowns.[150] And suffragists made the case that the only way to wipe out white slavery was to enable white women to vote. Such arguments greatly contrast with the discourse about Chinese and U.S.-Mexican sexual slavery: Chinese sex slaves were denied legal status and any rights to migrate to the United States, and Mexicans were seen as zones of tolerance when citizenship was denied. Nineteenth-century sexual slavery discourses produced a gendered image of exploitation that led to the interchangeable usage of "white slave trade" and "human trafficking."

To discuss sex and trafficking in the anti-trafficking movement is to describe a movement divided. In 1973 Call Off Your Old Tired Ethics (COYOTE) formed in San Francisco under the leadership of Margo St. James.[151] COYOTE and its followers espoused the belief that prostitution should be a legitimate form of labor; that stigmatizing and prohibiting it create the problems associated with sex work. In response to the sex worker rights movement, feminists argued that prostitution and all forms of sexual exploitation exist due to men's violence against women. On April 6, 1983, in Rotterdam, a workshop attended by various feminists commenced—the International Feminist Networking Against the Traffic in Women: Organizing Against Female Sexual Slavery. Editors Kathleen Barry, Charlotte Bunch, and Shirley Castley published a collection of essays in 1984 that drew on Kathleen Barry's definition of female sexual slavery: "Present in all situations where women or girls cannot change the immediate conditions of their existence; where regardless of how they got to those conditions they cannot get out; and where they are subject to sexual violence and exploitation."[152] The workshop signified a rebirth of the abolitionist movement as a movement against all forms of sexual exploitation. The definition of female sexual slavery is significant because it illustrates that violence is not individual but, rather, systemic. This reinvigoration of the abolitionist movement perseveres today against the decriminalization of prostitution. In this regard the movement is similar to its predecessors in the 1800s led by Josephine Butler—its advocates argue that legalizing prostitution only shifts whom the pimp is. The abolitionist movement connects various experiences of oppression. Their logic is one of universalisms: there exists "one" patriarchal oppression of women. Since the 1980s, scholarly contributions by Melissa Farley and Catharine MacKinnon, and the collection of contributions in the edited volume by Christine Stark and Rebecca Whisnant, are shaping the twenty-first-century landscape of abolition revitalized. They continue to "connect radical feminist critique of pornography and prostitution with a broader social justice agenda."[153]

As U.S. feminists critiqued patriarchy as being the central axis of power, the scholarly contributions of transnational feminists characterize the limitations of an assumed singular patriarchal oppression. Kamala Kempadoo and Jo Doezema call for a more complex analysis of prostitution beyond a voluntary/involuntary dichotomy. As such, contrasting with the abolitionists, they view prostitution and sexual economies as an "income generating activity or form of labor for women and men."[154] Some scholars see critiques of sex work as a "moral panic."[155] In particular, Sanghera critiques the attention paid to prostitution in the anti-trafficking movement by using the metaphor of cooking, arguing that "'too many cooks'"—that is, scholars and activists who argue against human trafficking through integrating migration, trafficking and "sex work"— have managed to "spoil the broth, " and sometimes end up "bonking each other with their spatulas."[156] Collectively, U.S. feminist points of view, and their polarization, shape how migrants are witnessed as trafficked in sexual economies— through dualities of choice and force.

CONCLUSION

Human trafficking is more than a legal definition. In revisiting the power of the law and Proposition 35, it is no surprise that, in tracing the genealogies of human trafficking legislation and relational policies, it would pass. It would not be the first time I engaged with legislation, or the last. However, it offered an important lesson: that although human trafficking is complex, movements are not organized around the complex, and that public participants in witnessing mechanisms are not beyond their own ideological orientations. In tracing labor economies, sexual economies, and immigration, I found that the arguments made by the opponents of Proposition 35 were not legible to a California public. The appeals to complexity were insufficient to galvanize an oppositional response, when on the simplistic level nobody is for trafficking. Instead, old arguments about sexual economies, and about the erasure of labor and migration, prevailed. And a nativist response that defines the anti-trafficking "wars" persevered, an argument critiquing anti-trafficking media discourse illuminated by Felicity Amaya Schaeffer.[157] Therefore, this chapter provided the genealogies of legal events that have shaped community understandings of slavery, labor, citizenship, gender, and sexuality, to understand human trafficking not as a singular phenomenon but rather as imbricated in multiple systems.

While witnesses are called to reduce trafficking to simplistic understandings of experiences with violence that require manageable and simplistic responses—for example, more training of law enforcement officers will lead to more identifications of survivors—to trace the unfolding of the different ways that human trafficking is defined by power relations, is to understand that it is not merely a power to name categorically what constitutes human trafficking or see it as solely a social construction: what is enabled through the law are the politics of witnessing.

3 "PERFECT VICTIMS" AND LABOR MIGRATION

TO UNSETTLE WITNESSING of transnational migrant laborers who experience violence is to unpack a discussion about victimhood. Therefore, this chapter offers a way to grapple with a particular site where trafficking for labor and sex has been seen as co-occurring—domestic work. On the National Domestic Workers Alliance (NDWA) website, there is an infographic where one can "learn about human trafficking and domestic workers."[1] The infographic describes how there are eight hundred thousand-plus domestic workers in the United States, of which a majority are female (fifty-three million worldwide). Domestic workers include nannies, housekeepers, and in-home caregivers for the elderly or people with disabilities, whose duties range in an industry where contracts are not typical. The workers range from visa holders, whose visas are tied to diplomats or international officials, to those who are undocumented. A story of heroism and vulnerability circulates in transnational discourse: gender inequality, discrimination, violence, and immigration status are overlooked by law enforcement, and migrants must overcome these adversities to participate in the global economy. The infographic walks the reader through a range of myths, including one in which "human trafficking is a problem faced only by women and girls in the sex trade." The polarizations in anti-trafficking discourse create invisibility for transnational migrant laborers—for example, domestic workers who experience a range of labor violations, including trafficking. The invisibility of domestic workers who experience forms of victimization, including trafficking, points to the tensions in the anti-trafficking movement surrounding what constitutes victimhood that shows up in the form of an absence in legal archives.

Some survivors who are seen as "victims" have become notable enough to
be archived in public archives as immigrants whose experience of servitude
led them to cross the threshold of invisibility into visibility as victim subjects.
I turn to a popular archive that was intended to shape policy and advocacy—
the Human Trafficking Law Project (HTLP) database. In 2011, the Human
Trafficking Law clinic at the University of Michigan launched the HTLP database, which held 420 cases at its launch. The law clinic envisioned the project's
goal to include providing "information for advocates, lawmakers, law enforcement, governments, nongovernmental organizations, and media to use in combating human trafficking. For example, lawyers could use the information in
the database to frame their cases and research what other tactics have been
most successful in the past."[2] This archive embodied what Derrida conveys as
a gathering together of signs. The sign being conveyed in this particular type
of public legal archive is human trafficking, where bodies, numbers, categories, and short descriptions give meaning to who is a victim. Overall, there is
a strong representation of sexual economies—nearly 70 percent of the cases include the trafficking of people into sexual economies, pornography, strip clubs,
and nightclubs. Also documented and archived are the economies beyond
those that fulfill dominant imaginaries of the trafficked person as sex trafficked,
including the trafficking of people into agriculture, domestic servitude, hair/
nail salons, the health industry, the hotel industry, military contracted labor,
peddling/begging rings, and the restaurant/bar industry, where open industry
in particular shows up visibly: domestic servitude represents half of all the
cases archived as labor trafficking. A singular industry that facilitates a care
economy, domestic work is an industry where trafficking is known to occur.
What are the perceptions of victimhood in industries where victims are commonly seen as legal industries?

On face value, the common perception suggests that trafficking into domestic servitude continues to comprise immigrant women of color. Although
the HTLP database was filled with diverse cases, people perceived of as victims of trafficking are predominantly from Mexico (13.6%), Indonesia (10.6%),
India (9.1%), the Philippines (9.1%), Nigeria (6.1%), Cameroon (6.1%), and Peru
(4.5%). And Asians and Latinas/os/x are trafficked to a diversity of states; however, such victims follow established survival circuits that are linked to major
global cities;[3] people trafficked into domestic servitude are visibly found in
California and New York, with the second highest representation in Texas
and Florida. This information is not surprising; it reflects existing, common

immigration routes. In spite of their diverse national origins, women continue to be represented predominantly as victims of human trafficking.

To further conceptualize victimhood and servitude, I draw upon discourse analysis of news, press releases, and media articles, legal analysis of court records, and notes from public court hearings. The two cases analyzed in this chapter represent domestic servitude and trafficking. I address how perceptions of victimhood impact understandings of human trafficking that are furthered by notions of choice. As a domestic worker's value is predicated on their ability to work in the shadows and behind closed doors, invisible to their employers, some have moved into visibility as victims of human trafficking.[4] What are the conditions that enable some victims of human trafficking to be seen as "perfect victims"? How does their valuation as perfect victims depend on a furtherance of the perception of domestic workers as nonhuman, devalued workers? Between 2000 and 2015, immigrants perceived of as victims trafficked into domestic servitude were primarily Asians and Latinas—a woman of color, "she" is defined by notions of "perfect victimhood." To make sense of the construction of the perfect victim, I examine three conceptions through case samples: (1) the "illegal" immigrant, (2) the victim whose narrative creates a disjuncture in the metanarrative of human trafficking discourse, and (3) the meaning of choice. The invitation to contend with victimhood does not mean that the goal of this chapter is to define true victimhood. Rather, it is to offer an applied way of analyzing how transnational migrant domestic workers are witnessed as victims in discourse and the law, where victimhood is predicated on the perception of their ability to enact choice. Transnational migrant subjectivities are dependent on notions of victimhood that further dualities and colonial logics. Therefore, this chapter offers two case studies as exemplars: one of coethnic violence (a Filipina trafficked by a Filipina) and the other of interracial violence (a Filipina trafficked by a Euro-American couple). In both case examples, the primary victim of focus in the media is a Filipina. This matters for understanding how notions of victimhood are constructed through an alleged (and in these cases, convicted) trafficker of the same national origins and racialization in the United States. Through the differing examples—a trafficker of the same national origins as the survivor in one case (the case of Cindy) and differing national origins between the survivor and trafficker in the other case (the case of Tess)—what is illuminated is how notions of "good" and "bad" immigrants are implicitly reified by the legal status and perception of the trafficker. It is central to pay attention to racialization and gendering in

human trafficking. Coethnic exploitation illuminates the complicity of violence within transnational economies—where the racial formation of the migrant laborers continues to operate through the normalizing of migrants in
low-wage labor industries. And what are reified are the racialized structures
that are furthered through perceptions of a "good immigrant" and "bad immigrant." This is further reified in differences surrounding class and legal status,
which should be contrasted with homosocial violence, when women traffic
women. While countries may depend on sending their citizens abroad, racialization in labor industries makes precarious migrant labor an everyday aspect
in the United States. Racialized migrant precarity is institutionally sustained
through laws, as well as an aspect of how racialized labor manifests in the
everyday. Sustaining such institutionalization and everyday-ness of migrant
labor precarity depends on community silence, and sometimes even community complicity. The cases explored here are named the case studies of Cindy
and Tess, which both are useful for microanalysis of the transnational structures
that facilitate human trafficking from the Philippines to the United States.

SERVITUDE, THE LAW, AND VICTIMHOOD

Differing concepts of victimhood exist in U.S. discourse include the notions
of the ideal victim, the pathetic victim, and the heroic victim. The 1960s witnessed the visibility of a particular type of victim—the vulnerable victim.[5] Diana Tietjens Meyers contends that two victim paradigms emerged in the
twentieth century due to the international human rights regime—the pathetic
victim and the heroic victim.[6] The notion of an ideal victim as a particular constructed type emerged out of the work of Nils Christie.[7] The ideal victim
maintains the binary assumption that some victims are undeserving of the
exploitation, and others deserve their victimization.[8] Walklate offers a sociohistorical development of the victim as tied to criminal activities, which suggests that individuals become victims through policy and social terms.[9] "Ideal
victims" are also constructed through narratives in the media. However,
I find legal scholar Jayashri Srikantiah useful for situating victimhood with
the language of "perfect." Srikantiah validates how the iconic anti-trafficking
victimhood is tethered to the perfect victim.[10] A perfect victim is perceived of as
lacking agency and as innocent of participating in criminal activity. The language of perfect victim is useful in that it automatically offers an assumption of
being a perfect victim, or not a victim at all. The "ideal" victim as passive does
not fit the current dominant discourses about human trafficking in legal and

media discourse. A perfect victim is not dependent on the victim's ability to construct a narrative of trafficking. The burden of proof falls upon the witness of victimhood (i.e., on the case worker, the law enforcement officer, or the health-care provider) to effectively identify this person as a human trafficking victim.

The categorization of a trafficked person as a "perfect victim" is signified by anti-trafficking discourse and has discursive power shaping an anti-trafficking movement. Here I draw upon Roland Barthes's concept of the semiological system. This system comprises language and metalanguages that give meaning to concepts such as "victim."[11] Trafficker, trafficked, and human trafficking are relationally described by and inextricably linked to other forms of violence. (Child abuse, physical/psychological abuse, and domestic violence intersect with human trafficking.[12]) And multiple institutions participate in anti-trafficking initiatives that solidify the perception of a perfect victim as a status quo so as to simplify and make sense of an already abstract image. As such, media images of physical abuse experienced by victims are problematic, in that they sustain simplistic understandings of human trafficking. For example, historian Micheline Lessard describes human trafficking at the China-Vietnam border and the image of kidnapped victims as not new and as historically defined.[13] To understand the constitution of a perfect victim calls for a critiquing of narratives and a situating of the multiple systems that impact meaning and the social and legal structures that further racialized and gendered experiences. Human trafficking is also facilitated by the push-pull factors that necessitate one to migrate: economic reasons, dislocations stemming from war, famine, limited employment, and cultural reasons.[14] These factors also impact domestic U.S. citizens trafficked within the United States who are pulled to migrate in search of love, work, family, and community. The push-pull factors of migration are useful for situating migrants in a transnational structure, even though they do not enable an understanding of individual desires, hopes, and concerns.[15] Push-pull factors of migration are also not static—they change constantly as the meaning and context of migrant lives shift.

In spite of the complex reasons why one migrates, an important disjuncture occurs with law enforcement officers' encounters with migrants. Migrants' narratives are dependent on their construction as innocent and therefore perfect. To be anything else is risky in a climate of anti-immigration. This is due to the conflation of trafficked migrants with "illegal" migration. Notions of legality/illegality are determined by the nation-state.[16] If the "illegal" migrant is contextualized by nation-states, then U.S. ideologies and practices create tension for victims of human trafficking by perpetuating an ideological standard of the perfect victim. For the international victim of exploitation, the stakes are high. The consequence of not being a perfect victim exacerbates vulnerabilities of being seen as a criminal (e.g., committing visa fraud is a felony) and therefore deportable or barred from reentry. Anti-immigration policies such as the IIRIRA 1996 affirm that the United States is tough on immigrants who commit acts deemed criminal under federal laws; these individuals risk being barred permanently from reentry to the United States.[17] Criminalization for the undocumented migrant means that Homeland Security Intelligence may subject them to conditions "as severe as we apply to our worst criminals."[18] Treatment of transnational migrants is then characterized by debates about moral character and proving that one is a perfect victim, not debates about human rights.

The case studies of Cindy and Tess illustrate the types of intimacy that are archived as perfect victimhood. They embody the commodification of intimacy, defined by Nicole Constable as "the ways in which intimacy or intimate relations can be treated, understood, or thought of as if they have entered the market: are bought or sold; packaged and advertised; fetishized, commercialized, or objectified; consumed or assigned values and prices; and linked in many cases to transnational mobility and migration, echoing a global capitalist flow of goods."[19] Intimate labor is work for an employer in which there is personal, face-to-face contact, and in which the worker fulfills the needs of the recipient.[20] For Cindy, it is as a domestic worker; Tess bridges the gap between domestic work and sexual economies. I have selected these cases due to the need to juxtapose similar yet different forms of trafficking within a single ethnic group (in this case, Filipina survivors). Their different public reception is due to the racializing logics of victimhood and criminality. Cindy's case, where her trafficker was also a Filipina, widely circulated in the media. In contrast, Tess's traffickers were white U.S. citizens, convicted for illegally harboring "an alien." This enables an understanding of perfect victims as racialized subjects even when their exploitation is homosocial, without reducing trafficking to a particular group—the same conditions that create victims, create traffickers. However, context is central to understanding how victimhood is deeply racial. Therefore, what follows is a setting of the context of the cases—U.S.-Philippine relations.

SETTING THE STAGE: THE SERVICE SECTOR, THE GLOBAL
ECONOMY, AND HUMAN TRAFFICKING

The Philippines is a major exporter of people. Filipinas/os emigrate for work to countries such as the United States, Japan, the United Arab Emirates, and Hong Kong.[21] How the Philippines figures into the global economy is historically shaped by relationships to locational centers in countries that are located in the Global North.[22] California frames the landscape of migration flows between the United States and countries in Asia and Latin America. The flow of Filipino migrants and material goods from the Philippines to East Asia, the Americas, and Europe dates to the 1500s.[23]

The Philippines has historical significance for the United States and its expansion of its territories, resources, and imperial nation building. U.S. colonial authority over the Philippines was solidified in 1898 with the signing of the Treaty of Paris, by which the Philippines, Guam, Puerto Rico, and Cuba became U.S. territories. This treaty redefined U.S. relations in the Asia-Pacific. At the turn of the twentieth century, the Philippines had a new meaning for the United States.

The passage of the 1934 Tydings McDuffie Act signified Philippines independence and also located Filipinas/os as perpetual foreigners in the United States. The treatment of Filipinos in the United States is connected to U.S. history of colonization of the Americas and treatment of people of color as second-class citizens in general. The treatment of Filipinos and the demand for their labor in the United States is reflective of what Aime Cesairé characterizes as the relationship between the colonizer and the colonized. The colonized are the "instrument(s) of production."[24] The United States no longer formally colonizes the Philippines; however, the manifestations of colonial relations persevere, where the "migrant flow of domestic workers suggests a contemporary colonial trade relationship with countries economically disenfranchised [like the Philippines], sending neither raw materials nor manufactured goods, but rather a [female] labor supply of [care] workers to richer countries."[25]

The twenty-first-century image of Filipinos is as transnational migrants— Filipinos are constantly on the move. In 1960, 104,843 Philippine-born individuals lived in the United States. By 2008, Filipinos in the United States numbered 1,684,802 (an increase of approximately 1,507 percent).[26] In 2014, the U.S. Census confirmed that California hosted the highest numbers of Philippine-born nationals—43 percent of the Filipino population in the United States.[27]

Analyzing the care chain of domestic work is useful, and I broaden it to include a chain that is determined by exploitation—the human trafficking chain. There is a demand for Filipinos in laboring industries. The production sites for Filipinos are traceable in global care chains, "a series of personal links between people across the globe based on the paid or unpaid work of caring."[28]

Domestic work and care industries, and the relationship such industries have to exploitation, is a part of the U.S. cultural ideological landscape. This is apparent in recent media representations. The media coverage of demands for the "helping hand" as caregivers, maids, and nannies is embedded in U.S. cultural productions such as films,[29] television shows,[30] and cartoons.[31] It is also manifest in "real-life" incidents that fall under public scrutiny in major newspapers and newscasts. In 2011, Dominique Strauss-Kahn, former chief of the International Monetary Fund, was accused of raping a hotel worker from West Africa in a New York hotel.[32] Celebrity cases such as Kobe Bryant allegedly raping a hotel worker,[33] and Arnold Schwarzenegger having a sexual relationship with a domestic worker during the worker's employment within his home, perpetuate images of women of color as laboring and sexually pleasing.[34] Maid cases illustrate the treatment of women of color in service sectors and the consequences when immigrant workers speak publicly about their experiences of sex/abuse. The image of domestic workers as a threat to their female employers or as passive and (sexually) available, evokes that domestic work is not merely about labor but also carries cultural norms and assumptions about intimacy and sex. This image of intimacy and sex demands of Filipinas stems from the 1980s. Neferti Tadiar describes the beginning of Ferdinand Marcos's authoritarian regime in the following terms: "In this misogynist, homophobic and racist worldview, pussy is not only what the Philippines *has,* it is what the Philippines *is.*"[35] The United States' presence in the Philippines led to the development of sexual economies around U.S. military bases.[36] Tadiar describes U.S.-Philippine relations as the "prostitution of the nation" (i.e., the Philippines) through feminized labor.[37] The "prostitution of the Philippines" is not simply about Filipina women working in sexual economies; it is also symbolic of the status of the Philippines in the global economy and its relation to other countries, where such labor is sexualized and bound to notions of criminality. Although sex work is criminalized in the United States, it is contained by zones of tolerance. Likewise, migrant domestic workers are bound to notions of legality and criminalization due to their legal status and informalized work. It is illustrative of the feminized commodification of migrant and Filipino labor.

Similarly, the prostitution of Hawai'i as being equated with cultural dominance and commodification of culture through tourism has been used to describe colonial relations in the late twentieth century.[38] Because the term "prostitution" has varying meanings and constructs, I situate it as being deeply tied to gendered labor, transnational economies, and power relations that unequally shape individuals and collectives. In some contexts, it is criminalized; in others, it is tolerated or legalized. Filipinas represent feminized labor through their participation in informal economies such as domestic work and sexual economies.

The discourse surrounding Filipinas/os working abroad is bound to contrasting images as heroes to the Philippine global economy[39] and as subjects vulnerable to exploitation in global markets. E. San Juan Jr. provides a snapshot of the scope and the dangers: "Over four million more leave, without proper/legal travel and work permits, for unknown destinations. About 3–5 coffins of these [Oversea Filipino Workers] arrive at the Manila International Airport everyday. Obviously the reason is not for adventure or tourism, or even for an exciting, less constrained life."[40] The number of Filipinas pushed to work abroad increased due to the lack of viable opportunities in the Philippines. In 2009, seventy-one thousand Filipinas left the country to work as workers or helpers in private households; they made up 21 percent of the newly hired in the top ten job categories abroad.[41] As Filipina migrants filled jobs demanding cheap labor, U.S. anti-immigration sentiment solidified, as represented in the passage of policies such as Senate Bill 1070, the IIRIRA 1996, and California's Proposition 187, suggesting that migrants were free to work in the United States (and were desired as laborers), albeit with limited rights. The lack of support systems in U.S. governmental and nongovernmental institutions creates and sustains vulnerabilities for workers and immigrants traveling abroad. These vulnerabilities have led to notable trends of immigrants experiencing violence such as maltreatment, sexual harassment, rape, and human trafficking. Not only are individuals impacted by transnational violence; their families are too, when workers sustain separation from their family—there are two million children left behind in the Philippines without mothers. In particular, these vulnerabilities are apparent in limited upward mobility and lack of diverse job opportunities. Some migrants are exploited anew after initially having left their trafficking experience because the industries they are trafficked into are the same industries they are recruited into and/or demanded for as cheap, affordable, exploitable labor.[42]

Exploitive industries produce what is referred to as a "slavery footprint" across nation-state boundaries. A slavery footprint is a pattern of systemic violence that may be traced transnationally through multiple ideological institutions. It is similar to other systems that map footprints, such as the carbon footprint of U.S. militarisms. The imprints are not merely the acts of violence; like a footprint in the sand, the legacies may be viewed where traces of a perceived origin may be tracked in some cases, and in others wash away. Some steps are so patterned and systematic that they produce a clear path. These footprints are exemplified by global economic industries (i.e., sex and labor). According to the 2011 TIP report, a strategy for countries to prevent human trafficking occurs through "acknowledging and addressing its own 'slavery footprint,'—government procurement of goods made and services provided on the backs of forced laborers—each government can drastically shift the economic policies that perpetuate modern slavery."[43] However, to address the conditions leading to human trafficking, policy impacting local and global economies is only one strand of the matrix of conditions that lead to exploitation. The status of a country's human rights policies cannot be separated from the multifaceted constitution of practices that also create vulnerabilities surrounding labor and migration.

Beginning each year, the United States evaluates countries for their response to human trafficking.[44] Countries placed in Tier 3 are ranked as such because it is ascertained that they do not comply with the minimum standards of addressing human trafficking and are not making meaningful attempts to do so.[45] The U.S. Department of State perceives the Philippines as a top ten country of origin for victims of human trafficking. In fiscal year 2010, the Philippines was listed as one of the top ten countries of origin for foreign victims.[46] In 2011, the Philippines moved up in the TIP ratings from Tier 3 Watch to Tier 2. Although the Philippines is improving in its anti-trafficking responses, the country's success depends on how it is figured in the global economy in an era when it is referred to as a postcolonial state. The current Philippine regime, the Duterte government, is perceived of as stamping out trafficking.[47] While the Duterte government is perceived as sympathetic to addressing violence abroad, the government's "war on drugs" has led to 6,200 deaths, unexplained killings from police operations, and vigilantes being reported in 2017.[48]

What follows is a nuanced reading of systemic violence through different forms of trafficking—labor and sex. Both cases are exemplary of transnational violence that is normalized by a pattern of U.S.-Philippine relations; however, within the U.S. context, they differ in how their victimhood as trafficking subjects is constructed.

CINDY AND TESS

The two cases analyzed (Cindy and Tess) in this chapter illuminate how immigrants are constructed as perfect victims.[49] Cindy and Tess are both recognized as human trafficking victims, and both survivors were recognized as human trafficking victims by federal authorities. (Law enforcement recognized Cindy's victimization, and Tess received immigration relief as a victim of human trafficking.) The outcomes of the two cases diverged greatly: Cindy's abuser was recognized as a trafficker, while Tess's abusers were recognized as human smugglers. In the legal sense, human trafficking differs from smuggling: trafficking is legally understood as a crime against a person, whereas smuggling is an evasion of a country's immigration laws.[50] As Cindy's narrative became headline news, Tess's story was altogether invisible to the public at large, as there was no media coverage of her trafficking. In the public profile of Cindy's case, where a Filipina trafficked a Filipina, I examine Cindy and Tess and their experiences of exploitation as a *perfect victim* and an *imperfect victim* respectively. Both cases offer insights into how the law and media produce racial constructions.[51]

THE CASE OF CINDY: THE "PERFECT" VICTIM

Thelma Gutierrez, CNN Correspondent (voice-over): From New York to Los Angeles, a secret labor force is hard at work in the fields, garment shops, restaurants, even in some homes. We're not just talking about undocumented workers.

Dan Stormer, Ruiz's Attorney: Slavery is alive and well. Trafficking of slaves is alive and well.

Gutierrez: We're talking about modern-day slaves living and working in this country without pay and against their will.[52]

The interview between Dan Stormer, one of the prosecuting attorneys who represented the human trafficking survivor Cindy,[53] and CNN correspondent Thelma Guttierrez portrays human trafficking as impacting the United States from coast to coast. In this high-profile human trafficking case, a married couple (whom I will refer to as the Jacksons) fell under public and legal scrutiny.

They were prosecuted for trafficking a Filipina, Cindy, into domestic servitude. Their case made headline news in 2004.[54] Mr. Jackson was the former vice president of legal affairs at Sony Pictures. Less visible in the media was his wife, Mrs. Jackson, also a Filipina; in a survey of the media coverage, Mrs. Jackson's national origin is only identified in Filipino media networks.[55] In contrast, Cindy is clearly described in the U.S. media as Filipina. Cindy is a former schoolteacher who was brought to work in the Jackson's home in Culver City, California, in 2001.[56] Her migration to California led her to leave her children behind in the small village where she had grown up in the Philippines.[57] Cindy embodied a transnational motherhood that is transformed for migrant laborers, whose spatial and temporal separations from family lead them to create new meanings about motherhood.[58] Although Mrs. Jackson was also a Filipina, she differed in her class location to Cindy; this class difference between the employee and the employer exacerbated the power dynamics and exploitation.[59] In 2018, Cindy published her own story in *The Atlantic*, where the power dynamics between herself and her employer are delineated through words describing Mrs. Jackson as "influential" and "prominent."[60] Michael J. Gennaco, a member of the board of directors of the Coalition to Abolish Slavery and Trafficking (CAST), the organization that aided Cindy, describes the significance of class: "Class differences . . . are used by traffickers to exploit victims."[61] Cindy left her abusers a year after her employment in 2002. Thereafter, in 2003, a lawsuit was filed by Cindy's attorney against the Jacksons for involuntary servitude, violation of the California Labor Code, false imprisonment, and invasion of privacy.

Cindy fits the bill of a "perfect victim" due to the visibility of force, fraud, and coercion in her trafficking experience. The fate of the Jacksons in 2004 depended on whether a jury would find them guilty for exploiting sixty-year-old Cindy into domestic slavery through force, fraud, and/or coercion (the elements needed to legally prove human trafficking). On August 25, 2004, a front-page headline in the *Santa Monica Daily Press* read, "'Slave' Case Rests in the Hands of Jury." Cindy's experience encompassed all elements of force, fraud, and coercion. She had been brought to the United States on false pretenses. Originally, she had been offered a job as a traveling companion and caretaker for the Jacksons' mother. Instead, she had been immediately transferred to the Jackson home to be a maid.[62] A central part of her story that circulated, even in her own narration of her experiences, was how she had been forced to "sleep on a dog bed and work long hours"[63] and how, after a year during which she had toiled for eighteen hours a day, she had been paid only three hundred dollars. In the sentencing of the Jacksons, U.S. District Judge Dale Fisher opined, "It seems [Mrs. Jackson] treated her dog much better than she treated her victim."[64] Cindy's victimization is central to the power dynamics that impact the relationship between traffickers and trafficked. Their difference is portrayed in media coverage of the court hearings: "[Cindy] dressed in a blue suit, looked down through most the closing arguments on Tuesday, while [Mrs.] Jackson sat upright and seldom glanced at the jury."[65]

The use of force and coercion, central factors of human trafficking, were described in the case. Cindy's experience also constituted force, in which she underwent other abuses, including never being taken to a doctor[66] and being physically abused by Mrs. Jackson, who was said to have regularly slapped and pulled her employee's hair.[67] Additionally, Cindy was coerced to stay in her exploitive situation. The Jacksons frequently threatened to call the police and immigration authorities, telling Cindy that she would be "locked up" and would "never see her family again."[68] Cindy's experience embodied the image of exploitation. During her employment with the Jacksons, she was neither mobile nor free to move without surveillance, and she was isolated—talking with other people was discouraged.[69] The turning point for Cindy occurred in February 2002, when she was hit in the mouth with a water bottle during an incident with Elizabeth Jackson, after which Cindy fled to a neighbor's house to ask for help.[70]

Cindy is perceived of as a "perfect victim" because the prosecutor was able to convict one of her traffickers on human trafficking charges (forced labor), which suggests the case was without a doubt human trafficking. The image of a perfect victim is dictated by assumptions about immigration, and how the experience fits into a larger anti-trafficking narrative. The fact that prosecutors are able to close a human trafficking case like Cindy's with human trafficking charges implies that the legal system sees such cases as perfect-victim cases. The charges against the Jacksons sent a message about acceptable and unacceptable exploitation: certain illegal types of exploitation lead to heavier penalties, while acceptable exploitation results in a lower conviction or in no conviction or, in some cases, in fines. Charges against Mr. Jackson were dismissed except for charges of illegal harboring of an alien,[71] reifying that acceptable forms of exploitation encompass hiring a domestic worker at exploitable wages. However, harboring an undocumented person in your home is a crime. The penalties for Mr. Jackson illuminated that while it was crime, it was a crime of white benevolence. That is, Mr. Jackson was ordered to perform two hundred hours' community service and to pay a fine of five thousand dollars, illuminating that his only crime was to have aided an undocumented migrant.[72] Mr. Jackson was convicted for allowing Cindy to work in their home, even though he knew that Cindy's visa had expired. It was the relationship between Mrs. Jackson and Cindy that defined the experience as trafficking.

In contrast to the community service Mr. Jackson received, Mrs. Jackson faced forty-six months in prison on charges of forced labor.[73] Mrs. Jackson's identity and criminality were absent from the U.S. media coverage, which focused on her role as wife and her origins from Tacoma, Washington.[74] This contrasted with the images of her circulating in Philippine news, which described her as a Pinay (a Filipina).[75] In the civil case, Cindy was awarded $825,000 in damages.[76] Her lawyer is quoted as saying in response to restitution, "You can't give her dignity back, but our system deals in dollars. Can it be $1 million? Yes. Can it be $2 million? Yes." Although it could have been $2 million, Cindy was awarded less. Prior to the case going to trial, the Jacksons filed for bankruptcy,[77] so Cindy is not guaranteed to see any of the money, as there are no assets or money to pull from. After two and half weeks of trial, the case was closed.[78]

Not only is Cindy constructed as a perfect victim; she is also the heroic victim. The *Manila Times* placed a positive spin on the outcome by declaring that "the decision puts exploitative employers on notice that their abuse of domestic help will not be tolerated."[79] Her case is symbolic of the standards to which other employers are held—those who traffic, like Cindy's employers, will not be tolerated. But not only is Cindy a model for employer-employee relations (and what happens when one goes against the terms of agreement), but also her figuring is defined by nationalist discourse. Cindy, as a transnational migrant laborer, would have been a hero even if she had not won her case. Cindy is an overseas Filipino worker, and the Philippine government sees workers like her as "new national heroes" due to their essential role in the economic and political stability in the Philippines.[80] In 1974 the Philippines enacted an official policy to combat domestic unemployment through supporting overseas Filipino workers. In 2008 it was estimated that 8.7 million migrants from the Philippines sent back to the Philippines more than twelve billion dollars.[81] The focus on statistics renders migrants abstract, faceless objects of study, an objectification that disables an understanding of migrants as multidimensional agents. Cindy is positioned as a heroic victim because of her role as a "new hero" for the Philippines, and as a hero for other survivors trafficked in the United States.

In the *Sacramento Bee* she is quoted as saying, "Slavery still exists, and I want to tell victims they should not tolerate it and should not be afraid to seek help."[82] Cindy participates in anti-trafficking discourse and the movement's call to rescue victims. Survivor testimonials are central to events where the self-witness can testify about their experiences to a public, whether in court, in the news, or in a public forum such as a conference. Albeit an important mechanism of witnessing, survivor testimonials are also politicized when they serve as central figures in nationalist discourse for both their countries of origin and the destination country. The heroism of the survivor turns transnational migrant laborers into superhumans who are expected by the dominant society to be able to persevere through a range of conditions. As they send remittances home, they do so at the cost of their own safety, never quite belonging in the United States.

Cindy is portrayed as a perfect victim because her narrative is dependent on her portrayal as being helpless at the time of victimization—law enforcement officers and NGOs are portrayed as her rescuers, even though she fled her own exploitation. Similar to other trafficking narratives, the role of law enforcement in combating human trafficking is clear. Julie Myers, Homeland Security Assistant Secretary for ICE, says that her agency's goal is to "send a message to those who traffic in human beings that ICE is committed to protecting those who cannot protect themselves." And CAST has made visible their role in helping Cindy to become a certified nursing assistant (CNA).[83] Such retraining for another occupation is depicted as crucial for survivors of human trafficking to take steps towards healing. However, Denise Brennan has described CNA training as improper and nursing assistant as a job that is perceived to lead "nowhere"—where migrant laborers "break [their] back for minimum wage. . . . They could be making more money and getting benefits at Starbucks!"[84]

Trafficking to the United States is rendered visible by cases that are able to fit the definition of involving individuals whose "choices" have been denied. Cindy's lack of choices made her a perfect victim. Her visible lack of choice was dictated by the force, fraud, and coercion she experienced, which kept her in her exploitation for a year. Immigration status impacts whether one is seen as a perfect victim; Cindy's age and her limited English set the stage for her to be seen as a perfect victim in need of rescue.[85] The case was dependent not only on the violence that Cindy experienced but also on the fact that she was constituted as an illegal migrant. She was able to illustrate how she illegally migrated, even though it was not by her own volition. As the story unravels, it is clear that what is integral to Cindy's narrative is her victimization.

Cases like Cindy's are exemplary of the normalization of a laboring third-world poor existing in major U.S. cities. Annalisa Enrile, Gabriela Network USA chairperson, best describes the systemic nature of the transnational dynamics of exploitation flow when she says, "I think it's to our benefit that we are made aware that things like this are not only done by menacing foreigners."[86] Discussions about transnational mothering are absent in Cindy's narrative in the media and legal discourse. Her physical absence from her own home and children necessitates new modes of showing a motherhood through remittances and gifts, telephone calls, and long-distance support systems.[87] Scholarly illustrations of migrant mothers focus on transnational motherhood through the context of migration, separation, and reunification. For someone like Cindy to leave her children behind as a means to support her family by increasing her income through remittances, reifies perceptions of her being an even "better mother" who is willing to go to great lengths to support her family. Cindy, therefore, is not only a survivor of human trafficking, but her story furthers a narrative of a sacrificing migrant. To understand perfect victimhood is to frame a narrative where absent mothers and family separation are a central part of the transnational migrant experience. The normalization of the separation of transnational migrant laborers from their families furthers what Cecilia Menjívar describes as "legal violence." In 2018, the image of the Trump administration forcibly separating migrant children from their parents was part of a larger practice of the cumulative effects of injuries from the law.[88] Cindy, and survivors like her, are not set up for automatic job success as decontextualized laboring migrants. This creates the conditions of vulnerability when they migrate. However, it is through transnational ties within communities and connections that a life after trafficking is possible.

In 2018, Cindy told her own story, "I Am a Survivor of Human Trafficking," in *The Atlantic*, a multiplatform United States-based magazine.[89] It was when she was introduced to Pilipino Workers Center (PWC) that her "life then changed." She received housing, food stamps, access to a doctor, a bus pass to navigate the city, and support from CAST. The public learns about Cindy's life after trafficking—eventually she became a CNA, and by the time she was seventy-four, she retired in the Philippines and remained an active member of PWC, raising awareness about workers' rights. But her happiest moment was "in 2013, years after [she] left the Philippines, [she] was finally reunited with

[her] husband, [her] children, and [her grandchildren]."[90] The life of struggle that transnational trafficked migrants face continues after a life of trafficking—forging ties where they live, work, worship, and volunteer to form a social network that many do not have.[91] As illustrated in Cindy's testimony in *The Atlantic*, the narratives of the affective space to create community and cultural membership for transnational migrants as a resistant strategy to exploitation are highlighted in the ability for migrants to collectively facilitate adaptive and resilient strategies. Although Cindy's community was in the Philippines, she fostered a new one in the United States through PWC. Although she could not belong in the United States, she did nurture a form of belonging, through her connections with Philippine organizations, and she maintained transnational ties to her family. To highlight her resilience and complex identities even after trafficking is to witness beyond her victimhood, even as the narratives continue to frame her as a "perfect" victim. Therefore, while Cindy figured into perfect victimhood, Tess represented the antithesis of a perfect-victim narrative.

THE CASE OF TESS: CHALLENGING THE PERFECT-VICTIM STEREOTYPE

Even as Cindy embodied a perfect victim, a hero, and a subject of struggle and resilience, Tess illuminates the complexity of what it means to be a "victim." The case that will never make headline news is the case of the *United States v. Lundbergs*.[92] In a survey of the media coverage, to date, no media coverage of the case exists. This case highlights the ongoing invisibilities of sexual exploitation and servitude of domestic workers, in which the Lundbergs allegedly trafficked a Filipina, "Tess," into California but were convicted on charges of illegal harboring of an alien.

"The Lundbergs" are a married couple and have been married since 1969.[93] Prior to being convicted, the husband was an attorney and former police officer and his wife, a schoolteacher. Upper-middle-class whites living in the Bay Area of California, they also had what the courts referred to as a "sexually extroverted lifestyle." As sex tourists to the Philippines, the Lundbergs recruited Tess to work as a domestic worker in their home in California for a nominal amount of money.[94] Tess grew up in an impoverished town in the Philippines that necessitated her working in karaoke bars to support herself and her family.

The case of Tess departs from common narratives of labor exploitation and domestic servitude in the public discourse, where choice determined victimhood. The defendant's Sentencing Memorandum suggested that sexual contact with Tess was "consensual" and should be stricken from the record. Consent and sexuality create contested meanings surrounding human trafficking into laboring economies that are tied to sex. While the United Nations' definition of human trafficking conveys that one can be trafficked regardless of consent, U.S. understandings reinscribe choice into human trafficking. Whether a person is sex trafficked, labor trafficked, or sex and labor trafficked, perfect victims are historically understood as those who lack choices. As part of their evidence, family members of the Lundbergs submitted supporting documents to show that Tess was treated "like part of the family" and that her experience with coercion was "doubtful." In the closing of the case hearing, it was judged that:

> In spite of backgrounds that suggest they should have known better, the defendants fraudulently brought [Tess] to this country for the nominal purpose of performing domestic duties in the defendants' home. While [Tess] had advance notice of the defendants' sexually extroverted lifestyle, the defendants took advantage of the situation and quickly and frequently integrated [Tess] into their sexual lifestyle. The government recognizes that there exists considerable dispute as to the frequency of these sexual interactions and the degree of pressure placed upon [Tess]. The defendants' actions were undoubtedly exploitative, especially when considered in the context of [Tess's] background and the defendants' stature in the United States. Nevertheless, it is *not* accurate to characterize the defendants' actions as coercing the victim to partake in their sexual activities through force or threats.

That they "should have known better" suggests competency, familiarity with the law, and even intention. However, they were never convicted of human trafficking, only of "illegally harboring an alien," leading one to read the problematic lesson at hand—the Lundbergs should have known better than to harbor an undocumented immigrant in their home. In the judgment of the case, the facts are described as "lurid and indicative of exploitation," and a picture of Tess's participation as someone who was "integrated into their sexual lifestyles" muddied the boundary between a victim and someone complicit in their treatment. Tess's exploitation could not be proven in the criminal case, and the Lundbergs were never convicted or even charged with trafficking charges. Even though Tess received a T-Visa,[95] which is a visa that victims of human trafficking are able to apply for, the decision to prosecute for human trafficking or not is dictated by the evidence: careful interviews of witnesses and survivors,[96] photos,[97] signifiers of exploitation that are captured and held onto by a survivor, whether it is marking the day of abuse on a calendar[98] or the paper tracking of money owed and not paid. T-Visas are received through immigration legal systems, whereas the Lundbergs were prosecuted through a criminal legal system, where the decisions of a criminal court are not dependent on whether a survivor received immigration relief as a trafficking survivor. Seemingly contradictory, the case illuminates the multiply complex legal systems that transnational migrant survivors may navigate—legal systems surrounding immigration, civil law, criminal law, and family law. On August 5, 2009, the Lundbergs pled guilty to one account of harboring an illegal alien for the purpose of private financial gain, and the survivor was awarded $2,400 in restitution.[99] The case of Tess and the Lundbergs is not a legal trafficking case; it is an immigration case. The plea could have emerged for a variety of reasons—it was not whether or not trafficking had occurred, but rather, whether or not it could be proven criminally without a doubt. The doubt painted by the defense was enough for the trafficking case to fall into a quasi-status.

What is illuminated by this particular case study is that while a person may be considered a trafficking victim for their immigration case, it does not guarantee them a successful criminal or civil case. Research on human trafficking prosecutions affirms that in spite of the legal attention paid to human trafficking, low numbers of prosecutions persist,[100] although here I am not making a case for increasing anti-trafficking prosecutions. Rather, I am pointing to the reality that there is a disjuncture—even when "victims" are found, prosecutions are not guaranteed. Amy Farrell et al. attribute the low numbers of prosecutions to a lack of awareness by law enforcement agents and attorneys and to ongoing issues with law enforcement and prosecutors "victim" blaming or dismissing survivors as not credible.[101]

If restitution is a representation of the severity of money owed for wages and the harm from abuse, for Tess, the money appeared not to add up. Tess experienced fraud, in that she was promised employment as a domestic worker for a salary of $200 per month for domestic housekeeping duties.[102] The $2,400 Tess was awarded was for "the loss of wages for her partner because of the child care situation, and a BART-related expense."[103] Although Tess was identified as a "victim" of human trafficking by the Office of Refugee and Resettlement, the criminal proceeding could not prove that her sexual exploitation was coercive. Therefore, the only area of contention in the eyes of the courts was back wages owed her for her work as a domestic worker and the possibility of money for mental health services. It was never questioned that had she worked full-time, forty hours a week, and the wages owed were not just nominal, they were below the minimum wage of $8 an hour for $1,280 per month;[104] $200 per month of pay was never questioned and only referred to as "nominal." Human trafficking is not merely abuse, because oftentimes another person is profiting off of the labor, sex, or servitude of another person. In cases involving restitution for labor, restitution cannot be defined merely by wages owed for labor. A financial reparation for wage labor is limiting, especially for cases in which there is no labor to compensate for, just the psychological trauma that follows exploitation and the loss of connection to community and time. Jessica Goldsberry, a probation officer, supported the defense and prosecution by stating that "she doesn't want to talk to anybody right now. She doesn't think it will help right now." Goldsberry summarized Tess's statement: "I don't want people to know all of my problems. No one in my family has received counseling or therapy. They can't afford it." Tess's statements did not assert that she did not want therapy; rather, they implied a cultural disconnect with what therapy meant and her financial inability to access therapy even if it were offered.

Sex played out in Tess's case in ways that reified notions of who counts as a victim—survivors who can show without a doubt that they have been sexually coerced. While the goal is not to reinscribe Tess as a victim, the questions this chapter grapples with is whether she could ever be witnessed as a "perfect victim," and what the constraints were on witnessing her experience with exploitation as victimization. Tess did not represent "perfect victimhood," because of her ability to "choose" to migrate and her knowledge of the Lundberg's "sexually extroverted lifestyle" prior to her moving in with them to work as a domestic worker. Their sexually extroverted lifestyle became code for their expectations of Tess with regards to sex and intimacy—she was expected not only to clean for the Lundbergs; as a Filipina who had worked in sexual economies in the Philippines, her relationship with her employers was also expected to be sexual. Her case hinted at sexual servitude tied to domestic servitude, but its stricken record reinforces the notion that rather than being a crime, her integration into the Lundbergs' activities implied choice. Tess's experiences as a sex worker in the Philippines impacted the legal outcomes of the case. In the United States, the criminalization of sexual economies means that sex workers may find it difficult to report abuse—in San Francisco, only in 2018 were sex workers able to report rape, sexual assault, robbery, extortion, and witnessing a crime without fear of being arrested.[105] The fact that Tess was a sex worker from the Philippines and her employer a lawyer and former law enforcement agent, illustrates the power of enforcement in creating more invisibilities for migrant laborers, who also may experience rape or sexual assault, or both, by law enforcement officers. Research shows that people in sexual economies experience coercive behaviors from law enforcement, including verbal harassment, sexual exploitation, extortion, and lack of responsiveness when sex workers experience violence.[106] Tess received a T-Visa. But in the legal case, her employers were convicted of illegal harboring of an alien, suggesting that it was only documented status that was legible to the courts.

The case did not move into the media realm, I argue, because it did not fit into the simplistic imagining of human trafficking as noncontradictory, where heteronormative ideologies persevered. Tess had worked in the karaoke bars in the Philippines, where the bars are associated with sex for sale, and the issue of choice became one that made defining sexual slavery no longer simple. Under the IIRAIRA 1996, participating in prostitution is a crime of moral turpitude and grounds for deportation and a ten-year bar on reentry into the United States for those convicted. One's role as a sex industry survivor prior to entering the United States makes sex exploitation suspect. Testimonies implied that Tess "was happy" with the Lundbergs.[107] In contrast to Tess, a migrant laborer, the Lundbergs were portrayed in the Sentencing Memorandum as family oriented and as leading an "entirely unblemished life," with "numerous letters of support." Although it is unclear in court records if the Lundbergs are white Americans, one need only to undertake an online search for "Lundberg" to find that it is of European ancestry.[108] The family orientation of the Lundbergs was notable in the husband's image as having a close relationship with his sisters. Mr. Lundberg was a survivor of testicular cancer, who had "proceeded to father two more children together" with his wife. The picture painted in the court records is one of a heteronormative couple whose benevolence in supporting an undocumented migrant led to their demise, raising the questions: can one smile and still be exploited for labor or sex, or both? And do racial constructs haunt the case of Tess, where her racialization as a Filipina is clear, in contrast to the absence of race in the Lundbergs? Human trafficking is traumatic, and understanding how one survives is not easy; survivors of sex trafficking oftentimes exhibit posttraumatic stress disorder.[109] Trauma breaks a person's safety and connection.[110] For the survivor of exploitation, a smile may be the only way to survive, because to not smile leads to worse consequences.

Differing definitions of human trafficking have meant that numbers are difficult to identify. Older numbers from the 1990s conveyed that annually 150,000 women are trafficked into Japan's sex industry. The numbers circulating about how many Asians are trafficked annually varies from the thousands to the millions.[111] Within the Philippines, it is estimated that 100,000 children are trafficked into sexual economies.[112] These numbers differ radically from the 2015 TIP report numbers, which included Inter-Agency Council Against Trafficking (IACAT) reporting of 1,089 trafficked individuals, and also from numbers from the Department of Social Welfare and Development (DSWD), which reported 1,395 trafficked people in 2015.[113] Although it is difficult to assess prevalence, because understandings of what constitutes human trafficking vary, as do perceptions of what counts as human trafficking, there has been a growing movement to address human trafficking into sexual economies through policy implementation. The movement to combat human trafficking has sparked important changes to legislation in the United States. The cases analyzed in this chapter fall outside the labor-trafficking and sex-trafficking divides, even though expectations of Filipinos and sexual services are defined by U.S. perceptions of the Philippines.[114] Cases that become visibly newsworthy are those that bear headlines like "Two Swedes Jailed for Life over Philippine Cybersex Den."[115] In that case, Bo Stefan Sederholm and Emil Andreas Solemo were found guilty of trafficking charges. While such cases of transnational sex trafficking have made news headlines, they eventually are forgotten and located as elsewhere. This is due in part to what some refer to as the McSexualization of the sex industry,[116] where sex is increasingly sold fast and cheap, but it is also partly due to historic and ongoing fantasies of the Asia-Pacific that can be traced to colonial and military histories.[117]

DISCUSSION: CHOICE, AGENCY, AND FREEDOM

There is a need to relationally situate labor human trafficking cases with those where labor and sex trafficking intersect. The goal in doing so is not to conflate trafficking into sexual economies with that of other forms of labor exploitation. Cindy and Tess complicate notions of choice, where victims are seen as perfect and lacking choice and imperfect because of their ability to choose. The stereotype of human trafficking survivors as passive is embedded in the discourse to differentiate victims from unlawful economic migrants, and it is effective for a prosecutorial story.[118] Currently, a victim of human trafficking is identified when there is force, fraud, or coercion in their experience.

Tess was a victim of human trafficking, even though her history of participating in a sex industry made her victimization questionable. As the courts described, "There exists considerable dispute as to the frequency these sexual interactions and the degree of pressure placed upon [Tess]."[119] Tess wrote a victim impact statement to the judge; however, her statement was never read out in the court hearings, and any allegations or inferences of any improper sexual activities were "stricken from the final report."[120] The inability to see Tess's experience as rape, sexual exploitation, or sex trafficking personifies what is referred to as "prostitute myths"—the misperception surrounding characteristics of women in the sex industry. An interdisciplinary study of the perceptions of prostituted people describes the "prostitute myth" as: (1) prostitutes are un-rape-able; (2) no harm is done to prostitutes when they are assaulted or harassed; (3) workers in sexual economies deserve to be raped; and (4) all prostitutes are the same.[121] Rape myths permeate in legal cases and in assumptions that are made about individuals in sexual economies. The attitudinal bias toward people in sexual economies is palpable.[122]

The debates about choice are informed by U.S. understandings of perfect victims as innocent and noncontradictory. Even with limited options or a complete lack of choice, people have agency. And choice is always present, even when this means choosing to be exploited over something worse (i.e., death). Anti-trafficking strategies must target the underlying conditions that impel people to accept dangerous labor migration assignments.[123] Regardless of the choices that leads to one's exploitation, no one chooses to be exploited.

Domestic workers are organizing to increase their rights as workers in households through pan-ethnic solidarities,[124] as delineated in the California Household Worker Rights Coalition, whose lead organizations comprise Filipinos,[125] Latinas/os,[126] and immigrant-based organizations.[127] Cindy's case greatly contrasted with the case of Tess, whose ability to show choice in working in exploitative industries (i.e., the sex industry) mattered as a means to diminish the perceptions of exploitation.

To look for narratives of perfect victimization is to fail to see the complexities of experiences that weave between exploitation, agency, and change.

CLOSING: BEYOND APPEALS FOR VICTIMHOOD

While some advocate for countering how women's bodies are the last colony of patriarchy,[128] the imbrication of colonial legacies in the present makes its way across the Pacific to the United States. Colonial legacies give shape to present-day constructs of victimhood that also make invisible agency, action, and choice. This is best described in the discourse of "perfect victims." Central to the establishment of victimhood is immigration status, how the individual's narrative figures into the metanarrative of human trafficking, and whether or not they are able to exert choice, which is problematically equated with agency. Therefore, to examine human trafficking beyond dominant imaginings, I offer, in closing, an appeal for decolonial conceptualizations beyond choice. Choice is oftentimes seen as a Western ideal about personal freedom and the ability to "choose." However, what does it mean when one chooses, but one's choices are governed by a collective notion, a community, a family? Therefore, rather than move toward defining victimhood, I call for a decolonial maneuver that seeks a kind of witnessing beyond the logics of choice. Take, for example, Cindy and Tess. Rather than ask whether they were free to choose, one might consider the contexts and the sociocultural understanding of choice that shaped their experiences. Contexts are multiple for transnational migrant laborers. Additionally, one may exhibit choice in the context of limited options. Therefore, victimhood is not about the choices one makes but about the consequence of having limited options. Cindy and Tess's immigration status and racialization and gender are the same; however, their narratives differed, in that Cindy's story figured well in the metanarrative of human trafficking, where her lack of choice was portrayed as clear by liberal and U.S. standards. Her choice was portrayed as one that was clearly denied; she fit the prototype of a human trafficking narrative of being in indentured servitude, and her traffickers facilitated her migration—Cindy is an example of the "perfect victim." However, her choice to labor in low-wage labor is decentered—it is normal and maybe even expected. Knowing that Cindy was a schoolteacher in the Philippines, unable to maintain her area of expertise while in the United States, suggests that the choices afforded her were always constrained. Tess differed greatly from Cindy, in that her narrative of choosing to work in sexual economies did not figure well in the possibility that she could have been trafficked for both her labor and sex (even though she received a T-Visa). Choice was up for debate in Tess's narrative, in that it was assumed she chose to migrate, and her vulnerability was not legible when her agency was more apparent to witnesses. To be seen as smiling, even in the face of limited options, is to be intelligible as a victim. Therefore, she was deemed an imperfect victim in the courts. The intercontextuality of Tess's choices was also transnational; how one conceived of economies (sexual and domestic), resources, and transnational migrants, impacted how Tess was witnessed. And agency is the ability to act—in the everyday or even within structures. Tess's narrative did not fit the metanarrative of human trafficking: she had worked in sexual economies in the Philippines prior to her migrating to the United States. In the eyes of the prosecutorial law, she was not seen as a perfect victim. Tess exemplifies imperfect victimhood, due to her having chosen to migrate to the United States and her history of participating in sexual economies. However, the goal may be for some to recover Tess as a perfect victim. To do so is to reinforce colonial dualities. Rather than reinscribe perfect-victim narratives, I ask what the contexts are of choices that are made available so that one can be seen (or not seen) as a victim, a criminal, and a trafficking subject. How do various systems, individuals, and collectives witness these choices? What are the choices that are furthered through the witness's action or inaction? Due to colonial legacies, the imagining and legal implementation of victimhood reinforces dualities that even perpetuate the iconic visualities of human trafficking.

4 WITNESSING LEGAL NARRATIVES, COURT PERFORMANCES, AND TRANSLATIONS OF PERUVIAN DOMESTIC WORK

IN 2010, IN *UNITED STATES V. DANN*, Dann was convicted for trafficking "Liliana"[1] into domestic servitude from Peru to Walnut Creek, California, on five different counts: conspiracy to commit visa fraud, visa fraud, forced labor and attempted forced labor, unlawful conduct regarding documents in furtherance of servitude, and harboring an illegal alien for private financial gain.[2] *United States v. Dann* embodies homosocial violence between coethnics: Dann, a Peruvian (naturalized U.S. citizen) female employer, and Liliana, a Peruvian female (migrant) domestic worker employed by Dann, were both propelled into the public eye of the media and the law when the district attorney charged (and then convicted) Dann on trafficking-related violations. The case received national and international media coverage as the "first" in Northern California legal history to have jury trial ensue for a human trafficking case in the region.[3] In spite of sharing national origins and gender, Dann and Liliana's racialization in Peru carried over into a U.S. context, interacting with U.S. ideologies of race. Regardless of the complexities of race and class, the case reinforced legal definitions of human trafficking, and it was prosecuted "successfully" as such.[4] From the earliest media coverage of the case to its closing, headline news included titles such as "Peruvian Nanny Exploited in Shocking ICE Case,"[5] "Walnut Creek Woman Convicted of Enslaving Nanny,"[6] and "Coco Real Estate Agent Convicted of Forced Labor."[7] Dann's seemingly upper-class status in the United States as a real estate agent contrasted the invisibility of her race. As Dann's profession mattered, so too did it matter for Liliana. However, in addition to being described as a nanny, Liliana's migratory status and victimization also mattered, where descriptors of her experience included slavery and exploitation. Human trafficking is an elusive concept.[8] It is determined by legal definitions,[9] defined by concepts of victimhood,[10] contextualized as a problem that must be interrogated and recognized in structures of race and citizenship,[11] seen as a contemporary slavery issue,[12] and understood as a problem of labor and migration,[13] of gender,[14] and of rights.[15] In spite of the varied definitions and meanings of human trafficking, I argue human trafficking is both determined by modern transnational economic structures that are reified through local settings (i.e., performances in the courtroom) and also embedded in perceptions of the particularities of the industry one is trafficked into, the industry in the case of *United States v. Dann* being servitude.

At what point does an experience become witnessed as trafficking—how does one cross into being seen as "trafficked"? How do migrants, their employers, and actors in the legal system perform expectations of race, gender, and class to enable a witnessing of trafficking (or not)? Examining *United States v. Dann* as coethnic violence enables witnessing beyond binaries (victim/criminal, illegal/legal, citizen/noncitizen) and shifts away from Othering who the trafficker/trafficked person is. For migrants working in a culture of servitude, their ability to cross into being seen as trafficked/the trafficker cannot be separated from perceptions of citizenship, social movements, sociopolitical processes, and culture. Focusing on the process of witnessing how one is determined as trafficked or a trafficker through court cases like *United States v. Dann* enables seeing migrants for their complex personhood and the limits (and possibilities) of what can be witnessed. In many ways Liliana represents the benefits of prosecutorial discretion.[16] While she had participated in visa fraud (a criminalized act), the humanitarian efforts of immigration attorneys and homeland security allowed her to be seen as a person to be protected from removal.

This chapter begins with a summary of the theoretical underpinnings regarding the witnessing of migration, gender, and servitude. This is followed by a transnational narrative of the *United States v. Dann*, to decenter U.S.-centric perspectives. I actualize an unsettled witnessing of migration into (involuntary) servitude within the U.S. context through examining the "Othering" that occurs in U.S. law and media (as also countered by migrants themselves), the performance of translation (and what is unknown), and the significance of breaking moments as events (like crying) that produce legibility as trafficking.

THEORETICAL FRAMING: WITNESSING LABOR MIGRATION
INTO SERVITUDE

Servitude, "to be at one's service," in the United States is at times viewed as analogous to slavery and trafficking, albeit it is distinguished through language of voluntary versus involuntary.[17] And it is codified through legal industries that carry various names—babysitter, nanny, caregiver, domestic worker, domestic service, and housekeeper. Servitude, or domestic work, is a form of reproductive labor.[18] Reproductive labor has been divided historically along racial and gender lines, where minority groups (due to sociopolitical inequalities) find themselves working in reproductive care. Domestic work must be studied because it raises a challenge to "sisterhood."[19] An analysis of domestic work, gender, and work is vital for understanding the complex social relations between public and private lives that cut across racial and national lines in homosocial relations. This chapter builds upon existing research on race and gender, where gendered migration and global capitalism and global flows are understood through micro- and macroanalyses.[20] A race, gender, and global economic lens enables one to make sense of how a visible number of women who work as paid domestic workers are from Mexico, Central America, and the Caribbean.[21] Influenced by the sociological work of Glenn, Hondagneu-Sotelo, Parreñas, Rollins, and Romero, I am interested in examining the complex dynamic in which servitude for a migrant laborer becomes witnessed as involuntary servitude. For some scholars, domestic work is a part of the cultures of servitude, the belief systems and practices that govern a society's practices, policies, and attitudes to service. As described by Qayum and Ray, a "traveling culture of servitude" impacts migrant laborers and their employers, as the laborers carry with them to the destination country cultural perceptions of servitude derived from their "homeland."[22] Likewise, the countries migrants enter into as laborers shape their experiences and understandings of domestic work.[23] If, as Nicole Constable frames it, globalization defines new spaces, meanings, and expressions of intimacy, what can be learned from understanding homosocial relations and servitude that cross into visibility as trafficking? And how may one understand servitude in the context of transnational circuits? U.S. legal responses to domestic service reflect dominant ideologies about service in the modern economic world order[24]—some laborers are in need of rescue, whereas others continue to be marginalized as fulfilling affordable labor demands in capitalist industries. But, the process of moving from being seen as trafficked (in this case, from involuntary servitude) must be further examined. To capture the nuance of a witnessing, I examine *United States v. Dann*.

To examine how human trafficking is witnessed is to situate this particular case in the context of multiple anti-trafficking narratives. The voices through which human trafficking is narrated occur in a rhizomatic fashion. The survivor, the witness, and the nonwitness collectively create a rhizome. Gilles Deleuze and Felix Guattari explain that a rhizome, unlike a structure, is an assemblage connected to another assemblage through lines where connections are made possible through semiotic chains and power.[25] A rhizome cannot be reduced to the one or the multiple. Therefore, a rhizomatic narration of human trafficking connects one story to another through semiotic chains (i.e., the legal system, the media, history, academic publications, anti-trafficking trainings, etc.), and is defined by multiple power relations (i.e., race, gender, class, nationality, ability). And, like ants, the chains can be broken but will reemerge elsewhere, still connected. I situate anti-trafficking narrations as a rhizome that can be mapped through individual and collective cases; the rhizomatic narration of human trafficking informs popular understandings of human trafficking (i.e., labor, migration, criminal justice, human rights, gender, and citizenship), whereby the semiological affects are transnationally deployed. As such, to witness a laboring experience as trafficking is to understand how it is relationally constituted.[26] Nonprofits, governmental agencies, law enforcement, academics, community-based organizations and their members, and religious entities act collectively as translators; it is never the survivor alone speaking, but rather the multiplicity of a movement speaking about the trafficked experience across time/space. During the trial for *United States v. Dann*, the audience comprised law students, lawyers (immigration and civil), social service providers, DHS agents, FBI agents, family members, friends, advocates, students—a diverse group, whose common circumstance was to witness the development of the case. The case traveled into news networks, is archived in court records, and is reinforced by the spaces in which it does not appear. Human trafficking is exploitive, socially and legally defined as such, where an advocate, a lawyer, a community member, and all the other components that together comprise an anti-trafficking movement, define that person, a person like Liliana, as "trafficked."[27] And in the case of *United States v. Dann*, Liliana also then sees herself as trafficked and narrates her story as such. The affirmation of a person as trafficked solidifies the definition of human trafficking and the "anti-trafficking movement." Liliana was defined as trafficked when she "met [her] caseworker at SAGE."[28] She later describes her relationship with SAGE in the cross-examination: "The organization SAGE helped me, helped me with the basic things, morally, doctor, food, clothes, because that was the most important thing right then."[29] At this point Liliana's story shifts into being named and witnessed as human trafficking, interpreted by a myriad of witnesses, including myself. However, I argue it is important to further understand that how one becomes witnessed as trafficked is a multifaceted process.

Multiple forms of witnessing take place in this chapter—the witness who takes the stand in a legal system, my role as a witness to the case, the reader's role in reading my witnessing, and so forth. However, I am calling for a particular type of witnessing, specifically an unsettled witnessing of experiences determined as human trafficking. An unsettled witnessing is an invocation of María Lugones's concept of "faithful witnessing," or a witnessing against power.[30] However, in witnessing through the legal system, I call attention to the possibility of a decolonial witnessing, but also to a reconciliation of what seems impossible with witnessing, whereby memory of violence is "approachable and unmasterable."[31]

TRANSNATIONAL PERSPECTIVES

There is a story that unravels before the story in the United States, and that is the transnational histories that have defined the relationship between the United States and Latin America, in particular Peru. Beginning in 2002, Dann frequently asked Liliana to move to the United States to be a nanny for Dann's children.[32] Liliana repeatedly refused. However, she eventually agreed when Dann started to experience difficulties in her marriage, and pled with Liliana to migrate to the United States. Dann promised Liliana the opportunity to learn English and learn how to drive, both important skills for Liliana, who wished to succeed in Peru's tourist industry. Dann was a naturalized American citizen of Peruvian descent who had graduated from the Haas School of Business at the University of California, Berkeley.[33] A divorcee, she began her relationship with Liliana long distance, as delineated in a letter she sent to Liliana:

> I hope you are well. Here, I'm trying to do everything possible to get ahead all alone with the responsibility of three children. As you probably know, my divorce will be finalized very soon. Now the judge has ordered that I must go out and work. And I need more help than ever. . . . I'm going try and see how to bring you over here. As you probably know, a man that my brother is acquainted

with is going to get in touch with you very soon and will try to bring you. Don't tell anyone from your family.[34]

Although Dann needed Liliana, their relationship was defined by a power dynamic surrounding class and race, even before Liliana entered the United States. The sociohistorical development of racism in Peru shapes the lives of Peruvians both in Peru and in the United States. Racist perceptions of indigenous peoples associate them as "backward" and rural, in contrast to whiteness, which is associated with modern and urban areas, solidifying the need to take into consideration race, class, and migrant status.[35] Liliana was relegated to a racialized lower-class migrant originally from Cuzco, Peru, who had internally migrated to Lima, Peru, to attend high school, landing her a job as domestic worker for Dann's sister. When Liliana migrated to the United States, she is described as coming from "limited means."[36] Dann was reported as referring to Liliana in derogatory ways as a "little girl" and "shit"—derogatory terms that were a reminder of their difference. And when challenged about worker rights, Dann was quoted in court records as telling Liliana, "You're a peasant. I'm giving you an opportunity here in this country."[37] In contrast to Liliana, Dann, originally from Lima, migrated to California to attend the University of California's business school. Dann became a real-estate agent, promoting that she spoke three languages: Spanish, French, and German.[38] Where she migrated from did not matter for the prosecution, but rather what she became perceived as—upper class, educated, someone who should have "known better." However, it is necessary to situate their raced and class difference in a transnational context to understand the significance of their relationship in the United States as raced, classed, and determined by different legal statuses (citizen/noncitizen).

Like many migrants, Liliana's reason for emigration was economic. She was promised six hundred dollars per month, the equivalent of three dollars and seventy-five cents per hour. Liliana continued to stay with her employer, Dann, even though her below-minimum-wage pay "ballooned" to a debt of fifteen thousand dollars.[39] A majority of the women in domestic service reflect a lower class of women.[40] Peru has reduced its poverty rates by 15 percent[41] since 2002 and opened trade internationally,[42] yet large numbers of Peruvians live and work abroad, suggesting that there is a need to go abroad to work to send home remittances. In 2010, approximately 10 percent of households in Peru had a family member who worked abroad.[43] Peru is increasingly dependent on migrants sending home remittances. During a ten-year period (1999–2009), re-mittances increased from 670 million dollars to 2.4 billion dollars. The Interna-tional Office of Migration attributed this increase in remittances to imbalances between supply and demand for jobs and to large wage disparities. It is esti-mated that 70 percent of Peruvians who have migrated in the last decade have done so for economic reasons. The need to send remittances to family members impacts why one migrates; sending remittances changes a migrant's social sta-tus in their home country, even if that labor is devalued in the other country.[44] As migrants are figured in the United States as laborers, they exist in "shadows of affluence," in which globalization is creating "new regimes of inequalities."[45] However, reasons to migrate and the industries one migrates into are not merely economically determined, but also defined by raced/gendered ideologies.

I refer to Liliana and Dann as Latinas, not to homogenize their experience but rather to illustrate the diverse making and meaning behind racial catego-ries in homosocial relations. Latina/o/x is a geographic reference that begins with Mexico and ends with the tip of Chile.[46] The shared geographic history is one that is defined by complex interpretations of race that travel and interact with U.S. perceptions of race. Latinas/os/x are historically situated in a com-plex relationship with migration and colonization as a complex group; Latinas/os/x are heterogeneous, multiple, and hybrid.[47] Cases like *United States v. Dann* point to how Latinas/os/x are homogenized and seen as all the same. Othering perceptions and the historic raced and gendered archetypes of Lati-nas/os/x, specifically of Peruvians, are a part of ongoing colonialism that may be traced back to U.S. romanticization of Peru as a tourist destination in the early twentieth century. The discovery of the "Lost City of the Incas" led to the Western imagining of Machu Picchu as "mythical" and a "must-see" on the South American grand tour.[48] The "mystery" of Peru and Latin America per-petuates the Latina/o/x as exotic. After the 1980s economic crisis, the Peru-vian economy relied on exporting labor to the United States and other parts of the first world.[49] Therefore, not only is Peru exoticized in the global imagi-nary, but also the Othering of Peruvians has reimagined Peruvian Latinas/os/x as homogeneous, racialized brown bodies for cheap labor in the United States. Some scholars refer to this as the Mexicanization of other Latinas/os/x.[50] Colonial racisms homogenize Latinas/os/x as all the same, in spite of their unique histories and identifications.[51] And, Spanish is assumed to be the language all Latinas/os/x speak, ignoring indigenous languages spoken by many of the people who live south of the U.S. border.[52]

The homogenization of Latinas/os/x reinforces racialized modes of production that siphon them into low-wage industries. Immigrant labor in the United States, although valuable, is devalued, enabling the United States to reap the benefits of unequal relations of power in the modern global economic system. The devaluing of domestic work is not unique to migrant domestic workers; rather, it reflects sociopolitical realities within and between particular nation-states. The demand for cheap, flexible labor augmented by social constraints (race and gender glass ceilings) explains why migrants work in laboring industries in the United States and carry low status. Currently, 24 percent of undocumented laborers in the United States are from Central and South America.[53]

Dann and Liliana migrated to the United States with Peruvian ideologies of race and class. Liliana worked as a "nanny" for Dann's sister in Lima. Liliana, originally from Cuzco, identifies as a mestizo. "Mestizo" in the United States carries a meaning very different to in Peru. In the United States, it represents the intermixing of Spaniards and American Indians, as a new culture that is a product of the "transfer of cultural and spiritual values."[54] *Mestizo* represents a hybrid identity that challenges identity itself[55] that even is fetishized and privileged in U.S. discourse.[56] In contrast to Chicanas/os/x, in which "mestizo" is inextricably tied to culture, in Peru it is characterized as "a terrain of political contestation and dialogic reformulations in which elite and grassroots intellectuals dispute meanings of identity labels and rights to equal citizenship."[57] "Mestizo" refers to an indigenous person as literate, as enjoying job success, and as having a ranking that differs from *indios*, who in contrast to mestizos are indigenous individuals who are rural and illiterate. As the *mestizo* connotes a shift toward a different class, a movement toward being educated and having job access, a *limeño*, a person from Lima who is not indigenous, is a class situated as socially white. Therefore, the *mestiza/o* and *limeña/o* are cultural interpretations of race. Although they are both racialized subjects in the legal case, their class formation was also essential in reifying their difference.

Liliana and Dann's raced and classed differences persevered in the U.S. context. In the United States, the relationship between Liliana and Dann is defined by normalized power imbalances, even if superficially, their racialization is similar—as Latinas. However, it is not merely a story about transnational economies that produce and give rise to the construction of a human trafficking subject.

UNITED STATES V. DANN: AN ANTI-TRAFFICKING STORY
AND LILIANA AS THE ANTI-FROG

Migrants cross not only national borders but also the spheres of public and private life. Many cases like *United States v. Dann* are referred to as "hidden behind closed doors."[58] However, domestic work does not solely occur in the private sphere; workers move out of the private into the public physically, culturally (e.g., in filmic representation), and politically (e.g., nannies as lovers,[59] as trafficked, or as political activists[60]). In 2005 Liliana migrated to the United States to work for Dann. For two years Liliana dropped off Dann's children at school. Because she was able to leave the house, in spite of Dann's requirements that Liliana not speak to anyone, Liliana was able to build a relationship with employees at Dann's children's school. And in 2007, with the help of eight community members, Liliana was able to leave her employer. Liliana's departure from the Dann home was facilitated by the connections she built with other individuals outside of the home, individuals who worked at Dann's children's elementary school (a gardener and a custodian) and another parent. A bilingual custodian reached out to speak with Liliana, and eventually Liliana left items with the custodian, things she wanted to keep safe: newspaper clippings, phone cards, postings, and money she made on the side by secretly selling chocolates to survive.

The court's portrayal of Dann and Liliana produce two diverging images. The U.S. attorney, the prosecutor, constructed for the courts an image of Dann as a person who went to great lengths to exploit Liliana, violating immigration, labor, and criminal laws. The U.S. attorney's opening statement summarized the case as a story about "exploitation and betrayal."[61] The day Liliana left Dann she hid under a blanket in the back seat of a car: "[Dann] never pays her. She only has to keep [Liliana] scared enough so that she does not leave." He continued to describe Liliana's journey from Cuzco "to the back seat of a car in Walnut Creek," where Liliana "cower[ed] under a blanket and in fear of the defendant [Dann]."[62] As described in the closing statements made by the U.S. attorney, "both claim Peru as their homeland, but you can't think of two more different kind of people."[63] The story of Dann and Liliana reinforces their difference in the United States, in spite of their shared national origins—a dichotomous imagining of good and bad migrants. In contrast, the defense portrayed Dann as a person who treated Liliana like a family member and as a victim of Liliana's lies and attempts to receive immigration relief at Dann's expense: "This is a case of an overworked, stressed out, single mother and a nanny with ulterior motives."[64] In general, Dann's defense depicted Liliana as a person whose character was to lie; Liliana lied to enter the United States in 2004, and therefore she also defrauded the government to receive immigration relief via a T-Visa.[65] A T-Visa provides immigration relief to migrants identified as trafficked. Dann's public defender described Liliana and Dann's relationship as a sisterly bond:

> Ultimately they came to live together, to work together, and even play together as a family. Not as master and servant, not as dominator and slave, but almost as sisters. . . . One did betray the other. But as you listen to the evidence in this case, what you're going to discover is it was the nanny with ulterior motives that betrayed Dann, not the other way around.[66]

Neither the prosecution nor the defense resisted a simplistic narrative of good/bad migrants; in fact, both depended on perpetuating dichotomous images of immigrants. At the closing of the case, the prosecution's representation of Dann through the witnesses and supporting evidence produced a conviction on all five counts.

In order to facilitate a narrative of victimhood, the defense focused on the fraudulent means by which Liliana entered the United States; therefore, *United States v. Dann* is a story not only about trafficking and forced labor but also about immigration. In 2004, Dann arranged to have Liliana enter the United States by fraudulent means. Liliana arrived in Northern California by fraudulently obtaining a B1 visa, a visitor/tourist visa.[67] Her intention was to stay and work for Dann without proper work authorization, a process orchestrated by Dann.[68] Dann created a narrative according to which Liliana was to pretend to help a friend of Dann's, Silvana. Silvana, who also was in on the fraud, pretended to be frail with cancer and in need of Liliana's caretaking to convince the U.S. government to issue a tourist visa for Liliana to enter the United States. The prosecution emphasized that the scheme was Dann's design; Liliana's participation in visa fraud was of Dann's design and a central part of Dann's scheme to ultimately traffic Liliana, even though Liliana was fully complicit. It was made clear in the court hearings that the plan was Dann's. The need to disaggregate perpetrator/victim or criminal/victim often breaks down in actual cases. Central evidence in the court proceeding was the federal investigation's discovery of Liliana's passport hidden in Dann's drawer, reinforcing Liliana's claim that her identification had been withheld. Although Dann herself is a migrant, her immigration story was less central to the narrative produced in the court hearings. To focus on Dann's complex subjectivity as also including her immigration history was marginal in the legal case. Dann's story was only acknowledged by her origins and a brief reference to her family in the presentencing hearing.[69] Although the courts produced an image that the scheme to be smuggled into the United States through visa fraud was Dann's design, the inability to see Liliana as an active agent is problematic and limiting, and also emphasizes the passivity of victims.

To commit to witnessing Liliana and Dann's complex-personhood necessitates a recalling of how, in spite of efforts to raise awareness about the dehumanizing nature of human trafficking, anti-traffickers are also complicit in such rhetoric (intentionally or not).[70] Liliana's experience was described by one of the prosecuting attorneys as a slow "cook of a frog." Describing what he meant by this, he likened the case to a question his mentor had posed during a government-facilitated training on human trafficking: "How do you cook a frog?"[71] He had responded, "You put it in a pot." The mentor had clarified that to cook a frog, the frog is placed into a pot. But if you put the frog in a hot pot, it will jump out of the pot. Therefore, the "trick" is to place the frog in a cool pot and raise the temperature slowly until you have a cooked frog. The assistant U.S. attorney described the slow cook of a frog as similar to the dynamic between the trafficker/victim in cases such as *United States v. Dann*. The cook is the trafficker, and the frog is the trafficked.

Using nonhuman images of trafficked people is a common strategy that reinforces the point that human trafficking is dehumanizing. The discourse reinforcing the dehumanizing imagery of human trafficking is illustrated in the reproduction of language to describe groups of trafficked people as a "stable";[72] in the reinforcement of images that refer to the sex trafficking of people as "fresh meat";[73] and in images of trafficked people shackled, bound, gagged, or behind barbed or cage-like bars, or of disembodied body parts placed on display. Not only are trafficked people Othered, so too are people convicted as traffickers.[74] The prosecuting attorney's comparing Liliana to a frog reflects dominant understandings of human trafficking and the trafficked through subhuman descriptors—human trafficking is viewed as dehumanizing, and the discourse that paints human trafficking (intentionally or not) also reproduces dehumanizing logics of individuals who figure in anti-trafficking narratives. Liliana's experience epitomized a slow cook, until she was able to leave; therefore, while Liliana was painted as a frog, I call her the anti-frog. Because even though the

U.S. attorney's interpretation of the case suggests that a slow cook describes her, Liliana left the pot. And, as the public consumed her story in the news, Liliana also participated in her own public display through her testimony in the court and her public shots in news coverage.[75]

Although victim narratives are used in anti-trafficking strategies (the images of force, fraud, and coercion),[76] violence and abuse experienced by domestic workers like Liliana is not new.[77] In fact, no one asked why Liliana was seen yet not *seen* for two years, and not paid (from July 2006 through April 2008).[78] Therefore, what was it about Liliana's experience that moved it from conventional domestic work to unconventional or conventional human trafficking? The prosecution's emphasis included reminding the jurors that Dann instilled fear (coercion) in Liliana through threats by showing her newspaper clippings that highlighted what the United States does to undocumented migrants; that Dann forced Liliana to stay in her service by tearing up Liliana's return ticket to Peru (preventing her from leaving) and also by withholding Liliana's passport; and that Dann forced Liliana to labor without pay and to "toil" under "intolerable conditions" for fifteen-hour workdays[79] by controlling Liliana's communication with the outside world,[80] and by instilling fear in Liliana by describing what would happen to Dann's children if Liliana left her services.[81] The story of Dann's inhumane treatment of Liliana extended beyond the courtroom into the media. Newspaper coverage of the case emphasized how Liliana was forced to sleep on the floor in the living room next to the window. Her food was rationed; Dann would weigh meat purchased and keep "a strict count of fruit in the house."[82] Eggs and bread also were counted, to ensure that Liliana did not eat "more than her ration."[83] Stories of Liliana's resistance to her own exploitation were painted by the prosecution through a narrative of resilience, in spite of experiencing destitution. In order to survive, Liliana picked fruits from trees on the way home from walking the children to school. In spite of being starved by her trafficker, she found ways to subsist, even if it was still insufficient.

Liliana's first public appearance for her testimony during the trial best illustrates how one may witness her active role in the legal system in being presented as trafficked; however, she also resisted the expectations of the legal structures. During her employment with Dann, Liliana was witnessed as looking disheveled. She wore poorly fitting clothes, she smelled because she was not able to regularly shower, and her teeth were rotting. She testified to the stigma and shame in wearing the ill-fitting clothes. On the day Liliana testified in court, she wore her hair in a ponytail, a bright striped sweater with pink, black, and yellow, with a fitted denim skirt and black stiletto shoes, even though it was recommended that she dress down rather than up. Liliana dressed in a way that went against even the recommendations of the prosecution.[84] The story narrated regarding Liliana's two years of employment included the absence of pay, malnutrition, and isolation from the wider community. After leaving Dann's employment, Liliana embodied a person who looked well and healthy—one would never have known that she was someone who had been "put in a pot." Although the legal system emphasizes narratives of victimhood that are performed, and even though Liliana narrated a story of exploitation during her testimonial, she also resisted perpetuating what one would expect a "victim" to look like.

THE SIGNIFICANCE OF TEARS, A LEGAL FRAMING, AND BREAKING MOMENTS

Sara Ahmed conveys that in affective economies, "emotions do *things*,"[85] aligning individuals with communities that are more than psychological dispositions. Therefore, crying is also a form of an affective economy salient in anti-trafficking and human rights discourses. There was only one physical altercation between Liliana and Dann during the two years of Liliana's employment. The court evidence shows how Dann's abuse of Liliana was primarily verbal. Liliana marked on a calendar the verbal abuse she suffered at Dann's hands.[86] But an aspect of the story, as subtle as it seemed to the prosecutors during their early interviews of Liliana, offered a major turning point in the story—the breaking of a radio. Dann broke Liliana's radio. It was at this point that Liliana was described as crying during her interviews with law enforcement. Roland Barthes's *A Lover's Discourse* is useful here for examining tears:

> By weeping, I want to impress someone, to bring pressure to bear upon someone ("Look what you have done to me") . . . By my tears, I tell a story, I produce a myth of *grief*, and *henceforth* I adjust myself to it: I can live with it, because, by weeping, I give myself an emphatic interlocutor who receives the 'truest' of messages, that of my body, not that of my speech: "Words, what are they? One tear will say more than all of them."[87]

Through fragments of discourse (called figures) supported by texts, friends, and his own memory and philosophical insights, Barthes offers an understanding of the lover at work. The nuance of Barthes's lover's argument for crying conveys that there is a complex repertoire of images at work when one cries. Tears have the ability to say more than words, even to speak in ways that words are unable to. The manifestation of a crying survivor is a necessity in creating a successful anti-trafficking narrative and performing victimization. *United States v. Dann* illustrates how anti-trafficking discourse includes in the meta-narrative of human trafficking the significance of subtle methods of control as characteristic of human trafficking.[88] In *United States v. Dann*, the defining event was when Dann broke Liliana's radio, one of the few objects that Liliana personally owned. The legal recognition of a breaking point, the breaking of a radio, makes legible how a witness like the district attorney determines an experience as trafficking. Without these moments, the juror's ability to understand how one's lived experiences are traumatic as trafficking is elusive and impossible; therefore, even Liliana participated in performances of recounting the specificities of traumatic moments and performing through crying the significance of such moments.[89]

Although crying can be a solitary act, to have witnesses to one's crying matters in an anti-trafficking narration. Whether the crying is tears caused by having to narrate one's own experience (as in the victim's case) or tears of empathy (as from a witness), crying is not merely an emotional response to something traumatic. This is especially true when words may mask a person's experience or are inadequate for describing it. Human trafficking invokes emotional and physical responses to trauma and traumatic events. Crying makes legible to the nonbeliever, the witness, and the anti-trafficker, an experience of violence whereby tears enable abstract series of events (human trafficking) to become legible to the nontrafficked person through understandings of sadness and grief. And it is also performed in the courtroom; a natural response or a forced act invokes the witness (the jurors, the judge, the attorneys, and the audience) to empathize with the narrative. Tears produce a performance of believability and truth in a narrative. Liliana describes a specific moment when she cried and when others witnessed her crying. It was the day she told the other witnesses about her experience (who exactly, it is unclear). It was the day that Liliana learned that Dann was going to open a day-care center, and she expected Liliana to work there. This meant that Liliana would never leave the house. As Liliana described during her court testimony, "I told them that day, 7th [April 7, 2007], I went there crying. And I went there and I told them the whole truth. By then, I didn't care if . . . everybody looked at me. . . . I was always discreet. . . . At that time, there were more people there. And they started seeing—they started seeing me crying." Just as crying mattered for the U.S.

attorney to pick up the case, it also mattered for the witnesses who saw Liliana working as a domestic worker—to recognize one's working conditions as abusive necessitates the witnessing of sadness. Can a witness understand sadness without the presence of tears? In *United States v. Dann,* the answer is no.

Understanding how one crosses into visibility as a trafficked person necessitates an examination of breaking moments for the witness (in the legal case, the U.S. attorney). According to prosecuting assistant U.S. attorney, the breaking moment in the case for the U.S. attorney arrived when Liliana narrated losing access to a radio. When the AUSA described the case, he emphasized how he did not witness Liliana cry until she described what happened with her radio, emphasizing that the tears came pouring down as she said, "And then she [Dann] broke my radio." The U.S. attorney submitted as evidence the significance of the breaking of Liliana's radio: "The complainant alleges Dann smashed [Liliana's] radio and a television set, to prevent her from listening to Spanish language programs that would, quote 'put ideas in her head.'"[90] After the breaking of the radio, Dann told Liliana, "When you come to the United States, you must suffer."[91] The district attorney/prosecutor has the power to create meaning for individuals witnessed as trafficked; therefore, it is essential to understand the breaking moment, the moment in which it is clear to the nonbeliever that what Liliana experienced was "suffering." The radio signified the last connection Liliana had with a Latina/o community, with the outside world. It was also the only item she was able to buy while living with Dann. The break of communication with the outside world perpetuated Liliana's social isolation. And, for Liliana, it was at this point that the tears fell, for despite the fact a radio is only an object, it was her last means of knowing anything about the "outside" world. For the prosecutor, the incident was moving enough to compel him to take the case to trial. However, just as compelling are the moments that Liliana did not cry—an absence of tears is just as central to an anti-trafficking narrative. Throughout much of Liliana's testimonial during the hearings, she did not cry. Instead, her story was narrated through dips and rises in the loudness of her voice, and a shifting pace, suggesting urgency, movement, and an intention to move the story forward. And yet, while crying reinforces an assumption of authenticity, the moments in which one does not cry accentuate that which is "sad." However, whether her tears were natural or forced, does not matter. What matters in *United States v. Dann* is that Liliana cried. Affect is a central part of translation work—where emotions, sentiments, and experience are translated—from the self-witness to the witness of the story. Affect in the court is also performed. The challenge is that people respond differently to traumatic events, where not all feelings of sadness translate into tears. Sometimes, a person can respond with a smile, laughter, apathy, anger, and a range of responses that can in some instances signify pain, loss, and suffering.

COURT PERFORMANCES AND TRANSLATIONS

The testimony and its translation are vital to conceptualizing human trafficking in *United States v. Dann*. The testimony is narrated by Liliana and represented in translation. Language translation takes place from Spanish to English. Liliana's testimony is performed in Spanish. However, her Cuzco origins and the diversity of languages in Lima (where Dann and Liliana were connected) invoke the possibility that Liliana's native language may not be Spanish, but rather Quechua.[92] Regardless, the court proceedings occurred in Spanish and English. Translation involves fragments of a "greater language."[93] The greater language in this narration contributes to the metanarrative of human trafficking. Translation is a mode by which the meaning of an "original" is conveyed. And, through the translator, the receiver of a translation learns to understand not only the "Other" being translated but also the translator as "self."[94]

The testimony is situated as legally authoritative, in that the witness is sworn to/affirms to tell the truth. To testify is to know one's story, a story that otherwise would be buried. The significance of a testimony is that it creates a sequence of events, a history. This type of oral history, which forms part of the public record and state archives, is one of the many forms of testimonials or *testimonios*.[95] John Beverly describes the *testimonio* as a form of autobiography, autobiographical novel, oral history, memoir, confession, diary, interview, eyewitness report, life history, novella-testimonio, nonfiction novel, or "factographic" literature. Testimonials include sound and video recordings that cannot take place in solitude, where "the witnesses are talking to somebody."[96]

It is impossible to summarize in a courtroom two years of labor trafficking.[97] The narrative is constructed over time as information is lost, remembered, and forgotten again, and some details are never recounted. Liliana's testimony is in itself new: it is her ability to recount in a linear narrative that which she may want to forget, or that which she remembers in too many significant details, a sequence of events in her life becomes a part of a larger narrative of an antitrafficking movement. Liliana's testimony enables her narrative as a survivor to enter into historical record,[98] with the possibility that information is lost in translation.

During the *United States v. Dann* trial, a male interpreter translated Liliana's story. In fact, the jury was instructed to base their decisions on the translation—even if some of the jurors understood Spanish, the English translation was the authoritative text, so as to have all jurors consider the "same evidence."[99]

The interpreter's credibility was heightened by his ability to mimic Liliana's intonation, gestures, and pace. The illusion and attempts to delineate the real were often disrupted during the court hearing by the translator interjecting when Liliana spoke. The interpreter repeatedly stated throughout Liliana's testimonial, "Your honor, the interpreter needs to ask for a repetition," "Your honor can we slow down a bit," and even during Liliana's narration of the breaking point, the interpreter exclaimed, "Wait, wait!"[100] These moments included the point in Liliana's narrative when she was asked to describe how things had changed a year after living with Dann; the point in Liliana's narrative when she described the increase in her tasks after Christmas (a list was created that Liliana needed to complete);[101] when she described what happened when she was witnessed speaking to a schoolteacher; and the moment she decided she could no longer stay at Dann's home.[102] The interpreter often paused, asking Liliana to wait for the translation to take place. Multiple times he requested the judge order Liliana to slow her testimony down, thus breaking the storytelling with pauses and shifts in voice. Robert Wechsler likens the process of a literary translator to that of a musician taking a composition and performing it in his/her own special way. Like the literary translator, the court translator has one performance.[103] Through the male voice and in English, Liliana's narrative is made legible and intelligible to a non-Spanish-speaking audience. During *United States v. Dann* voices shifted, Spanish to English to English to Spanish—a back and forth. For those who did not understand, the authoritative voice was not Liliana's but rather the interpreter's. The untrained ear does not catch any slippages. And to solidify the legitimacy of court translations, in this case, the interpreter's skills were not on trial and were never questioned. In fact, all evidence examined was to be done through the translation (even if one knew Spanish and noticed a slippage in translation).

What does it mean to translate that which someone may or may not desire to forget, and memories that are haunted by hyper memory and forgetting? The testimony is constructed out of memories that are at best fragmented, misremembered, and then constructed as linear. The time-space of memories is dependent on a visual, sensory, and conceptual recollection of moments in the *past*. Suppressing memory of violence so that one can avoid living in the past of traumatic memories, or the desire to live in such memories through hyper memory of a past, impacts the narrative of a testimony. The testimony is a frozen document that has weight in the legal sense, as a means to construct a narrative of trauma and memories of human trafficking. The testimony may be written or oral, and when performed for trial, the facts in the oral testimony must correlate with the written. What counts in the courtroom is the proper construction, even if memories are fragmented and distorted and include (re)envisioning. The trafficked person can be a self-witness. Their testimony in court, however, disciplines their memories through a narration that requires the retelling of events linearly, with no contradictions, no points of disjuncture. Memories that are unclear, fragmented, and filled with gaps are forced into a neat, linear narrative. How does one remember that which one has survived by forgetting? How does one remember in a climate in which a particular type of remembering—a story of exploitation—is necessary for one's survival (otherwise, Liliana and migrants like Liliana face deportation, imprisonment, or are forgotten because of the devaluation of immigrants in the United States)? The court performance in *United States v. Dann* leads to questions surrounding not only authority but also the process of translation.

The defense's closing statement in *United States v. Dann* suggests that there is a limit to translation beyond language, but even across ideological institutions. Dann's public defender's closing statement is useful as a point of departure for what can be translated within and what one can never translate:

> You'll recall that my colleague, Mr. Smock, cross-examined agent Vergara on the stand about Agent Vergara's involvement in the special smuggling and forced trafficking unit. It was their goal to spread it far and wide this type of crime going on. They utilized all means available to them. They contacted local law enforcement to say, 'be on the lookout, this type of stuff is going on. You need to be aware of it.' They tried to make the public aware of it. The media was used, television, radio, newspapers. They did outreach . . . when [Liliana], she came onto their radar screen, that was their opportunity. That was what they needed to show that they could make one of these cases stick. And once they got into the case, prodded by the immigration attorney that [Liliana] hired to go forward, she's got something to say, 'please take this thing forward,' they ran with it.

As the defense attorney called the jurors to recognize the politics of an anti-trafficking movement as translating for the masses that "This is trafficking," and to acknowledge the role of the government in such initiatives, the jurors could not see within legal structures, as they were also called to use the structure to decide justice for Liliana or an acquittal for Dann. The limits of translation are not merely across language; the translation (and the opportunities of mistranslation) are also inclusive of one being able to make a particular set of meanings legible across experience; it encompasses an array of translating meaning.

CLOSING: (IM)POSSIBLE RECONCILIATIONS

In examining Liliana and Dann's legal case as a witness interrogating witnessing, I am left with recognition of my own limits of witnessing, and of the process of witnessing in general. However, to examine witnessing and homosocial violence has multiple interventions in anti-trafficking discourse, feminist theory, and practice; what it means to witness cannot be taken for granted or naturalized. What is at stake for feminisms, theories in decolonization, and transnational framings is that to move beyond victim/criminal paradigms is to interrogate the mode of witnessing in itself and call for a new form of witnessing—an unsettled witnessing.

As Liliana's story is made visible, and legible, to those who witnessed her story in the legal system and in the media, an unsettled witnessing informed by decolonial practice begins with recognizing the boundaries of witnessing within colonial structures. In the anti-trafficking narrative, how Liliana matters is always, and only, in relation to her experience of human trafficking. Liliana's history in Cuzco, her transnational relationship with her boyfriend, her family (to whom she sent remittances), and her life in the United States, as well as other aspects of one's life that illustrate the complex humanity that one inhabits, are absent in the media, suggesting that what mattered was how Liliana was exploited, not how she lives.

To close, I end with a Dann who never speaks—therefore what was witnessed was her silence and mediation through other actors. Dann is an immigrant, a *limeña* Peruvian, a mother of three children, a divorcee, a former real-estate agent, a Berkeley alumna, and now a convicted felon who served time in jail. (January 2010 was the start of her five years in jail.) Dann's story is always mediated through other actors—through the U.S. attorney, the public defender, and the witnesses who took to the stand such as Liliana, a homeland security agent, an interviewer for the U.S. embassy, a senior security representative for American Airlines, officers of Walnut Police Department (two in total), a computer forensic agent, parents from the school her children attended (two in total), the head custodian at that school, a gardener, the gardener's employer, a property manager for the apartment building Dann, her children, and Liliana resided in, Dann's ex-boyfriend, her brother, and her brother's girlfriend. The courts never heard Dann's narration of her own story, even though witnesses described moments of choice even at the moment of arrest: prior to her arrest, Dann requested to be taken to the hospital to have a medical checkup.[104] Although she was arrested, it was on her terms, albeit limited. Similar to Liliana, Dann is always represented through other witnesses. But in contrast to Liliana, Dann never takes the stand. In a way, although problematic, how the media described Dann best illuminates how she is witnessed: "On Monday, Dann saw KTVU's camera and covered her face with what appeared to be a ski mask and goggles as she took her children to school."[105] A person attempting to live a life beyond the eye of the public, she was always in it and interpreted by it—covered yet on display.

Through an unsettled witnessing of *United States v. Dann,* I am left with a witnessing that is bound to possibility and irreconcilable tensions. As the Department of Justice has taken the center in the anti-trafficking movement with prosecuting human trafficking cases, *United States v. Dann* highlights that an anti-trafficking narrative is equated with the legal system—arresting trafficker(s). However, how this has enabled rights for Liliana is unclear. By the time of her trial, she only made $1,100 a month and lived in a shelter.[106] Although she is owed money, it is not clear if Liliana will ever see the restitution and civil claims ordered by the courts.[107] Liliana conveyed during her testimonial that she wanted an "American justice." Dann's arrest and conviction may or may not represent justice for Liliana, but it is an American justice, leaving one to wonder what is a Peruvian justice, a woman-of-color justice, or even a decolonized justice. As anti-traffickers are called to witness Liliana and Dann, one is left with a contradiction surrounding how one witnesses the legal system and how individual experiences are framed by U.S. perceptions of victims/criminals and colonial limitations. However, the possibility of what seems impossible—reconciliation with the limitations, and an imagining of a witnessing beyond what is seen—is an important decolonial maneuver because in the global modern economic system, working for a radical witnessing within the confines of colonial systems must be imagined and enacted. This matters where human trafficking is witnessed regularly through a range of contexts: on the Internet, in film, in the news, in schools, even in conversations where stories are passed down from one witness to another, both locally and transnationally.

5 (LIVING)DEAD SUBJECTS

Mamasans, *Sex Slaves, and Sexualized Economies*

IN 2018, AL JAZEERA COVERED THE EVICTION of Korean sex workers from Cheongyangni 588 district, a red-light district in Korea. The demolition of the red-light district has led to sexual economies being pushed underground and online, "making things more dangerous for sex workers."[1] Highlighting the complex lives of the women surviving in sexual economies in Seoul, South Korea, doomsday images accompanied the doom-filled narrative of danger, lack of resources, income displacement, and invisible voices—the voices of the women who work in the economies. The images included abandoned buildings and messages left by the sex workers in abandoned bathrooms. The absence of people in all but one of the images, which showed a single woman sitting alone in her sex shop, the last remaining sex shop, portrayed a picture of people in sexual economies as dead—long gone, no longer part of the present. The images were reminiscent of apocalyptic films. Unpeopled, their haunting nature manifests through the objects left behind, through the trash that surrounded the zoned-off construction site, and through the broken mirror with a message on the wall, "Big brothers! and uncles. Thank you during all this time. 588 representatives!" (see Figure 4), reminiscent of "millennial zombie" films. If a zombie is perceived of as incapable of examining itself, lacking consciousness, an object, dead, and perceived of as an "other,"[2] then Korean women who are tied to sexual economies are treated as zombified figures.

In 1992, Yoon Geum-ee (Yun Guem-i) was murdered in a U.S. military camp town. Her murderer was twenty-year-old Private Kenneth Lee Markle III, stationed at Camp Casey. The graphic images of her murdered body continue to be circulated: blood oozing from her head, a coke bottle inserted into her

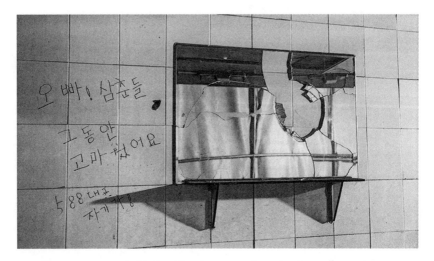

FIGURE 4.   A message left behind by the sex workers thanking the customers.
Al Jazeera.

vagina, an umbrella insert in her rectum, matchsticks in her mouth, white detergent over her body, and her blood on Markle's shoe.[3] In 2015, Markle was arrested for drunk driving in Maryland. The comments posted included, "This!@#$%tard is a murderer," "Brutal murderer," and even a link to a website describing the case.[4] Grace Cho describes how the murder of Yun represented a turning point for women in sexual economies: "A symbol of a colonized nation was transformed from the shameful sex worker in exile to the nation's daughter welcomed home."[5] Yun was not a trafficking survivor, but the case represents how Korean women's sexualities are resurrected in transnational discourse. Like the trafficking subject, the Korean sex worker, prostitute, "Yankee plaything," "comfort woman's" death embodies how Korean sexualities as dead or dying are resurrected for contemporary movements. Human trafficking survivors are not only iconic, but, when their death or dying status is central to how they matter for the living, this leads one to interrogate the resurrections of trafficking subjects as living(dead) subjects. It is important to think about the ghosts of earlier Asian women in a book on trafficking—the figures of the comfort women and wartime sex slaves are bound to twenty-first-century figures of the trafficked person. Although they are historically and contextually specific, collectively they illuminate the multiple colonialities in Asia (from Japanese to U.S.) and how sexuality, the body, and migrant subjects come to matter discursively and materially. To witness migratory subjects is not only to examine the present but also to see as productive a form of witnessing through an unsettled witnessing of subjects that are resurrected from the past for a contemporary moment. An example of the resurrections of the trafficked subject is best delineated through the figure of the "comfort woman." In 2003 and 2004, publications furthered the linkages between the sexual slavery of "comfort women" and human trafficking.[6] And by 2007, House Resolution 121 was passed, where it explicitly states:

> The government of Japan should: (1) formally acknowledge, apologize, and accept historical responsibility for its Imperial Armed Force's coercion of young women into sexual slavery (comfort women) during its colonial and wartime occupation of Asia and the Pacific Islands from the 1930s through the duration of World War II; (2) have this official and public apology presented by the Prime Minister of Japan; (3) refute any claims that the sexual enslavement and trafficking of the comfort women never occurred; and (4) educate current and future generations about this crime while following the international community's recommendations with respect to the comfort women.[7]

In this resolution, the U.S. government explicitly names the sexual slavery of the "comfort women" as "trafficking," even though human trafficking as we know it today was only legally codified in 2000.

However, not all Korean women who have been shaped by sex, sexual economies, militarisms, and coloniality will be relegated to the status of resurrection and memory. Some are relegated to dead status, forgotten by many. In Dongducheon there are unmarked graves. And as described by Katharine Moon, the murder of Yun Geumi did not inspire a movement.

Therefore, I call for an unsettled witnessing of how death matters in the circulation of Korean subjects as trafficked. As illuminated by Priest, "They [the dead] tell us both that the broken [racialized] body, central to the making of individual and collective power, must inevitably fail to produce a 'truth' that can recompense for the crime and that it will rise before us again and again."[8] The remembering of racialized figures who are resurrected, such as the sex worker, the comfort woman, and the sexual slave survivor, offers important lessons for diasporas and the witnesses of diasporic subjects. How they are remembered and how they "can be called upon, fed, and remembered" illuminates how sex and sexual economies come to matter in a praxis of witnessing. The figure of the comfort woman as a living(dead) subject who haunts the twenty-first century enables forms of remembering, but it also is a reminder of what is reconstituted—imperialism, militarisms, and nationalism. Her subjectivity can never be translated beyond the efficacy of her dead body. What kinds of methods may one invoke to make sense of her in relation to other forms of violence that surround Korean women diasporas? It is through an unsettled witnessing where multiple meanings and (im)possibilities of Korean diasporic sexualities may be conceptualized. An unsettled witnessing is a commitment to the complex. It invokes seeing and moving toward actions that encompass the plural, the multiple, without losing sight of how the multiple is tethered to individuals. An unsettled witnessing is a commitment to witnessing without being settled with what one is seeing. To commit to being unsettled in how one sees is to raise questions about normative aspects of events, to pay attention to the performances occurring in institutions, and to examine the politics of representation of victimhood, citizenry, race, and gender. Such witnessing enables seeing the complex humanity that the multiple witnesses embody, and even the complexity of dead and dying subjects.

Testimonies like Ha Koon's brought into Korean national consciousness the war crimes against the women.[9] They also awakened the international community to conceptualizing sexual slavery as a war crime with long-lasting and generational effects. As described by Sarah Soh, "More than sixty years have passed since the end of World War II, but the wounds of Japanese colonialism and war still fester in . . . East and Southeast Asia. . . . Thanks to social movements that began in South Korea, Japan, and elsewhere in the early 1990s comfort women survivors are now represented as "sex slaves" of wartime imperial Japan."[10] Comfort women are survivors of wartime atrocities during World War II. The "comfort woman" has many names: in Japanese she is *Jūgun ianfu* (military comfort woman). She was expected to provide comfort to Japanese military personnel during Japanese expansion throughout the Asia-Pacific prior to World War II and during the war period. The original translation of *ianfu* is the euphemism "comfort girl." In the everyday, military personnel used slang such as *pi* to refer to the women, which might be translated as "cunt"[11]—she was reduced to the derogatory and denigrated. The "comfort women" have many names. In Japan they are referred to as *Jūgun ianfu*, which translates to "comfort women." In Korean, *Chŏngshindae* translates to "Women's Volunteer Labor Corps" or *wianbu* (comfort women), illustrating the coercive elements of their recruitment—recruited Chŏngshindae assumed they would work in Japanese factories but encountered an experience they did not agree to—a narrative of trafficking. They are also referred to as *halmoni* (grandmother) as a form of respect. And, similarly, in the Philippines they are called *lolas* (grandmother). They are also referred to as "sex slaves" due to the mass mobilization that began in the Asia-Pacific, spreading to the Americas and Europe, raising awareness surrounding the exploitation of the comfort women in militarized systems. For those who lived to testify to their experiences, death was a part of their lives in the comfort stations. Koon-ja Kim, a former comfort woman, is cited as stating that if they resisted they "would be punished, beaten, or stabbed by the soldiers."[12] As the women were shaped by their lives as former comfort women, sex slaves, and survivors, it was their death, their aging status that served as the precipice for international actions surrounding reconciliation, a turning point in the international movement. In 2007, Representative Mike Honda urged the U.S. House of Representatives Foreign Affair Subcommittee on Asia, the Pacific, and the Global Environment to support HR 121, stating, "The urgency is upon this Committee and the Congress to take quick action on this resolution. These women are aging and their numbers dwindling with each passing day."[13] But the comfort woman, sex slave, *Chŏngshindae*, *lolas*, trafficked victim, militarized prostitute, and the many names she carries are not simply shaped by death. As a dead and dying figure, *she* is continually reanimated through the specificity of her status as slave and victim. This chapter grapples with a particular trafficking subject that has been located in the past, resurrected for the present of the twenty-first century. As the formerly captive,[14] the fallen,[15] comfort women are living(dead) subjects.

To examine the resurrection of figures, this chapter first frames a theory of the living(dead). Following this framing, a historical tracing of the comfort women and sexual slavery during World War II is highlighted to illustrate how the comfort woman is resurrected and how she is resurrected through discourses surrounding sexual slavery and *mamasans,* through the exemplars of Mi Na Malcolm and Kyong Jackie Roberts. The chapter ends with a discussion of how subjects are bound to dualities in twenty-first-century filmic representations.

THEORY OF THE LIVING(DEAD)

Death is physical, social, and civil,[16] where the figure of the living(dead), the undead, the zombie points directly to a struggle between life and death. A theory of the living(dead), or zombie theory, may for some be tied to a history of vodoun and the zombie in Haitian culture.[17] To examine zombified figures is to see them as intersectionally constructed subjects—racialized and gendered.[18]

While it was not until the twenty-first century that the millennial zombie in television was popularized, the grappling with death frames the living.[19] To discuss comfort women as the living(dead), this chapter is inspired by the work of Myisha Priest, who describes Emmett Till as a living(dead) subject. Emmett Till was brutally murdered at the age of fourteen in 1955 for allegedly flirting with a white woman. Priest conveys how Mamie Till, Emmett's mother, and his relatives held an open-casket funeral. They sought a particular type of justice, one that revealed the "untold story" of Emmett Till, by exhuming his murdered and mutilated body:

> Public recognition of the untold knowledge of the body, not necessarily legal action, would bring about justice. In making suffering visible and audible . . . is also to hear "what cannot be conveyed." Justice, then, is not a matter of compensation and closure but the creation of a mechanism for the continued enunciation of pain . . . a way of remembering and reckoning with the pained subjectivity of Emmett Till that makes him a part of the "living dead," one who "can be called upon, fed, and remembered."[20]

Like Emmett Till, the body of the comfort woman is a resurrected dead figure; she is the living(dead). The resurrection is symbolic, the breaking of silence. It is also a resurrection of those who have passed away or died, and their lives as former slaves are called upon by people living in formerly occupied zones and zones that continue to be occupied, by diasporas, and by an international human rights community to point to a history of Japanese imperialism, to reveal an untold story, a history ignored, reified by the Shinzo Abe administration, which denies the history of comfort women. Therefore, in an effort to call for justice, the comfort woman continues to be called upon, fed, and remembered. She, too, is a resurrected figure, whose life is shaped by her sexual slavery and a death of the person she once was. She is a plaque on a stone where the image is of a woman huddled in front of an ominous soldier in Palisades Park, New Jersey;[21] she is signified by boulders with two butterflies as benches in Fairfax, Virginia;[22] and she is frozen in time as a life-sized bronze statue of a comfort woman sitting on a chair in Glendale, California. In San Francisco, she is a contested figure—a column of strength where three women representing China, Korea, and the Philippines stand in a circle, holding hands.[23] An iconic figure, she travels from Asia to the Americas and beyond. And in the actions to reclaim her, she too is the living(dead), in which an enunciation of pain continues to be transmitted transnationally from formerly and ongoing occupied countries and beyond.

The figure of the comfort woman who represents the fallen women, *wianbu*, as sex slaves, is positioned in contrast to the heroes of war—the soldier. The U.S. flag draped over caskets, the image of white crosses for headstones, and the sound of a bugle playing "taps" collectively reinforce the sounds, images, language, and even collective sentiments that death inscribes in a militarized context. Death during wartime as encompassing civilian or soldier casualty is naturalized.[24] If the soldier is the masculine hero, a comfort woman is the victim who the twenty-first-century witness is also called to rescue. She represents the collateral of war. But one cannot contend with the comfort women without thinking through death. Death is material and symbolic, and has ideological power. Death inspires social movements. It also encompasses the use of weapons to enact destruction—what Mbembe calls the creation of "death worlds,"[25] where populations are subjected to conditions of a social life where their status is one that constitutes them as the "living dead."[26]

Those who continue to live—not dead, not resurrected—are relegated to a social death. Lisa Marie Cacho's definition of social death is useful here: "To be ineligible for personhood . . . it not only defines who does not matter, it also makes mattering meaningful. For different reasons, undocumented immigrants, the racialized poor of the global South, and criminalized U.S. residents of color in both inner cities and rural areas are populations who 'never achieve, in the eyes of others, the status of living.'"[27] Therefore, what are the meanings that continue to have valence with the transnational circulation of Korean women as dead and dying subjects, and how are such meanings invoked to address Korean women's sexuality in the twenty-first century?

How does one remember subjects who are highly sexualized, whose meaning is shaped by nationalist discourses, neoliberal economic realities, militaristic, and imperialist legacies, and whose lives encompass both the horror of slavery and the resiliency of being human, of which, they continue to be resurrected through a discourse that reproduces a tethered subjectivity? It is through theorizing the figure of the comfort woman as a living(dead) subject, one who is called upon, summoned, and resurrected, that we are able to unsettle witnessing. But the witnessing, the unsettling of witnessing must not be contained. Grace Cho links the configurations of Korean women's (dis)embodiment that haunt the diaspora beyond the comfort women and sex slave: "*Yanggongju*. Yankee whore. Western princess. GI bride. *Yanggalbo*. *Yangssaekshi*. GI's plaything. UN lady. Bar girl. Entertainment hostess. *Wianbu*. Fallen woman. Formerly a comfort woman. Formerly called a comfort woman. Daughter of a comfort woman. Camptown prostitute. Military bride."[28] For Cho, the *yanggongju* vacillates between hypervisibility and invisibility, haunting the diaspora. On the one hand she is a victim, and on the other she is positioned as morally corrupt, bound to images of criminality as a bar girl, hostess, fallen woman, and even "madam."[29] This bounded enfiguring of transnational migrants is a tethered subjectivity. As the multiple understood sexualized meanings of comfort woman, *Chŏngshindae*, sex slave, militarized prostitute, sextrafficked victim, sex worker, and madam finds their way into popular culture and the media, dualities continue to persevere where such imaginings of sexualities reify the opposing image of Asian women's sexualities as "dragon lady" and "lotus blossom." She is a figure who is continually resurrected, especially when modern colonialities manifest in a pacific pivot, in a military turn to the Asia-Pacific, and in neoliberal capitalism in the form of transpacific partnerships. Korean women's sexualities, as a resurrection of the living(dead), are an invocation of Orlando Patterson's concept of the social death, where the representation of social death is when socially dead subjects are positioned as the enemy on the inside—the domestic enemy (the intrusive mode of representing social death) and forever an outsider who does not or no longer belongs.[30]

RESURRECTING THE LIVING(DEAD): COMFORT WOMEN

Comfort women have historically been relegated to a dead status through efforts to erase their experience and the silence surrounding what occurred in occupied countries during World War II. A theme that continues to shape contemporary discourse surrounding Japanese systems of sexual slavery during World War II is silence. However, due to the absence of evidence, known comfort stations are the "tip of the iceberg." According to a report by Nakayama Tadanao, director of the Nakayama Institute of Japanese-Chinese Medicine, "when the Japanese army advances, the officers' primary concern is the transportation of the 'girl army.' The reason Japanese troops don't rape Chinese women is precisely because they have the girl army.' So they are not merely prostitutes!"[31] As the "girl army" was envisioned as a central aspect of wartime efforts, how this "girl army" was raised was at the center of debates most visibly in the international community in the 1980s. The women were described in Japanese documents as "camp followers," so they were already absent in their documentation.[32] After nearly fifty years of silence, the comfort women began to demand justice. And through their testimonials, they resurrected the dead, testifying to experiences that had been buried, and testifying to the dead who had been silenced for decades.

Testimonial narratives are a mechanism of summoning the dead and are central to breaking the silence surrounding wartime crime. These are the life stories and published personal accounts of the comfort women's experiences.[33] The comfort women's narrative testimonials expose that their experiences were diverse, including physical abuse, verbal abuse, rape, hard labor, and even murder.[34] Those who survived live with physical markers such as scars and disfigurement from rape and other forms of physical torture; venereal disease, including gonorrhea and syphilis; an inability to give birth; and posttraumatic stress disorder and other mental disorders from rape and physical traumas experienced as military comfort women. The testimonial narrative has been central to propelling the "comfort woman" experience into the public eye and unveiling an invisible history. In many ways, testimonials have been important recovery work serving a historical function: "Only through these women's testimonies can we discover the stark realities that never appear in military government documents, reports, or statistics."[35] The former comfort women's narratives were central to organizing the international community to respond to the war crimes committed by the Japanese government; they were the central evidence. By the 1990s, Korean activists organized to call for reconciliation for the comfort women as a human rights violation. Comfort women became equated with war crimes of sexual slavery.[36] And the international circulation of the testimonial narratives was made possible by organizations such as the Washington Coalition for Comfort Women Issues. Beginning in 1994, they interviewed fourteen women and collected five testimonies from North Korea and another from an international symposium.[37] The circulation of the Korean women's testimonial was characterized by *han*, a painful, invisible knot that an individual carries in their heart over a long period.[38] However, what is lost in translation? Whose experiences were not represented and are, in effect, a life history that the public can never come to know and witness? In the 1980s, dying comfort women began organizing for redress; their movement was internationalized.

In 1991, the Asian Women Human Rights Council, a Manila-based NGO, hosted a conference in Seoul. The conference discussed the trafficking of Asians, and it was here that Filipina *lolas,* or grandmothers, also began to name their experiences during Japanese occupation as "comfort women." This led to the establishment in 1992 of the Task Force on Filipino Comfort Women (TFFCW).[39]

The TFFCW made a radio announcement asking former comfort women to
come forward—169 women came forward. In 1992, Maria Rosa Luna Henson,
also known as Lola Rosa, was the first Filipina to come out in public about her
experiences of wartime rape as a comfort woman. Lola Rosa went public because
she believed her "role was to serve as an example to other survivors of wartime
sex slavery who may still be ashamed to come out with their experience."[40]

Beginning in the 1990s, the calls for justice went hand in hand with cultural narratives in the form of novels to grapple with death and truth in
regards to the comfort women's experience. Her dying status meant that with
her death her story would disappear. The pressures for reconciliation in the
1990s were also due to a fear that former comfort women would never witness
a formal apology. They called the Japanese government to apologize formally
for the World War II war crime. The backdrop of truth is shaped by silence,
which is taken up by creative writers like Nora Okja Keller in her novel *Comfort Woman*. *Comfort Woman* tells the story of a former comfort woman, Akiko
Bradley, and her mixed-race Korean American daughter, Beccah. The reader
learns that Akiko's real name prior to being forced into wartime sexual slavery was Soon Hyo. Silence is a central theme in the novel. Soon Hyo rarely
speaks. (Her language was controlled during the war—she was forbidden from
speaking Korean, and even after the war in her marriage she only speaks in
English.) Her endeavors to speak are literally covered, in which her husband
covers her mouth, stating, "I ask you to protect our daughter, with your silence,
from the shame."[41] The multiple aspects of silence are metaphorical, historical,
and ideological.[42] As the novel illustrates, the silence is both forced and
embraced by the figure of Akiko as comfort woman and survivor. And the
centralizing of the comfort woman experience and her generational implications in creative works is illustrative of how women's bodies come to stand for
the national body, reproducing national subjectivities. The comfort woman
signifies, as a figure in history (i.e., comfort women), the nation (i.e., Korea,
Japan, and China).[43] She is a figure that must be understood not only by historical context and through frames of silencing but also through theories that
make sense of structural power, sexuality, and nationhood. In search of reconciliation through war crimes, the polarized events that have occurred between
Japan and the former "comfort women" are a battle of truths in history. Although Abe and others have attempted to deny the experience of comfort
women, the goal should not be denial. Rather, it should be to understand how
a lack of complex personhood makes it difficult to see survivors of sexual

slavery as also encompassing contradiction, agency, choice, and even pleasure and life, in the context of violence (both systemic and physical violence). By examining the comfort woman as contradictory, one may understand how it is that through other figures—the *mamasan*, the sex slave, and the trafficked person—she continues to be resurrected through colonial systems that depend on militarisms and racialized sexualities.

RESURRECTING THE DEAD THROUGH DISCOURSES OF
SEXUAL SLAVERY AND *MAMASANS*

The terms of visibility for women in sexual economies in the U.S. legal system are shaped by how the comfort women are resurrected and circulate. The dichotomous figure in the legal record—victim of human trafficking/criminalized sex worker—is tethered to dualities. And when victimhood is called upon, it is also a resurrecting of the comfort woman as sex slave. Take, for example, the two "Jane Does" who were material witnesses in *United States v. Kyongja Kang* (2005). Wun Hee Kang and Kyongja Kang, a married couple, owned several nail salons on Long Island and a bar known as Renaissance in Queens, New York. In April 2003, Kyongja traveled to South Korea to recruit young women to work at Renaissance. The women were promised pay of $40 per day, plus tips, and would not be required to have sexual relations with the customers while working at the bar. Instead, they found themselves in debt of $20,000, sexually abused, assaulted, and forced to prostitute by Wun Hee, who threatened them death. In a case where a migrant becomes a sex-trafficked victim, to see her victim status, one must resurrect the figure of the comfort woman, calling upon her pain, and therefore the pain of Jane Doe. Jane Doe's experience is shaped by threats, kicks, screams, unable to leave, and being held captive in a basement. Her ability to move on without a public eye on her life is central to her healing. But, as she moves, her status as "Jane Doe" is forever a part of the repertoire of living(dead) subjects who are resurrected. To be a living(dead) subject means that Jane Doe is effaced from a public narrative where her hopes and pleasures as a person whose life extends with and beyond a trafficking one are absent to the public. Her socially dead status is necessitated, where she will always be Jane Doe the outsider who does not belong, a victim, a sex-trafficked victim. In contrast to the sex-trafficked victim as a socially dead subject is the *mamasan*.

Kyong "Jackie" Roberts, also known as the Dallas "madam," or notable *mamasan*, represents another common polarized image of the Asian female—the "dragon lady" who circulates in anti-trafficking narratives. The resurrection of the victim, the slave, also reifies another figure—Asian women who utilize their sexuality and participate in sexualized economies. The story unfolds in the *Morning Dallas News*: "Madam's Fall Offers Window into Lucrative Sex Trade Federal Agents, Police Team Up to Put Dent in Dallas Prostitution." The news coverage summarizes Jackie's career. She came to America as the "Korean bride of a U.S. servicemen more than twenty years ago and climbed from dress shop owner to modeling studio proprietor to queen of Asian brothels."[44] The brothels that Jackie and her co-conspirator, Mi Na Malcolm, operated included massage parlors, spas, baths, saunas, modeling studios, and nightclubs.[45] In a single day, Dallas police, ICE, and the FBI seized almost $500,000 in cash and more than 138,000 condoms. Millions in assets were seized through the raids. Robert's partner Malcolm was sentenced to ten years in prison with a fine of $460,000 after pleading guilty to "conspiracy to hold or harbor illegal aliens for purposes of prostitution, harboring illegal aliens for commercial advantage and private financial gain, and bulk cash smuggling."[46] In contrast, Roberts and her husband, Cho, were convicted of conspiracy to structure large currency deposits and monthly rents from individuals operating prostitution and other businesses. In 2007, law enforcement received $367,356.20 in forfeited assets from Roberts and Cho, and they were sentenced to 37 months and 30 months in prison respectively.[47] Neoliberal responses to human trafficking have made assets (and asset forfeiture) a central aspect of anti-trafficking efforts. And the complex personhood even of traffickers is denied, as they are reduced to villainy and a threat to the U.S. economy, disconnected from the complex economic, political, and social structures creating and sustaining the need for migrants to participate in informal economies. Complexity and the ability to commit violence are not mutually exclusive.

Roberts is imagined as lacking a complex history—she is reduced to being a criminal migrant to which the victimized migrant is tethered. The history of Roberts's relationship to her husband is absent in the media coverage of the case; all that is known is that she went from military bride to a Dallas madam.[48] Absent in the media depictions of Jackie (and migrants like Jackie who participate in or facilitate exploitation) are the societal conditions that compel such individuals to survive by participating in criminal networks in the United States. Instead of a complex story, the crackdown on a criminal enterprise of Dallas's most infamous madam held the center of the story. Roberts became the figure of the threatening madam, and law enforcement, the triumphant hero.

The image of Asians as a threat is reminiscent of Yellow Peril discourse. Journalist Tim Wyatts, who covered the story, quotes Roberts as saying in response to whether or not she knew prostitution was occurring in her spas, "I don't have to answer that. . . . You know what goes on in those places. I have to make money, like everyone else."[49] As Roberts pled ignorance, the money uncovered in the sting operations and Roberts's role with smuggling migrants was positioned as a threat to U.S. formal economies and border security. What mattered in the portrayal of the case in the media was the scale of her operations in the media narrative; Roberts was positioned as a threat to U.S. territoriality and was described as operating criminal networks, in the United States from Texas to California, and transnationally from South Korea to the United States via Canada and Mexico. The *Dallas Morning News* cites the "fall of the madam" as being part of a larger federal effort involving large-scale raids and indictments in Los Angeles and San Francisco.[50] In many ways, Roberts was tethered to familiar iconic images of the "dragon lady" who uses her sexuality to get what she wants (i.e., through complicity in sexual economies) and who is a threat to the United States. Her migrant status bound her to a discourse surrounding undesirable migration. The homosocial forms of violence continue to be uncontested, and the survival circuits within which migrants continue to survive, naturalized. Although Roberts is constructed as a villain, a danger, and a threat, she is also part of the same manifestation that constructs Jane Doe, the perfect victim.

Although the story was painted as a human trafficking one, only five of the forty-two arrestees were eligible for human trafficking benefits and the T-Visa, which enables survivors to stay in the United States legally, work, and receive cash-aid and medical assistance through the Office of Refugee & Resettlement. Even though the women who worked for Roberts and Malcolm were described as working in debt, as having had their passports taken (to guarantee they pay back their debt), as enjoying limited mobility, and as being under constant camera surveillance,[51] thirty-four of the forty-two were deported, reinforcing the polarized identities that continue to define migrant women who survive in sexual economies as victims and criminals. Invisible in media discussions about human trafficking is the vulnerability migrants face when they are identified not as victims but as criminals during law enforcement raids of potential human trafficking rings. These migrants are at risk for deportation and criminalization. Political scientists Rebecca Bohrman and Naomi Murakawa assert that immigration and crime control "have not only grown in parallel fashion, they have become more interlocking."⁵² In fact, this is not unusual, as migrants caught in federal raids are required to testify against their employers/traffickers. (If they do not do so, they are deemed uncooperative, undesirable, inassimilable subjects who are deportable.)

Like Emmett Till, the knowledge that the comfort woman, sex slave, and *mamasan* embodies destroys her; "it penetrates the white male subject and is absorbed, constituting him. . . . [Like Till, her] subjectivity can never be translated beyond the efficacy of [the] dead body . . . collapsed upon itself, this density of meaning, and splintered a million ways at once."⁵³ The haunting nature of what the comfort woman represents and has come to represent in the United States surrounding racialized sexualities of Asian women also manifests in filmic representation.

EDEN: YELLOW PERIL, TETHERED SUBJECTS, AND
ANTI-TRAFFICKING FILMS

How are Korean Americans making sense of the legacies of the comfort woman who is resurrected as a living(dead) figure? It is here that I turn to the film *Eden*. Films in the United States recirculate narratives about migrants in transnational sexual economies that occur in the Greater Mekong subregion, from Cambodia in the documentary *Redlight* (2009) or *Call + Response* (2008), to Thailand in *Sacrifice* (2007), as well as South Asia of India through films like *Born into Brothels* (2004). The perception of Korean sexualities, vulnerabilities, and exploitation is tethered to Asia. Collectively media productions, from film to the Internet, shape the visual terrain of raced/gendered subjectivities, but they also reinforce consumer activisms that naturalize racial, national, and gendered assumptions of subjectivities (victims, rescuers, criminals; first world, third world; women and children) and what constitutes a desirable response to violence.⁵⁴ Human trafficking iconographies in the twenty-first century reproduce fears and anxieties about the Asian migrant as "Other," as well as circulate ideologies of fascination and fixation, a phenomenon that is reminiscent of Yellow Peril discourse. Yellow Peril discourse is theorized in media studies (i.e., Gina Macchetti, Kent Ono, and Vincent Pham) as being tied to migration, citizenship, and the circulation of images, policies, and texts that reinforce the perception that Asians are a threat to whites and to American citizenry.

An example of the complex ways in which Asians are tethered to the polarized images of the lotus blossom and the dragon lady (but are also complicit in such imaginings) is best delineated in the film *Eden* (2012), directed by

Megan Griffiths. The film is based loosely on the experiences of Chong Kim, a Korean American who publicly speaks and writes about being trafficked in the United States. *Eden* stars Jamie Chung as Hyun Jae, a nineteen-year-old Korean American who finds herself in the trunk of the car of a man in uniform she befriends at a bar during a night out with a girlfriend (Abbie, played by Tracey Fairaway). The viewers watch Hyun Jae experience being trafficked from her hometown in Arizona to a warehouse that functions as a brothel trafficking girls as young as twelve for sex (Hyun Jae, at eighteen or nineteen, is one of the oldest girls), facilitated by Bob Gault (a marshal played by Beau Bridges, who is a "dirty cop").[55] Jamie Chung's character is tethered between two subjectivities: the passive lotus blossom and the threatening dragon lady. Hyun Jae symbolizes the passive Asian—raised by Korean parents in Tucson, Arizona, and with a common Korean name meaning wisdom and respect. From a respectable common Korean girl, Hyun Jae, she is renamed "Eden," which she is told is the Hebrew word for "delight"—as Eden, she is complicit in trafficking, she murders her traffickers, and she is even shown to be performing Orientalism on screen—as Eden she symbolizes the dragon lady. The film moves the viewer through a protagonist who begins, sex-trafficked, behind a cage but who eventually becomes a complicit participant in the brothel system, and whose departure is facilitated by her killing her traffickers. As the film redeploys racialized meanings of the trafficked person, the viewer is never called to actively participate in witnessing violence, only to witness what is implied.[56] However, the viewer sees Eden and the other girls she is trafficked with handcuffed, beaten, verbally abused, psychologically abused, and behind cages. To leave the brothel, Eden participates in sexual economies and the trafficking of other girls. When she leaves, Eden calls her mother and refers to herself as Hyun Jae, restoring the image of who the viewer is being called to rescue—the lotus blossom who becomes the dragon lady but who can be restored to the figure of the passive Asian. Such a dynamic is a tethered subjectivity that anti-trafficking iconographies reproduce about Asian Americans and Asian migrants trafficked within the United States.

The story developed in *Eden* represents the variety of images in the visual economy of human trafficking and human rights that reinforce citizenship and national belonging. (Theoretical framings on human trafficking and human rights are further examined by Wendy Hesford and Julietta Hua.) The film's images are mired in anti-trafficking iconographies of trafficked people as bound and caged, reinforcing liberal desires to free the trafficked subject (and migrants who are viewed as desirable). The *New York Times* review of the film conveys what viewers are left with: "After watching 'Eden,' you may worry that the cargo in any innocent-looking white van streaking down a highway may not be furniture and home appliances but a group of chained sex slaves being taken from one hell to another in a sadistic warlord's fiendish underground network."[57] Eden is the sex slave, monolithic, chained; and the fear is that she lurks in our everyday. As Asian migrant tethered subjectivities are bound to identities as passive victims and criminals, Asian migrants participate in such logics through yellow-face. In one particular scene, Eden is taken into a room lit with red lights. Eden faces an older white American who wears a suit, whose dress contrasts greatly to the dress Eden wears with flower prints that mimic Orientalist perceptions of Asian silk, and her hair is pulled into a bun—she embodies the trope of the *yonggangju*, the Western princess who has sexual relations with Americans.

Chung's character, Eden, is also an American; however, she is an American performing Orientalist desires of the exotic Other, pretending to be Chinese, with an exaggerated accent. During a visit to one of their sites, Eden is in a private room with an older white man. She approaches the man, placing her right hand on his shoulder as she walks around him. Standing in back of him, she helps him take off his jacket, asking him in an Orientalized accent that is docile and sweet, "So mistah? What's your name?" He responds, "Uh, Bill." Eden continues, "You have such nice eyes Bill. So handsome." As Bill sits down, he responds, "You say that to everyone." Eden replies, "No, I like you Bill," as she moves in front of Bill and lowers to her knees, helping to remove Bill's tie. Bill asks, "What's your name?" Smiling coyly, she responds, "Eden." Bill asks, "Where you from?" which leads Eden to respond "China." Bill follows with a question, "Oh yeah? Where?" Eden smiles at Bill, saying, "Just China." Leaning in toward Bill, as Bill moans, she then lowers herself in relation to Bill asking, "Okay Bill, you want me to take control or you take control?" as she performs what is assumed to be fellatio. Bill breathes out and the viewer never hears his answer. *IndieWire* describes the scene as a "moment of humor and humanity."[58] Regardless of whether one is laughing, Eden calls attention to Orientalism and the dualities that construct Asian women's sexualities. Additionally, she points to Asian American complicity in racial performance as means of survival. Contextualizing complicity in racializing logics as survival leads one to consider what the conditions are of such participation: for Eden it was violence, or worse, death.

The complex manifold in which Asians are constituted in the United States is situated through binary images of threat and assimilation. Yellow Peril discourse (the belief that Asians are a threat to U.S. and Euro-Americans) manifests in the portrayal of China and North Korea, where the geopolitics of Asia as a threat stems from Cold War logics. Yellow Peril discourse is dependent on metaphors of Asians as perils, pollutants, and contaminants to the United States and its citizens[59] and is theorized as linked to Asian exclusions. Scholars in media studies have theorized the gendered imaginings of Asian Americans; in particular, Renee E. Tajima offers language to describe the polarized gendered imaginings of Asian women as dragon ladies and lotus blossoms. The image of Asian women using their sexuality to get what they want, of the threatening Asian female figure, and of the lotus blossom as an innocent figure to be rescued, manifested in the twentieth century as Asians (and their representation) were produced on screen as a means to narrate U.S. preoccupations with peoples from Asia (and their exclusions from a U.S. citizenry). Such articulations of Asian/American women have transnational implications. Historian Erika Lee uses the concept "hemispheric orientalism" to describe the transnational nature of exclusions and anti-immigration policies.[60] The representation of human trafficking and its subjects, in particular Asian subjects, is one that is produced through yellow-face logics.

How Asians/Americans are portrayed on screen is solidified through yellow-facing. By yellow-facing, I refer on the one hand to where Asians are impersonated by non-Asian figures, blurring the Asian/American difference.[61] To participate in yellow-face logics is to exaggerate the visual aesthetic of "Asians," through the performance of Asian language as a distorted English, and a dress that is aestheticized as orient. Yellow-facing is a racial masquerade.[62] However, on the other hand, Asians/Americans also participate in yellow-face logics[63] that enable them to become visible, albeit limited, as subjects (even if raced, gendered, and classed) in a dominant society. Therefore, what is at stake in examining dominant constructions of anti-trafficking iconographies is the need to further understand and situate Asian/Americans as active participants in these imaginings, articulations, and practices that circulate about homosocial forms of violence. The complicity must be contextualized as survival in the face of erasure and social death. By tracing the comfort woman, the sex worker, and the trafficked survivor as resurrected figures, one finds that what is continually reified is the human/nonhuman divide.

THE HUMAN/NONHUMAN

Examining the living(dead) subject that shapes racial sexualities of Asian migrant laborers necessitates a discussion of the human/nonhuman divide that
shapes trafficking subjects. *Deadgirl* (2008) is a U.S. horror film directed by
Marcel Sarmiento and Gadi Harel. In the film, two high-school seniors, Rickie
and J.T., come across a naked, undead woman chained in the basement of a
psychiatric hospital. The zombie figure is named Deadgirl. In Steven Jones's
analysis of the film, the film exposes questions around whether a zombie can
suffer. And also consent.[64] These questions remind one of Yun Geumi. She was
not seen as a subject having a personhood that could experience suffering and
could be raped, even though the public knows she was raped and brutally murdered. Her rape and murder were so violent, it is a reminder of the human/
nonhuman status Korean women and their sexualities are relegated to. This
human/nonhuman status is reminiscent of Lisa Marie Cacho's definition of
social death, where it encompasses those who have been denied personhood.
Therefore, a zombie or a person relegated to social death status is denied a
personhood that enables them to be seen as a subject who can consent and
experience suffering and harm. Just as the large numbers of pleasure-bots blur
the human/nonhuman divide,[65] for the sex worker, the comfort woman, the
trafficked survivor, the human/nonhuman divide is bound to a narrative of
victimization and suffering. To be seen as human is to be a seen as a subject
who can suffer.[66] However, rather than reify human supremacy, this chapter
has sought to contend with human/nonhuman subjectivities that the figures
of the comfort woman, the sex worker, and the survivor inhabit.

CLOSING: CONTENDING WITH THE LIVING(DEAD) OF
ANTI-TRAFFICKING DISCOURSE

Drawing upon Lisa Marie Cacho's analysis of neoliberal ideologies of worth as
reproducing socially dead subjects, I examine how the representation of Korean sexualities reproduce living(dead) subjects that haunt the living. The resurrected status of the Korean comfort women shapes Korean diasporas in
general—that is, as the "comfort woman" is called upon time and again, she
matters not only for Korea but also for how Korean diasporas, in particular
Korean women's sexualities, circulate. While the resolve to address the
living(dead) is to kill it, one must enact decolonial visions, visions that believe
in redress and visions that reconcile with the need for coexistence while holding

radical visions. For, as illuminated by Jodi Byrd regarding zombie imperialism, it "is the current manifestation of a liberal democratic colonialism that locates biopower at the intersection of life, death, law, and lawlessness—what Mbembe has termed necropolitics—where death belongs more to racialized and gendered multitudes and killing becomes 'precisely targeted.'"[67] But how comfort women and similar figures are resurrected is part of the process of reconciliation. To remember is to reconcile and reckon with the horrors of a past and bring it into the present time and again. Saidiya Hartman and Stephen Best propose that the project of redress means that we concern ourselves with questions that prevent us from forgetting a "past that is not past" and that demand other modes of remembrance, modes that recognize that achieving justice will mean living in the knowledge that "what has been destroyed cannot be restored."[68] It is through conceptualizing the comfort women as living dead that one can also make sense of the living(dead) status of bar girls, sex workers, and trafficked people in the twenty-first century. The socially dead status normalizes their subjectivity as other, where transnational migrant laborers who are bound to sexual economies are also tethered to the logics that deny rights in the form of citizenship that allows one to fully participate in social life. The resurrected figure of the comfort woman finds herself in the figure of the sex worker, the prostitute, the "Yankee plaything," the *mamasan*, the Korean war bride, and the sex slave; these are the many names through which she is resurrected, that tether her experience from Korea to an international discourse of the living(dead). These figures are continually resurrected because their sexuality, gender, nation, and race, whose subjectivity is one that is relegated to social death, requires their living(dead) status to manifest for social, political, legal, and discursive purposes. The living(dead) status of the comfort woman is resurrected not only in her iconography and circulation but also through the narrative of the sex-trafficked victim. In effect, anti-violence movements see her rise again as a means to mobilize a movement through logics that continue the racializing, gendering, and nationalizing logics of pain and suffering.

CONCLUSION

IN THIS MOMENT, immigration clearly continues to be a central political and social issue in the United States, from immigration being perceived of as a security threat—where in 2017 President Trump signed an executive order restricting entry from countries considered "a state sponsor of terrorism"[1]—to immigration policies limiting family members from entering into the United States,[2] and policies that draw a more strictly defined line between the perfect victim and the imperfect one.[3] A project such as *Migrant Crossings*, therefore, where I examine how migrants are figured legally as (non)citizen subjects and as victims/criminals, is not only timely but also relevant for policy and practice that shapes real people's lives. In the opening of *Migrant Crossings*, I shared the story of Saul, a young person from Honduras, an undocumented youth. Next to Saul's story in the Freedom Network USA press release about undocumented migrants was the story of Pablo. It seems only fitting to close with how this journey of *Migrant Crossings* began: with a story of undocumented youth, but here I introduce Pablo.

> When Pablo was just 15 years old, Mara Salvatrucha (MS) gang members came [to] this high school and tried to force Pablo to join them. Pablo did not want to be part of a gang and repeatedly told the older boys he would not join them. But the gang would not accept "no" for an answer and told Pablo they would kill him if he refused. Terrified for his life, Pablo begged his parents, who had come to the United States when he was young, to bring him and his younger brother to the United States as well. He knew that he would never be safe in El Salvador because of the threats against him. Pablo's parents arranged for a

coyote to bring him and his brother to the United States. However, instead of bringing Pablo to the United States, they forced him to work for them in Mexico, making him spend long hours cultivating squash in the fields. Fifteen-year-old Pablo was denied food if he did not work, kept isolated and alone, and told that he would be arrested and deported if he did not do everything his traffickers said. Meanwhile, his traffickers attempted to extort additional money from Pablo's parents. After about six weeks of trafficking and abuse, Pablo's traffickers attempted to bring him to the United States, where they intended to make him continue to work for them against his will. Subsequently, Pablo was apprehended by Customs and Border Patrol (CBP). He was terrified of his traffickers and afraid to share his trafficking ordeal with them until CBP called his father, who encouraged him to share what had happened. Pablo spent a month at Southwest Key Detention Center for children before he was reunited with his parents in southern California. When Pablo was released, he was given a list of legal service providers and his calls for assistance eventually led him to the Coalition to Abolish Slavery & Trafficking (CAST). CAST helped Pablo re-report the crime against him to law enforcement, and he was then interviewed by Homeland Security Investigations (HSI) and the LAPD, who certified him as a trafficking survivor. CAST also helped Pablo and his family apply for and receive T nonimmigrant status (a T-Visa). CAST worked with partners to ensure that Pablo and his family had the support they needed to fully recover from their trafficking ordeal. Today, Pablo is about to start 12th grade and is doing well. However, he still has nightmares about returning to El Salvador, where one of his friends was recently murdered by the same gang members who had threatened him.[4]

At the time of time of circulation among members of the Freedom Network in 2014, Pablo served as a success story—he was able to receive legal support and social services through CAST. He is also a cautionary tale of the challenges the American public faces if the dualities that witnesses are called to see in continue. Migrants are mediators between the state and the community, where the future of "security" and "insecurity" is a central part of the nation-making project. Pablo's experience figures into being a survivor of organized criminal networks linking the Americas from countries to the south of the U.S. border to the United States. His experience tells more than a story of abuse by organized crime groups, in this case Mara Salvatrucha (MS). He worked in agricultural fields in Mexico, where Mexico is one of two leading suppliers to the

United States' horticulture industry.[5] At fifteen, Pablo was detained. Just by entering into the United States through being smuggled as an undocumented person, Pablo was seen as breaking immigration law. However, in his narrative the context of his story is more than about borders and crossing them. Pablo's experience also reflects how transnational economies and human trafficking are imbricated in notions of security. During the Obama administration, transnational organized groups like MS were seen as a national security threat.[6] Building on the narrative of the need to police borders. And, under the Trump administration, anti-immigration rhetoric and policies continue, where the building of a wall looms in national discourse and executive orders deny people entry. In many ways, to close, I end with the query: how are migrant crossings in the twenty-first century bound to U.S. ideologies surrounding governmentality and security? In this way, how have witnesses been called forward to witness in ways that further the state and notions of governmentality?

There is no doubt that a central ideology that circulates in the twenty-first century is one of security. In the United States, the passage of the Uniting and Strengthening America by Providing Appropriate Tools Required to Intercept and Obstruct Terrorism Act of 2001 shapes U.S. perceptions of security. In 2013, President Obama's speech on national security described the post 9-11 moment in the United States: "We strengthened our defenses—hardening targets, tightening transportation security, and giving law enforcement new tools to prevent terror. Some caused inconvenience."[7] But some caused more than an inconvenience. Take, for example, the expanded surveillance through biometrics scanning systems and of fingerprinting scanning systems, and Title II of the Patriot Act, "The Sneak and Peak Act," which has changed U.S. citizen relationships to the Fourth Amendment. All of these actions collectively raise difficult questions about the balance struck between national interests in security and individual values of privacy. The discourse on terror, surveillance, and security cannot be separated from human rights concerns. The directed ideologies of (in)security tie mobile subjects (the subjects of human rights such as human trafficking) to a discourse on terror. Pardis Mahdavi finds commonality between the war on terror and the war on trafficking, highlighting filmic representation such as in *Taken*, where Liam Neeson's character, an ex-CIA agent, must rescue his daughter from Middle Eastern traffickers in Europe.[8] Mahdavi contends that both the War on Terror and the war on trafficking fail to recognize that social problems are rooted in inequality in the new economic world order. Trafficking and terror are intertwined—post–9-11 security

programs have impacted mobility into the United State. This conclusion fo-
cuses on the linkages between the War on Terror and the war on trafficking,
which are most evident in the recent technologies of surveillance that shape
anti-trafficking efforts—the militarization and the normalization of U.S. hegemony at the domestic level in the name of security. The ability to cross into
being seen as a trafficking subject, or Otherness as a socially dead subject, is
deeply defined by not only a larger context surrounding modern colonial capitalist systems, but also by how these systems reinforce governance, securitization, and the unstable notion of insecurity. How anti-trafficking subjects
cross is due to technological innovations and the use of technology to sustain
normative practices of witnessing.

A discourse of terror, technologies of surveillance, militarized borders, and
conspiracy shape human rights endeavors regarding human trafficking. How
do technologies of surveillance—where these technologies secure the nation
and reinscribe the United States in the modern economic colonial system—
shape collective and individual witnessing of violence? In particular, how do
technologies of surveillance sustain narratives of security through militaristic
responses in the domestic scene?

OPERATION SYCLOPS

> In Homer's telling, the Cyclopes are a race of gigantic one-eyed
> cave dwellers, man-eating, barbaric, and easily fooled. . . . In my
> telling, the Cyclops story is a revenge story. She is the anti-her,
> anti-host. She wants to be left alone. Her enormous eye sees the
> deceptive Odysseus who feigns codes of hospitality to receive the
> sheep as gifts. . . . [Cyclops] walks the vastness of Odysseus'
> kingdom, slowly becoming a ghost. Her emptied socket becomes
> a mask. Her revenge feeds her, making her opaque, anti-gravity, a
> black hole
>
> —Eve Tuck and C. Ree, "A Glossary of Haunting."

Operation Syclops was a law enforcement operation in Seattle that began in
2004 and concluded in 2006. It comprised federal law enforcement investigations of a Seattle Asian "brothel." The early surveillance by FBI agents was described as typical, where the brothels had a network from Portland to Seattle
and San Francisco. The surveillance footage found that the women working in
the brothels were recruited from Asia, accruing debts ranging from $30,000

to $50,000. Women were recruited to work in "Apple Spa," which employed women from Korea, Malaysia, and China to be "prostitutes."[9] The arrest of Malaysian women as "material witnesses" illustrated their tethered subjectivity. An early investigation following an anonymous tip led to no charges being made. And the massage parlor closed. A new brothel opened in Portland. And in 2005, the owners made a return to Seattle. FBI surveillance led to the discovery of the sale of sex, smuggling, the harboring of aliens, and money laundering. Operation Syclops is a story of coethnic violence and a legal case called *United States v. Kang et al.*[10] The case exposed a larger network of brothels beyond the triangulation of Portland, San Francisco, and Seattle, to include Los Angeles, Chicago, New York, and Las Vegas, and additionally a mobile network where the women traveled through Texas to get to Seattle as well as across the Canadian border in shipping containers.[11]

In returning to the opening quote, how may one reread the figure of Cyclops/Syclops beyond its normative mythological frames? Like the monster Cyclops, the dominant narrative of Syclops depends on the particular ways in which the trafficking subject has become mythologized, Othered, and a spectacle of a past that is not part of a notion of a future. However, to take a familiar story, and to reread it with a decolonial lens, is to see the role of anti-trafficking technologies as reifying the colonial legacies of the present.

The technologies of surveillance include wiretaps, observing and following people, Global Positioning Systems (GPS) tracking devices, monitoring travel records, telephone records, state identification, following wire transfers of money and financial records, and the use of undercover officers. Reflecting upon Operation Syclops, the technologies of surveillance are multiple. Therefore, I draw upon Michel Foucault's definition of technologies as a matrix.[12] Technologies in anti-trafficking endeavors are shaped by productions—productions of power, of signs and systems, and by the selves, that collectively reify how people witness violence. *Migrant Crossings* explores the subjectivities that are constituted—what I call tethered subjectivities. Tethered subjectivities encompass the subjectivities migrants are bound as illegal/legal, citizen/noncitizen, and victim/criminal. To further new ways of seeing, throughout *Migrant Crossings* are appeals for an unsettled witnessing. To unsettle witnessing requires critiquing the normative scripts and constructs that give meaning to the actions/inactions one is called towards. As in the story of Operation Syclops, the all-seeing eye of the government in anti-trafficking endeavors draws upon technology as machinery and science to address abuse, violence, and trafficking. The wiretaps from Operation Syclops facilitate a particular type of witnessing through evidence, where the justice and legal systems come to know victims/criminals, legal/undocumented, citizens and noncitizens alike. Witnesses of Operation Syclops included law enforcement, attorneys, the judge, and those who read the legal and media discourse. The migrant women in Operation Syclops vacillated between being perceived of as complicit, not trusting law enforcement, refusing clients, and in some instances, fleeing their conditions of debt bondage. The women's victimhood, unlike other trafficking narratives, is never staged in the courtroom or in the media beyond narratives of smuggling and debt. And they are tethered to their victimhood and criminality—as trafficking victims in press releases and as "prostitutes" in the courtroom.

Popular discussions of human trafficking and technology view technology as either a medium of exploitation (i.e., the traffic of people into sexual economies through Craigslist or Backpage) or as a tool for addressing human trafficking. Technology impacts transnational economies, technocultures, and mobile subjects.[13] And mobile subjects shape technology. U.S. technocultures regarding human trafficking produce and circulate transnational narratives of (in)security; insecure subjects must be protected, the security of the nation must be furthered, and criminalized subjects sustain insecurities, so are deemed deportable or even to be eliminated by the state. Schaeffer examines how local and global discourses and technologies shape transnationally directed desires.[14] Likewise, local and global discourses and technologies in anti-trafficking efforts shape transnationally directed ideologies of a desire for security of the nation and its citizen subjects.

For if consumers speak to notions of identity,[15] as media consumers and spectators consume cases like *United States v. Kang et al.*, the surveillance summary suggests that they, the spectators, were not the only one's eating. Chinese nationals Yong Jun Kang, Kesheng Zhu, and Rujing Jiang (Jiang and Zhu are a married couple) were sentenced in 2007 by Seattle by District Judge John C. Coughenour.[16] Wiretaps exposed that clients calling the spa were ordering Asian delicacies such as pho, dim sum, or Kung po, pad thai, Malaysian curry, and kimchee, where the food represented the countries of origin, respectively Vietnamese, Chinese, Thai, Malaysian, and Korean. Women were brought from China, Korea, Thailand, Vietnam, Malaysia, Singapore, Hong Kong, Taiwan, and Laos. When clients arrived early, they were told that other clients were still eating. And, "no home deliveries" were offered code for there were no outcalls provided. Clients consumed an "international buffet." Other codes included merchandise, cars, and movies to describe the women working in the brothels. The women's departures and arrivals were referred to in reference to leaving shipping docks (brothels) and the supplies as women were coded as "torpedoes" or "seafood." The consumers were racialized: they were never white, because of the racialized assumptions that law enforcement is white. Therefore, diasporas or displaced peoples who are displaced economically, socially, politically, militarily because of the modern colonial economic system, requiring their displacement and new settlement, are shaped by systems where they eat each other up—or exploit each other. Surveillance and technologies of surveillance as mechanisms for securing subjects and the state are normalized and the state as white reinforced. But through surveillance comes control—and this control looks like big data. Because in anti-trafficking endeavors, the dominant (mis)perception is that if the United States can control numbers, it can control the problem.

CONTROLLING HUMAN TRAFFICKING IN NUMBERS AND BIG DATA

In 2015 the U.S. military's Defense Advanced Research Projects Agency (DARPA) used Memex, in collaboration with seventeen contractors, to find an effective way to monitor the dark web.[17] Memex is intended to find traffickers and online sexual predators through codes and language. The government sees this anti-trafficking software as eventually allowing for the surveillance and finding of those it deems "terrorists." The ongoing development of the tools is apparent. In collaboration with DARPA, IST Research Corp sought out 750 experts, stating, "Memex is developing tools that help investigators find and identify trafficking in online spaces. In order to make these tools accurate, they need to learn how experts like you find relevant data and answer investigative questions from online sites. The annotations that you provide will enable Memex tools to automate parts of the search/investigation process."[18] Current strategies in anti-trafficking efforts turn people into quantifiable numbers, code, nonhuman entities, whose security is dependent on carceral and militarized responses. These endeavors suggest that in a post–9-11 era, technology, anti-violence, and security are deeply intertwined.

Claudia Aradau illustrates how security and humanitarian efforts feed into each other, where humanitarian efforts further a "politics of pity," where emotions are used to restructure the situation of trafficking and govern it to the benefit of trafficked women. The security regime is synonymous with a "politics of risk," where the government governs the phenomenon of trafficking through technologies of risk management.[19] Risk management is a "family of ways of thinking and acting, involving calculations about probable futures in the present followed by interventions into the present in order to control that potential future."[20] To activate the spectators' pity, trafficked people must be specified as undangerous, and their future and possible futures must be defined by interventions that control that future. Categorical constructions of victimhood and trafficking further the control of mobile subjects, where in order to be legible as a victim, one must show promise of being an "ideal" citizen, because immigration laws link pathways to legality and citizenship to morality and class mobility. As illuminated in previous chapters, victimhood is also predicated on a notion of a subject who is to be rescued. This poses challenges in trafficking cases where crimes of moral turpitude such as drug sales or prostitution propel migrants into being seen in extremes—as criminals or as imperfect victims.

Human trafficking subjects are tethered to narratives that continue to further how trafficked people are nonhumans, or living(dead) subjects, whose resurrection is in the form of quantifiable data—numbers, like a quota system, that must be controlled. The discourse on numbers conveys varying understandings of the phenomenon—17,500 in the United States to two million in the world. The numbers show precedence for a response and a climate of insecurity. And the popular perception is that with big data comes the prospect of mitigating human trafficking. University of Southern California, Mark Latonero's Annenberg Center used data to explore trends on websites like Backpage .com. Their software led to the linking between illicit websites and organized crime contacts. The links between technology, militarized cultures, and anti-trafficking efforts are not a conspiracy theory. DARPA's Memex program hunts criminal networks in the deepweb / dark web—criminal networks involved in activities like human trafficking and hacking. The deep web can now be accessed because of Tor (The Onion Router), software created by the U.S. Naval Research Laboratory to allow for anonymous communication. Not only do anti-traffickers, investigators, and government bodies search, but they also track countries ranking them according to the Global Slavery Index.[21] Organizations like Free the Slaves quantify the improvement in communities with anti-slavery interventions. The use of technology in anti-trafficking efforts is highly valued. In 2011, Google gave $10.5 million to anti-trafficking organizations. Technologies are utilized to create a myriad of "securities"—to secure evidence collecting, to secure responses for prosecution, and to secure victims from criminals. As migrant victims becomes the center of security efforts of rescue, prosecution, and protection, their precarious status as migrants is tethered to dualities of criminal and victim, sustaining insecurities and mechanisms that reinforce securitization.

CONSPIRACY AND MILITARIZED BORDERS

Under U.S. federal law, conspiracy is an overt act (e.g., illegal harboring, money laundering, or furthering prostitution). Violating federal laws as a group is perceived to be a form of conspiring against the United States. In the twenty-first century, conspiracy is a knowledge-producing discourse.[22] The type of knowledge-producing discourse furthered in how traffickers are perceived to conspire is best delineated in the charges including immigration, prostitution, money laundering, fraud, and forced labor. In 2006, Kang and his co-conspirators were convicted on conspiracy charges: conspiracy to transport individuals in furtherance of prostitution, conspiracy to transport and harbor illegal aliens, conspiracy to engage in money laundering, and conspiracy to transport individuals in furtherance of prostitution. The convictions were not for the actual acts, but rather for the act of conspiring—even though they had done all of them at least once. Prostitution, money laundering, and the transportation and harboring of illegal aliens were solidified in how they talked about moving women in shipping containers. And money laundering is found in following the monetary paper trail—one only had to follow the paper trail. Federal conspiracy laws reinforce the notion that the partnership of individuals in crime is more "dangerous for the public" than individual acts. The legacy of U.S. conspiracy laws dates to the 1700s; however, U.S. statutes from that time focused on maritime laws—making a criminal act to conspire against the master of a ship or to engage in maritime insurance fraud.[23] By the 1860s, during a time of civil war and the eventual liberation of enslaved peoples, conspiracy became an act against the U.S. government. At present, dominant perceptions of conspiracy against the government cannot be separated from terrorism. Conspiracy theorists, unlike people convicted of conspiring against nations, are perceived to be paranoid, hypervigilant, and nonconformist.[24] While we are seemingly far removed from the McCarthy era, conspiracy continues to show up in the twenty-first century—those who conspire against the United States are oftentimes equated with terrorists; they are a threat to the nation-state. And conspiracy theory is oftentimes entangled with the perception or the paranoia surrounding the United States' role in creating the conditions for a climate of fear. The fear of the trafficker and the criminal is shaped by hypervigilance and the perception that these figures cannot assimilate. For the victim, "she" is tethered to this duality of failing to assimilate, but only when her victimhood matters. Conspiracy discourse and practices produce patriotic assent and dissent, which are reinscribed in the courtroom, where some acts that are perceived of as deviant are more punishable than others. Pardis Mahdavi illuminates how discourses on trafficking and terror, "infused with morality, have been socially constructed to create ideas about deviance."[25] The women working in the brothels were also shaped by these very ideas, interchangeably referenced as "prostitute" and "sex trafficked." This deviance for the Asian migrant is tied to sexuality, race, and national belonging. Kang was already under the watchful eye of the government—earlier investigations of his brothel had placed an ICE hold on him, and deportation proceedings (which he evaded by disappearing). But in tethering victims of human trafficking to an undangerous status as victim, the women who were on the menu, and all others who failed to fulfill such imaginaries, were deemed dangerous, deportable, and security threats. In reading Kang's (the convicted trafficker's) letter to the judge, one can't help but position him as not merely a criminal but also one whose conspiracy is also dictated by the need to survive in the world order:

> Honorable Judge,
>
> How are you?
>
> First of all, I want to thank you for giving me an opportunity to express myself. I want to say I am sorry for the crime I have committed. At the same time, I want to express my deep regrets.
>
> Because I have violated United States Law, I have lost the opportunity to stay in the United States. Thus, I cannot live together with my wife in the United States. Because I have violated United States Law, my mother has suffered a stroke. She has been lying in bed and unable to take care of herself. I am not a filial son. I really want to keep my mother company for the rest of her life. I have not seen her for twelve years.
>
> I really hope your Honor will give me a chance to start a new life all over again. I deeply appreciate. [Court translation from Chinese].

Kang, too, was tethered to the very same dualities that construct women in sexual economies as "prostitutes"—complicit, therefore deemed criminal. His closing letter offers insight into his own sufferings as surviving in survival networks of global economies. It did not highlight that his mother was also a cancer survivor (stomach therapy in 2004, at the peak of his criminal endeavors). Regardless, the letter reinforces that a good migrant is one who desires to come to the United States, is a family person, and shows remorse. He was sentenced to three years in jail. Convicted on federal offenses, Kang and his co-conspirators will be deported and, under the IIRAIRA 1996, will be ineligible for legal re-entry for up to ten years. Victim and criminal; these tethered subjectivities are central to a U.S. endeavor to secure the nation in a post–9-11 era. Their deportability when criminalized is the extreme of a militarized border—the elimination of anything that crosses into the boundaries of the nation-state that creates insecurities.

ENACTING AN UNSETTLED WITNESSING OF MIGRANT CROSSINGS

As national borders are militarized, furthering the belief that the world is a dangerous place, transnational migrants trafficked into the United States are also shaped by discourses of security. The technologies of surveillance in the name of securing the border, the state, and the U.S. body politic range from technologies of mobilizing a human rights agenda through apps to surveillance of Asian massage parlors. As the courts highlighted the consumption of the women in the economies, the media furthered the popular consumption of a trafficking narrative and a call to secure the rights of the victim through the state and technologies of surveillance. This climate has reinforced tethered subjectivities surrounding citizenship, legality, and victimhood. And, as anti-trafficking discourse and the reproduction of (in)security are furthered, new relations and subjectivities are also forged through and shaped by technological innovations and implementations to address violence and human trafficking.

While this conclusion tells the story of Operation Syclops, which included Asian migrants exploiting within their communities, one cannot help but think of the Cyclops (with a "C") from Greek mythology, that single-eyed giant. A species, monstrous and gigantic, with a single eye looking at a "you." The Cyclops, a creature that is to be feared, becomes metaphorical for the investigative operation to find trafficking. The naming of operations is a legacy of military covert operations, made localized through domestic law enforcement efforts. Therefore, Operation Syclops, regardless of intention, facilitates a story that it is through its single eye, or the perception of a singular eye of government, that fear is to be instilled in traffickers, alleged traffickers, and those who are to be criminalized. And in the search for security through U.S. hegemony and empire, what one may find, even in human rights endeavors, are the creation and sustaining of insecurities and the furtherance of invisibilities. What would a human rights endeavor look like for diasporic subjects who disrupt the U.S. empire, and its dominant notions of security, to create a kind of security defined by alterity, the subaltern, border crossers, and even the indigenous?

To begin to take the steps toward unsettling how settler and state governmentality shape anti-trafficking endeavors is to grapple with the manifold of witnessing that is being sustained.[26] It also means contending with diasporic subjects, those who have settled and maintain transnational ties as central to settler colonial critiques. Dominant forms of witnessing maintain dominant logics. Decolonial visions and possibility mean finding modalities to imagine witnessing and enact forms resistance. If my goal is to untether the subjectivities that are sustained in the modern colonial economic system surrounding victimhood, criminality, legality, and citizenship, one must look the giant in the eye and see it as a myth with material consequence that shapes how one witnesses even the most seemingly innocent places of human rights. And in light of this, I call for untethering subjectivities through unsettled witnessing.

ACKNOWLEDGMENTS

WRITING *MIGRANT CROSSINGS* encompassed a journey that began in 2005, and encompassed various iterations, audiences, revisions, and conversations. I would like to thank Evelyn Nakano Glenn, who is not only an exemplary scholar but also provided critical feedback, support, and scholarly discussions that were an invaluable component to the earlier stages of the manuscript. There are not enough words that can describe my deep appreciation for having Evie's support. In addition to Evie, Gary Glenn (Evie's husband) has been a behind-the-curtains supporter of my work, and I am deeply indebted to him for his commitment and the additional support he provided to me. I am also grateful for Laura E. Pérez, Catherine Ceniza Choy, and Paola Bacchetta, who offered vital feedback, shared scholarly insight through discussions and their teach-ings, and offered professional advice. They are amazing women-of-color schol-ars; I am honored to have worked with each of them through the years, and to receive such amazing support from faculty and students in ethnic studies and gender studies at University of California, Berkeley. Two colleagues I must highlight who have supported my work: Ethel Regis Lu and Dalida María Ben-field. Ethel Regis Lu was my writing partner and collaborator. I thank Ethel for supporting my writing from San Diego. Dalida María Benfield's collabora-tions informed the earlier thinking that went into the writing and the visual culture elements of the dissertation that has manifested in newer projects such as the Institute of (Im)Possible Subjects, which grew out of our earlier collabo-rations through the Visuality & Alterity Working Group at UC Berkeley. Other colleagues who have provided support throughout the years, intellectually and with their insightful conversations and feedback: Wanda Alarcon, Cindy Cruz,

Alejandro Perez, Joshua Troncoso, John Dougherty, Gabriela Erandi Rico Spears, Jennifer Jue-Steuck, Jennifer Reimer, Juan Herrera, and Maurice Rafael Magaña. And deep appreciation for the emotional support provided by my dear LLNs, Anna Lamson, Cecilia Kim, and Kari Unebasami.

Many people inspired the various changes that were needed to migrate the ideas, journeys, theories, and case exemplars into *Migrant Crossings*. The journey began during a position at Rutgers University with the Department on Women's and Gender Studies and the Institute for Research on Women. At Rutgers, mentorship received from Nicole Fleetwood, a brilliant scholar and mentor, opened up platforms for my book in progress to receive the kind of community it needed to become a fully fleshed out book manuscript. I am deeply appreciative of the readers whose input on various chapters enabled the book to embark on a new journey: Sarah Tobias and the IRW community, Thea Abu El-Haj, Patricia Akhimie, Ronald Cumings, Elin Diamond, Sylvia Chan Malik, Laura Fabris, Donna Gustafson, Nadia Guessous, Fakshri Haghani, Maria Hwang, Chie Ikeya, Temma Kaplan, Suzy Kim, Laurie Lambert, Ellen Ledoux, Preetha Mani, Susan Marchand, Ghassan Moussawi, Kathleen McCollough, Ferris Olin, Rheana Salazar Parreñas, Cyril Reade, Monica Ríos Vasquez, and Yana Rodgers. Other Rutgers scholars whose insights helped move this book forward include Allan Isaac, Kathy Lopez, Yolanda San Miguel Martinez, and Abena Busia. Martin Manalansan provided insightful feedback at my presentation. An important community was also provided by the Transnational Feminisms Summer Institute organized by *Frontiers: A Journal of Women Studies* editors at Ohio State University. In particular, Karen Wu provided important insights as a reader of my work. I also received incredible support from Karen Leong, Roberta Chevrette, Ann Hibner Koblitz, Heather Switzer, and the transnational feminist community. Blind reviewers for *Feminist Formations* and *Frontiers* also pushed the thinking of the manuscript. I am forever grateful to Julietta Hua, whose scholarly works inspire my own and have helped shaped this project, and I am deeply appreciative for the insights gained from Felicity Amaya Schaeffer, whose intellectual insights have inspired this project. Additionally, I am very grateful to Michelle Lipinski and the Stanford University Press team (Nora Spiegel, Stephanie Adams, Anne Fuzellier, and the amazing design team) and Westchester Publishing Services (Brian Ostrander and his team of editors), whose enthusiastic support of this book helped it cross the finish line.

Excerpts of the chapters were presented in a range of publics, which helped to further the intellectual thinking and rigor of the project—my colleagues who shared these spaces with me provided insight, questions, and feedback that were additionally needed to move the project forward: Marisa Fuentes, Leece Lee, Terry Park, Laura Fantone, Tara Daly, Crystal Baik, Ayano Ginoza, Edi Kinney, Gary Pak, Eddy Lee, Ellen-Rae Cachola, Tammy Ho, and the Center for Arts Design & Social Research (led by Christopher Alan Bratton and Dalida María Benfield), among many others.

My fieldwork (2006–11) influenced my theoretical framing of categorization, representation, and narration of human trafficking; countless people I met over the years inspired my scholarly thinking. In particular, I have to send a deep appreciation for my colleague and collaborator Cindy C. Liou (former attorney at Asian Pacific Islander Legal Outreach and current Deputy Director for Legal Services at Kinds in Need of Defense), whose conversations and collaborations shaped my own perspectives. I am also very grateful for my collaborations with community members Paniz Bagheri, Gwyn Kirk, Deborah Lee, Sophia Larrea, Lenora Lee, Elisabet Medina, Mollie Ring, Hediana Utarti, Allen Wilson, Susan Duggan, Francine Braae, Svetlana Pivchik, Celia Roberts, Yasmin Kaderali, Donna Sinar, Kristie Miller, Makiko James, and Rafael Cerna. Other organizations and people within them that have influenced my work include the Freedom Network USA members, Asian Women's Shelter; Asian Pacific Islander Legal Outreach, Legal Services for Children, Students & Artists Fighting to End Human Slavery, the End Internet Trafficking Coalition, Women for Genuine Security, the International Women's Network Against Militarism, and many, many other collaborators over the years whose conversations have encouraged my work and, where needed, shifted its direction. I am deeply grateful to the survivors who are able to share their stories publicly as experts and witnesses. I also appreciate survivors and survivor witnesses who have testified publicly and/or through sharing their stories with organizations and communities—their everyday witnessing inspired this project.

The research was made possible due to the financial support of the Ethnic Studies Department, the University of California, Soroptimist International, CAORC, and the Andrew W. Mellon Foundation.

And more recently, colleagues at the University of Utah, including the Ethnic Studies and Gender Studies Division, and Women of Color Academics. Additionally, I want to thank Sarita Gaytán, Leticia Alvarez Gutiérrez, Maile Arvin, Hokulani Aikau, Lindsay Gezinski, Edmund Fong, Ed Muñoz, Baodong Liu, Susie Porter, Wanda Pillow, Kathryn Bond Stockton, and Diana Leong. There are so many folks who have helped breathe life into *Migrant Crossings*— named and unnamed.

Migrant Crossings was birthed out of my own diasporic experiences and transnational ties of living in the United Kingdom, being raised in Hawaiʻi, and traveling to various contexts. I thank my family for their unwavering support. My parents, Kyung-Mi (Mimi) Fukushima and Harvey Fukushima, have provided the moral support and encouragement. It really is the migrant crossings of my mother that inspire my writing and my scholarly commitments. Through my mother I have traced a genealogy of strong women in the Min family. And, while I was less familiar with the migrant stories of my Mexican family while growing up, I willed to learn them. Like many diasporas, I learned to contend with the (in)visibility that defines the migrant experience. As a child born in Nebraska to a migrant mother, then raised in the UK, then Hawaiʻi, and eventually finding my journey taking me to California, New Jersey, and now Utah, this project has been shaped by earlier questions surrounding race, migration, and transnational processes. My extended family, past and present, are also inspirations for what it means to survive (ongoing) colonialities. Jonathan Wood helped to edit my manuscript and has supported me while I wrote and journeyed this project into a book. And, although she is unable to read, I would like to thank Artoo-Shihtzu for being the perfect academic dog—her emotional support has been unwavering in this journey, and she is a reminder of the range of interspecies support that is needed to live in this world.

SAMPLE LETTER OF CERTIFICATION FOR HUMAN TRAFFICKING, U.S. DEPARTMENT OF HEALTH AND HUMAN SERVICES

HHS Tracking Number

XXXXXXXXXXXX

DOB: XX/XX/XXXX

VICTIM NAME

C/O CASE MANAGER

NGO

ADDRESS

CITY, STATE ZIP

CERTIFICATION LETTER

Dear VICTIM:

This letter confirms that you have been certified by the U.S. Department of Health and Human Services (HHS) under section 107(b) of the Trafficking Victims Protection Act of 2000. With this certification, you are eligible for benefits and services under any Federal or State program or activity funded or administered by any Federal agency to the same extent as an individual who is admitted to the United States as a refugee under section 207 of the Immigration and Nationality Act, provided you meet other eligibility criteria. Certification does not confer immigration status.

Your certification date is **CERTIFICATION DATE**. The benefits outlined in the previous paragraph may offer assistance for only limited time periods that start from the date of this certification. Therefore, if you wish to seek assistance, it is important that you do so as soon as possible after receipt of this letter.

You should present this letter when you apply for benefits or services. *Benefit-issuing agencies must call the toll-free trafficking verification line at 1 (866) 401-5510 in the Office of Refugee Resettlement (ORR) to verify the validity of this document and to inform HHS of the benefits for which you have applied.*

The Department of Labor offers employment and training services for which you may be eligible. Call 1-877-US2-JOBS or visit www.servicelocator .org to find out about the nearest One-Stop Career Center.

You must notify this office of your current mailing address. Please send a dated and signed letter with any changes of address to: Trafficking Program Specialist, Office of Refugee Resettlement, 8th Floor West, 370 L'Enfant Promenade, SW, Washington, DC 20447. We will send all notices to that address, and any notice mailed to that address constitutes adequate service. You may also need to share this same information with state and local benefit-issuing agencies.

Sincerely,

Director

Office of Refugee Resettlement

GLOSSARY OF HUMAN TRAFFICKING–RELATED TERMS

COERCION

The Trafficking Victims Protection Act defines coercion in §1591. The term "coercion" means: (A) threats of serious harm to or physical restraint against any person; (B) any scheme, plan, or pattern intended to cause a person to believe that failure to perform an act would result in serious harm to or physical restraint against any person.

CONTINUED PRESENCE

Continued Presence (CP) is a temporary immigration status provided to individuals identified by law enforcement as victims of human trafficking. This status allows victims of human trafficking to remain in the United States temporarily during the ongoing investigation into the human-trafficking related crimes committed against them. CP is initially granted for one year and may be renewed in one-year increments. CP is authorized under provisions of section 107(c)(3) of the TVPA, which has since been reauthorized, and is codified at 22 U.S.C. § 7105(c)(3).

Source: *Continued Presence: Temporary Immigration Status for Victims of Human Trafficking,* Homeland Security, Blue Campaign, August 2010, accessed September 1, 2010, http://www.dhs.gov/xlibrary/assets/ht-uscis-continued-presence.pdf.

DEBT BONDAGE

Debt bondage is defined in the Trafficking Victims Protection Act under section 103 of Definitions as meaning: the status or condition of a debtor arising from a pledge by the debtor of his or her personal services or of those of a person under his or her control as a security for debt, if the value of those services as reasonably assessed is not applied toward the liquidation of the debt or the length and nature of those services are not respectively limited and defined.

FORCE

Force is not defined by the Trafficking Victims Protection Act. Force is described in the Congressional findings of the TVPA under section 3: "Victims are often forced through physical violence to engage in sex acts or perform slavery-like labor. Such force includes rape and other forms of sexual abuse, torture, starvation, imprisonment, threats, psychological abuse, and coercion."

FRAUD

Fraud is not defined by the Trafficking Victims Protection Act. Fraud is defined by state codes. Fraud is defined by the California civil code § 3294: California Code—Section 3 as: an intentional misrepresentation, deceit, or concealment of a material fact known to the defendant with the intention on the part of the defendant of thereby depriving a person of property or legal rights or otherwise causing injury.

HUMAN TRAFFICKING

Definitions, The Trafficking Victims Protection Act (2000)
(8) SEVERE FORMS OF TRAFFICKING IN PERSONS.—The term "severe forms of trafficking in persons" means—

(A) sex trafficking in which a commercial sex act is induced by force, fraud, or coercion, or in which the person induced to perform such act has not attained 18 years of age; or

(B) the recruitment, harboring, transportation, provision, or obtaining of a person for labor or services, through the use of force, fraud, or coercion for the purpose of subjection to involuntary servitude, peonage, debt bondage, or slavery.

(9) SEX TRAFFICKING.—The term "sex trafficking" means the recruitment, harboring, transportation, provision, or obtaining of a person for the purpose of a commercial sex act (Page 8).

INVOLUNTARY SERVITUDE

Involuntary servitude consists of two terms. "Involuntary means 'done contrary to or without choice' - 'compulsory' - 'not subject to control of the will.' [487 U.S. 931, 937].

"Servitude means '[a] condition in which a person lacks liberty especially to determine one's course of action or way of life' - 'slavery' - 'the state of being subject to a master.'

"Involuntary servitude involves a condition of having some of the incidents of slavery.

"It may include situations in which persons are forced to return to employment by law.

"It may also include persons who are physically restrained by guards from leaving employment.

"It may also include situations involving either physical and other coercion, or a combination thereof, used to detain persons in employment."

Source: United States v. Kozminski et al., 487 U.S. 931 (1988). Certiorari to the United States Court of Appeals for the Sixth Circuit, No. 86-2000. Argued February 23, 1988; Decided June 29, 1988.

Involuntary Servitude as defined by the Trafficking Victims Protection Act, Section 103: includes a condition of servitude induced by means of—(A) any scheme, plan, or pattern intended to cause a person to believe that, if the person did not enter into or continue in such condition, that person or another person would suffer serious harm or physical restraint; or (B) the abuse or threatened abuse of the legal process.

PEONAGE

Peonage is not defined by the Trafficking Victims Protection Act. It is always listed collectively with involuntary servitude and the slave trade. Peonage is defined by its legal abolition in U.S. code: 42 U.S.C. § 1994: US Code - Section 1994, Peonage abolished (1865). The holding of any person to service or labor under the system known as peonage is abolished and forever prohibited in any Territory or State of the United States; and all acts, laws, resolutions, orders, regulations, or usages of any Territory or State, which have heretofore established, maintained, or enforced, or by virtue of which any attempt shall hereafter be made to establish, maintain, or enforce, directly or indirectly, the voluntary or involuntary service or labor of any persons as peons, in liquidation of any debt or obligation, or otherwise, are declared null and void.

THIRTEENTH AMENDMENT: ABOLITION OF SLAVERY

Section 1. Neither slavery nor involuntary servitude, except as a punishment for crime whereof the party shall have been duly convicted, shall exist within the United States, or any place subject to their jurisdiction.

Section 2. Congress shall have power to enforce this article by appropriate legislation.

Appendix C
NONIMMIGRANT STATUS VISAS

T NONIMMIGRANT STATUS VISA

T Nonimmigrant Eligibility

To be eligible for a T-Visa, a noncitizen trafficking victim must demonstrate that he or she:

- is or has been a victim of a severe form in trafficking (as defined by the TVPA; see Appendix B);
- is physically present in the United States, American Samoa, or the Mariana Islands or at a port of entry on account of trafficking;
- has complied with any reasonable request for assistance in investigating or prosecuting trafficking (if eighteen or older); and
- would suffer extreme hardship involving unusual and severe harm upon removal.

The nonexhaustive list of such extreme hardship includes: the age and personal circumstances of the applicant; serious physical or mental illness of the applicant that necessitates medical or psychological attention not reasonably available in the foreign country; the nature and extent of the physical and psychological consequences of severe forms of trafficking in persons; the impact of the loss of access to the U.S. courts and the criminal justice system for purposes relating to the incident of severe forms of trafficking in persons or other crimes perpetrated against the applicant, including criminal and civil redress for acts of trafficking in persons, criminal prosecution, restitution, and protection; the reasonable expectation that the existence of laws, social practices, or customs in the foreign country to which the applicant could be returned would penalize the applicant severely for having been the victim of a severe form of trafficking in persons; the likelihood that the trafficker in persons or others acting on behalf of the trafficker in the foreign country would severely harm the applicant; and the likelihood that the applicant's individual safety would be seriously threatened by the existence of civil unrest or armed conflict as demonstrated by the designation of Temporary Protected Status, under section 244 of the Act, or the granting of other relevant protections. Legal citation: 8 CFR §214.11(i)(1).

Source: "Human Trafficking and the T-Visa," contributors Gail Pendleton, Marie Jose Fletcher, Florrie Burke, Lejia Zvizdic, Maunica Sthanki, and Lauren Polk, Grant No. 2000-WL-VX-K004 awarded by the Violence Against Women Office, Office of Justice Programs, U.S. Department of Justice. Points of view in this document are those of the author and do not necessarily represent the official position or policies of the U.S. Department of Justice.

U NONIMMIGRANT STATUS VISA

U Nonimmigrant Eligibility

To be eligible for a U-Visa, a noncitizen victim of criminal activity must demonstrate that he or she is:

A. a victim of criminal activity designated in section 101(a)(15)(U) of the Immigration and Nationality Act (the Act). Such activity is defined as being the victim of one or more of the following or any similar activity in violation of Federal, State or local criminal law: rape; Torture; Trafficking; Incest; domestic violence; sexual assault; abusive sexual contact; prostitution; sexual exploitation; female genital mutilation; being held hostage; peonage; involuntary servitude; slave trade; kidnapping; abduction; unlawful criminal restraint; false imprisonment; blackmail; extortion; manslaughter; murder; felonious assault; witness tampering; obstruction of justice; perjury; or attempt, conspiracy or solicitation to commit any of the above.

B. Has suffered substantial physical or mental abuse as a result of having been a victim of qualifying criminal activity;

C. Possess information concerning the qualifying criminal activity of which he/she was a victim;

D. A Federal, State or local government official investigating or prosecuting a qualifying criminal activity certifies (using Supplement B of this petition) that he/she has been, or are being or are likely to be helpful to the official in the investigation or prosecution of the criminal act of which he/she is a victim; and

E. The criminal activity of which he/she is a victim violated the laws of the United States or occurred in the United States (including Indian country and military installations) or the territories and possessions of the United States.

Source: "Instructions for Form I-918, Petition for U Nonimmigrant Status," Department of Homeland Security: U.S. Citizenship and Immigration Services, OMB No. 1615-0104, November 23, 2010, accessed December 15, 2010, http://www .uscis.gov/files/form/i-918instr.pdf.

Appendix D
DIFFERENCES BETWEEN HUMAN
TRAFFICKING AND SMUGGLING

Trafficking	*Smuggling*
Must contain an element of force, fraud, or coercion (actual, perceived or implied), unless under 18 years of age involved in commercial sex acts.	The person being smuggled is generally cooperating.
Forced labor and/or exploitation.	There is no actual or implied coercion.
Persons trafficked are victims.	Persons smuggled are complicit in the smuggling crime; they are not necessarily victims of the crime of smuggling (though they may become victims depending on the circumstances in which they were smuggled).
Enslaved, subjected to limited movement or isolation, or had documents confiscated.	Persons are free to leave, change jobs, etc.
Need not involve the actual movement of the victim.	Facilitates the illegal entry of person(s) from one country into another.
No requirement to cross an international border.	Smuggling always crosses an international border.
Person must be involved in labor/services or commercial sex acts, i.e., must be "working."	Person must only be in country or attempting entry illegally.

This chart does not provide a precise legal distinction of the differences between smuggling and trafficking. The chart is designed to illustrate general fact scenarios that are often seen in smuggling or trafficking incidents. Fact scenarios are often complex; in such cases expert legal advice should be sought. Source: "Fact Sheet: Distinctions Between Human Smuggling and Human Trafficking 2006," U.S. Department of State: Diplomacy in Action, January 1, 2006, accessed August 25, 2006, https://www.state.gov/m/ds/investigat/hstcenter/90434.htm.

Appendix E

CULTURE AND THE TRAFFICKED, THE TRAFFICKER, AND THE ANTI-TRAFFICKER

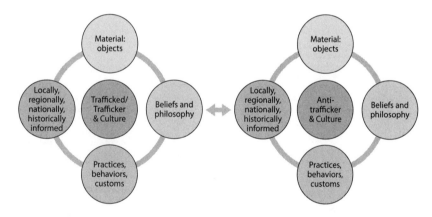

Annie Fukushima, "Cultural Awareness and Human Trafficking," *Ending Violence: Preserving Our Roots While Looking to the Future,* July 24, 2012, National Coalition Against Domestic Violence, Denver, Colorado.

NOTES

Introduction

1. Ana Gonzalez-Barrera and Jens Manuel Krogstad, "What We Know About Illegal Immigration from Mexico," Pew Research Center, March 2, 2017, accessed August 12, 2018, http://www.pewresearch.org/fact-tank/2015/11/20/what-we-know-about -illegal-immigration-from-mexico/.

2. C. Gallagher, "Adolescents and the Border Crisis: Unaccompanied Alien Children and Child Trafficking" (IOFA talk, 2014), accessed March 15, 2016, http: //freedomnetworkusa.org/wp-content/uploads/2014/03/UAC-blog-series.pdf.

3. Muzaffar Chishti, Faye Hipsman Muzaffar Chishti, and Faye Hipsman, "Dramatic Surge in the Arrival of Unaccompanied Children Has Deep Roots and No Simple Solutions," Migrationpolicy.org, March 2, 2017, accessed August 12, 2018, http://www .migrationpolicy.org/article/dramatic-surge-arrival-unaccompanied-children-has -deep-roots-and-no-simple-solutions.

4. "The Freedom Network's Response to the Current Influx of Unaccompanied Children at the US-Mexico Border," Freedom Network USA, August 2014, accessed September 15, 2018, http://freedomnetworkusa.org/wp-content/uploads/2012/05/FN -Statement-on-UACs.pdf.

5. Emmarie E. Huetteman, "U.S. Placed Immigrant Children with Traffickers, Report Says," *New York Times*, December 21, 2017, accessed August 12, 2018, https://www .nytimes.com/2016/01/29/us/politics/us-placed-immigrant-children-with-traffickers -report-says.html.

6. Ibid.

7. See Luibhéid 2002.

8. In Chapter 3, I provide a conceptualization of perfect victimhood and iconic victimhood status. Such notions of victimhood are predicated on binary assumptions

of underserving victims versus those whose victimization is imperceptible to a public.

9. Homeland Security, Deferred Action for Childhood Arrivals (DACA), https:// www.dhs.gov/deferred-action-childhood-arrivals-daca.

10. B. Fertig, "When ICE Shows Up in Human Trafficking Court," WNYC, June 22, 2017, accessed April 12, 2018, https://www.wnyc.org/story/when-ice-shows-court/.

11. Butler 2009, p. 31.

12. For example, Executive Order 13759: Protecting the Nation from Foreign Terrorist Entry into the United States (signed January 27, 2017) suspended the entry of migrants from Iran, Iraq, Libya, Somali, Sudan, Syria, and Yemen for ninety days. Executive Order 13780 replaced Executive Order 13759, requiring not only extreme vetting but also restrictions of migrants from Iran, Libya, Somalia, Sudan, Syria, and Yemen. Executive Order 13767: Border Security and Immigration Enforcement Improvements (signed January 25, 2017) called for the immediate repatriation of undocumented migrants.

13. Randy Capps et al., "Revving Up the Deportation Machinery: Enforcement Under Trump and the Pushback," Migrationpolicy.org, July 03, 2018, accessed August 12, 2018, https://www.migrationpolicy.org/research/revving-deportation-machinery -under-trump-and-pushback; Peter Slevin, "Deportation of Illegal Immigrants Increases Under Obama Administration," *Washington Post*, July 26, 2010, accessed March 1, 2010, http://www.washingtonpost.com/wp-dyn/content/article/2010/07/25 /AR2010072501790.html.

14. See "Human Trafficking in the Media" and "Culture (Art/Literature)" in the Bibliography.

15. Jaxon van Derbeken, "S.F.'s 'Sell Crack or Die' Defendant Convicted," SFGate, February 11, 2012, accessed August 12, 2018, http://www.sfgate.com/crime/article/S-F -s-sell-crack-or-die-defendant-convicted-3286004.php.

16. Jaxon van Derbeken, "S.F. Crack Case Highlights Immigration Dilemma," SFGate, February 10, 2012, accessed July 10, 2017, http://www.sfgate.com/bayarea /article/S-F-crack-case-highlights-immigration-dilemma-3217501.php.

17. See Fukushima and Liou 2012.

18. See Barry 1984. See also Farr 2005; Gallagher and Pearson 2010; Outshoorn 2004.

19. See Agustín 2007. See also Aronowitz 2001; Brennan 2014; Chin and Finckenauer 2012.

20. See Bales 2005.

21. See Van den Anker 2004.

22. See Shelley 2010. See also Stoecker and Shelley 2004.

23. See Brysk and Choi-Fitzpatrick 2012. See also Hua 2011.

24. See Hesford 2011.

25. See Gallagher 2010. See also Chacón 2006; Chapkis 2003.

26. See Lee and Lewis 2003–4.

27. See Office on Trafficking in Persons: An Office of the Administration for Children & Families, https://www.acf.hhs.gov/otip.

28. See "Anti-Human Trafficking Task Force Initiative," Bureau of Justice Assistance, U.S. Department of Justice, https://www.bja.gov/ProgramDetails.aspx?Program_ID=51.

29. Global Slavery Index, https://www.globalslaveryindex.org/methodology/.

30. See "FY 2016 ICE Immigration Removals," US Immigrations and Customs Enforcement, https://www.ice.gov/removal-statistics/2016.

31. "Request Blue Campaign Materials," DHS, August 3, 2018, accessed August 12, 2018, https://www.dhs.gov/blue-campaign/request-materials.

32. "Human Trafficking: Look Beneath the Surface," Department of Health and Human Services, accessed August 12, 2018, https://www.acf.hhs.gov/sites/default/files/endtrafficking/healthassessment_nov2016.pdf.

33. See Duggan 2002.

34. Rosaldo 1993, p. 244.

35. Cheng 2010.

36. Grewal and Kaplan 2006.

37. See Lopez and Miller 2011; Martinez and Lee 2000; Sohoni and Sohoni 2014.

38. Lawston and Escobar 2009–10.

39. Martinez and Slack 2013.

40. Originally, a person could remain for three years in the United States. In 2006, 8 CFR 214.11 adjusted this to four years.

41. See "USCIS Victims of Trafficking Form I-914 (T) (Fiscal Year 2017, 4th Qtr)," United States Citizenship and Immigration Services, data as of September 30, 2017, published January 19, 2018, retrieved April 19, 2018, https://www.uscis.gov/sites/default/files/USCIS/Resources/Reports%20and%20Studies/Immigration%20Forms%20Data/Victims/I914t_visastatistics_fy2017_qtr4.pdf.

42. Comparing the US Department of State's TIP reports, which is released every year, what is found is that the investigations and prosecutions between 2009 and 2017 increased and also became more complex across varying government investigating bodies. In 2009, the TIP report reported as follows: "FY 2008, the DOJ's Civil Rights Division and U.S. Attorneys' Offices initiated 183 investigations, charged 82 individuals, and obtained 77 convictions in 40 human trafficking cases (13 labor trafficking, 27 sex trafficking)." By 2017, DHS investigations alone outnumbered the total of investigations, charges, and convictions in 2009. The 2017 TIP report reported, "In FY 2016, DHS reported opening 1,029 investigations possibly involving human trafficking, compared to 1,034 in FY 2015. DOJ formally opened more than 1,800 human trafficking investigations, a significant increase from 802 in FY 2015. DOJ's ECM task forces

separately initiated 982 investigations, a slight decrease from 1,011 in FY 2015. DOS reported opening 288 human trafficking-related cases worldwide during FY 2016, an increase from 175 in FY 2015." U.S. Department of State, *Trafficking in Persons Report 2009*, June 2009, https://www.state.gov/documents/organization/123357.pdf, p. 57. See also U.S. Department of State, *Trafficking in Persons Report 2017*, https://www.state.gov /documents/organization/271345.pdf, p. 415.

43. Bernstein 2010, p. 58.

44. Fitzgerald 2015.

45. Ibid., p. 115.

46. Reilly 2009.

47. María Lugones contends that the logic of colonial modernity is categorical, dichotomous, and hierarchical. The logic of colonial modernity is shaped by human/ nonhuman dichotomies that are reinforced by distinctions of race, class, and gender. Lugones 2010.

48. See Rentschler 2004.

49. See Laub 1995.

50. See Caruth 2002.

51. A *testimonio* is a first-person narrativizing of an event and/or events. See Felman and Laub 1992. See also Beverly 2004.

52. A *differend* is a dispute or a disagreement in which the "victim" is silenced. See Lyotard 1988.

53. See Hesford 2011..See also Agustín 2007; Andrijasevic 2007; Aradau 2004; Soderlund 2011.

54. Sandoval 2000, p. 63.

55. "Colonial difference" is the classification of the planet in the modern/colonial imaginary by enacting coloniality of power, an energy and a machine to transform differences into values. Mignolo 2000, p. 13.

56. Lugones 2003.

57. Neil Smith illustrates, through the example of the Homeless Vehicle, how a political and artistic response to homelessness enables evicted people to jump scales—"to organize the production and reproduction of daily life and to resist oppression and exploitation at a higher scale—over a wider geographical field." Smith 1993.

58. I draw upon Althusser's notion of institutions as encompassing religion, family, legal, political institutions, trade union, communications, and culture. Althusser 2001.

59. Anzaldúa 1989, p. 68.

60. See Rentschler 2004.

61. See Laub 1995.

62. See Caruth 2002.

63. See Laub 1992, p. 57.

64. Berger 2016, p. 215.

65. Lather 1986.

66. See Appendix B and Appendix C.

67. See "Human Trafficking in the Media" in the Bibliography.

68. Feminist philosopher Uma Narayan specifically refers to third-world feminisms as feminist politics in third-world countries. Narayan 1997.

69. U.S. women of color collaborated with and continue to collaborate with women of color migrants and third world women to bring to the center a philosophy and practice that makes important interventions in American studies, ethnic studies, feminisms, and disciplinary programs such as sociology, the law, and the humanities.

70. Chicanas raised their voices beginning in the 1960s within the civil rights movement to bring to the center their struggles against racism and sexism. See Garcia 1997. Black American women organized to put forth a collective statement, the Combahee Collective Statement, to show their solidarity against interlocking systems of oppression: racism, sexism, heterosexism, and classism. See Combahee River Collective 1986. "Third-world" feminists, women of color, recognized the need to understand difference in social movements that became visible during the 1970s. Sandoval 2000.

71. United Nations Office on Drugs and Crime, Human Trafficking Knowledge Portal, https://sherloc.unodc.org/cld/en/v3/htms/index.html.

72. Garcia 2013.

73. Chin and Rudelius-Palmer 2010, p. 265.

74. Anzaldúa 1989.

Chapter 1

1. As part of my role as expert witness on the case, I interviewed the defendants and presented to the jurors information about human trafficking. Court-appointed interpreters translated English-Cantonese. Unpublished Opinion. The People of the State of California v. Yonghua Zeng (2015) 1 Cal 5d A138970 (San Francisco County Super. Ct. No. SCN219176-02).

2. Albert Samaha, "The Blessing Scam Suspects Will Be Extradited to NYC Following Sentences in California," *Village Voice*, July 2, 2013, accessed July 1, 2015, http://blogs.villagevoice.com/runninscared/2013/07/blessing_scam_suspects_extradition_california.php.

3. Erin Sherbert, "Would be Victim Outsmarts Suspects in Weird Asian Ghost Scam, Four Charged," *San Francisco Weekly*, November 16, 2012, accessed June 3, 2015, http://blogs.sfweekly.com/thesnitch/2012/11/ah_chung_liu_ying_liu_tam.php.

4. The People of the State of California v. Ying Liu Tam, Ah Chung Liu, Mudi Wu, Yong Hua Zeng, Cal 1d. S.F. (2013).

5. Bay City News Service, "Chinese Woman Suspected of Running Blessing Scams in San Francisco and L.A. Detained Attempting to Flee U.S.," *San Jose Mercury News*, November 4, 2014, accessed June 1, 2015, http://www.mercurynews.com/crime -courts/ci_26862623/chinese-woman-suspected-running-blessing-scams-san-francisco.

6. Albert Samaha, "Ghost Stories: Scams Targeting SF's Cantonese Community Reveal the Terrible Power of Belief," *San Francisco Weekly*, June 5, 2013, http://www .sfweekly.com/2013-06-05/news/ghost-scam-blessing-scam-cantonese-george-gascon -david-chiu/full/.

7. Mina Kim, "Chinatown 'Blessing Scams' Target Elderly Women," NPR, July 3, 2013, accessed June 3, 2015, http://www.npr.org/blogs/codeswitch/2013/07/18/197732751 /chinatown-blessing-scams.

8. Human trafficking cases oftentimes are found in three different types of court systems: immigration law, family court, and criminal courts (i.e., local at the district attorney level or a case at the federal level prosecuted by a federal prosecutor such as a U.S. attorney). An infraction is the least serious type of crime. A person may receive a ticket for speeding but will do not jail time. A misdemeanor is more severe than an infraction where a person may do jail-time up to a year. A felony is viewed as the most serious form of crime, where prison time is more than a year. These crimes range from murder to burglary.

9. Reilly 2009.

10. Hesford 2011, p. 10.

11. Gordon 1997, p. 8.

12. Ibid., p. 4.

13. 4:09-cr-00573-SBA United States District Court, N.D., California, Oakland Division, 2012.

14. Butler 2004, p. 43.

15. "Human Trafficking," Polaris Project, December 21, 2017, accessed August 13, 2018, http://www.polarisproject.org/human-trafficking/overview.

16. Hua and Ray 2014, pp. 17, 24.

17. Brennan 2014.

18. Schaeffer 2012, p. 7.

19. Kaplan, Alarcon, and Moallem 1999, p. 11.

20. Chouliaraki 2009, p. 217.

21. Fantone 2007, p. 10.

22. Laub 1995, pp. 61–62.

23. Caruth 2002, p. 436.

24. "Popular regimes of truth" are characterized by specific visual tropes, narrative genres, discourses, stories, and popular expertise about trafficked women. Galusca 2012, p. 3.

25. National sentimentality encompasses a rhetoric of "promise that a nation can be built across fields of social difference through channels of affective identification

and empathy. . . . The object of the nation and the law in this light is to eradicate systemic social pain, the absence of which becomes the definition of freedom." Berlant 1999, p. 128.

26. Carceral feminisms are a commitment to heteronormative family values, crime control, and the putative rescue and restoration of victims. Bernstein 2010.

27. Fukushima 2015.

28. Fleetwood 2011, p. 2.

29. For Román-Odio, Chicana sacred iconographies are emancipatory for Chicanas and a means to dismantle national and transnational projects. Román-Odio 2013. I, too, situate iconographies within the conceptual community from which they emerge (the specific historical and cultural experiences). Fukushima 2015.

30. Zoe Trodd uses the concept of abolition iconography. However, "abolition" privileges individuals and collectives who are committed to ending all forms of slavery. Not all participants deploying anti-violence iconographies are committed to abolitionist visions. Sex workers, who call for the legalization and legitimization of sex as work, greatly differ in their ideologies and practices and surrounding sexual economies, which, from a radical feminist approach, see sexual slavery as an expression of sexual violence against women. Both sex workers and abolitionist play on familiar motifs of the cage to comment on twenty-first century trafficking. Trodd 2013, p. 339.

31. See Kempadoo, Sanghera, and Pattanaik 2005.

32. Mediascapes encompass electronic capabilities, production, and dissemination. Mediascapes provide large and complex repertoires of images, narratives, and ethnoscapes to viewers throughout the world. Appadurai 1996, pp. 38–39.

33. Asian Americans are multiple, hybrid, and heterogeneous. See Lowe 1996.

34. Tuck and Ree 2013, p. 642.

35. Supra note 1.

36. "Vancouver Chinese Seniors 'Blessing' Scam Suspects Identified," *Huffpost British Columbia*, August 8, 2013, accessed June 3, 2015, http://www.huffingtonpost.ca/2013/08/08/vancouver-chinese-seniors-blessing-scam_n_3727972.html.

37. "Another 'Evil Spirit' Scam Targeting Elderly Women in Honolulu's Chinatown," *Angry Asian Man*, November 20, 2012, accessed June 3, 2015, http://blog.angryasianman.com/2012/11/evil-spirit-scam-targeting-elderly.html.

38. M. Wilson, "Scam Suspects Become the Victims," *New York Times*, June 7, 2013, accessed June 3, 2015, http://www.nytimes.com/2013/06/08/nyregion/in-chinese-blessing-scam-suspects-become-the-victims.html?_r=0.

39. Byrd 2011, p. 18.

40. Lowe 2015, p. 8.

41. Povinelli 2011, p. 13.

42. Supra note 1.

43. See Peffer 1986. See also Lee 2003.

44. Lee and Yung 2010.

45. Lowe 2015, p. 27.

46. Sess. II, Chap141, 18 Stat. 477, 43rd Congress, March 3, 1875.

47. See Takaki 1989. See also Hirata 1979.

48. 36 Stat 825 (1910), as amended 18 U.S.C.A. §2421(supp. 1992).

49. Jung 2006.

50. See Yun 2008, p. 21.

51. Jung 2006, p. 4.

52. Ibid., at p. 9.

53. Lowe 2006, p. 194.

54. Zhao 2012.

55. Immigration numbers were limited to numbers of births. H.R. 4075; Pub.L. 67–5; 42 Stat. 5. 67th Congress; May 19, 1921.

56. The Hart-Cellar Act abolished the national origins quota system from the 1920s.

57. Under 8 U.S. Code § 1226(c) detained migrants are deportable (C). A deportable migrant who is criminalized, is, under section 1227 (a)(2)(A), considered inadmissible (also see 1182 (a)(3)(B)).

58. Degenova 2002, p. 439.

59. Degenova and Peutz 2010, p. 14.

60. E.g., the Chinese Exclusion Act of 1882, the Asiatic Barred Zone Act of 1917, and the Illegal Immigration Reform and Immigrant Responsibility Act (1996).

61. See Pascoe 2009.

62. E.g., the Bracero Program. Ngai 2004.

63. California Alien Land Law of 1913.

64. E.g., California's Prop 187, which prohibited illegal aliens from using health care, public education, and other social services in the state (1994). Lee 2003; Ngai 2004; Park and Park 1999.

65. Chin 2013.

66. Johnson and Betsinger 2009.

67. Liang and Ye 2001, p. 187.

68. Chin 1999, pp. 13–14, 19–20, 21.

69. Siu 2005.

70. Gordon 1997, p. 17.

71. Colonial modernities cohere due to the production and sustaining of European paradigms of rational knowledge. Quijano 2007, pp. 168–78.

72. Supra note 1.

73. Ibid.

74. Martin 1991.

75. Ibid., p. 36.

76. Erin Sherbert, "More Victims Duped by Weird Asian Ghost Scam," *San Francisco Weekly*, September 5, 2012, accessed June 3, 2015, http://www.sfweekly.com /thesnitch/2012/09/05/more-victims-duped-by-weird-asian-ghost-scam.

77. "Four Arrested in Asian Ghost Scam," *Angry Asian Man*, November 19, 2012, accessed June 1, 2015, http://blog.angryasianman.com/2012/11/four-arrested-in-asian -ghost-scam.html.

78. "'Evil Spirit' Scammers Targeting Asian Women," *Angry Asian Man*, September 5, 2012, accessed June 1, 2015, http://blog.angryasianman.com/2012/09/evil-spirit -scammers-targeting-asian.html.

79. Mina Kim, "To Ward Off Ghosts, Chinese Seniors Give Up Life Savings to Scammers," KQED, June 21–23, 2013, accessed June 1, 2015, http://audio.californiareport .org/archive/R201306211630/d.

80. Reddy 2011.

81. Mike Aldax, "S.F. Officials Reach Out to Banks to Help Stanch Chinese Blessing Scam," *The Examiner*, July 29, 2013, accessed June 1, 2015, http://www.sfexaminer .com/sanfrancisco/sf-officials-reach-out-to-banks-to-help-stanch-chinese-blessing -scam/Content?oid=2525575.

82. Michael Finney, "San Francisco Warning Elderly About 'Blessing' Scam," ABC KGO-TV (San Francisco), May 14, 2013, accessed June 1, 2015, http://abclocal.go.com/kgo /story?section=news/7_on_your_side&id=9102731.

83. Beck 2002, p. 48.

84. Supra note 3.

85. Fan Ping Ding Case: United States of America v. Shen et al., 09-CR-00573 (N.D. Cal., May 27, 2010).

86. Amy is a pseudonym. Court documents refer to the migrant as GXK, most likely the acronym for her name. Ibid.

87. A culture of servitude is when domestic servitude joins the public and domestic spheres, where domesticity is assimilated into the public, and the structural inequalities of domestic servitude of difference are incorporated as well. Ray and Qayum 2009, p. 102.

88. Supra note 85.

89. Ibid.

90. 18 U.S.C. § 1592(a)(1).

91. 8 U.S.C. §§ 1324(a)(1)(A)(iii) and (B)(i).

92. Kathleen Speake, "Project to Promote Equality and Decent Work for Women," ILO, Beijing, China, http://www.ilo.org/wcmsp5/groups/public/—asia/—ro-bangkok /documents/publication/wcms_114256.pdf.

93. "China," United States Department of State, 2014, accessed August 13, 2018, http://www.state.gov/j/tip/rls/tiprpt/countries/2014/226700.htm.

94. John Ashcroft, "#012204: Prepared Remarks of Attorney General John Ashcroft Regarding Human Trafficking," United States Department of Justice, June 29, 2004, accessed August 13, 2018, http://www.justice.gov/archive/ag/speeches/2004/12904aghumantrafficking.htm.

95. 472 F.3d 638: United States of America, Plaintiff-appellee v. Kil Soo Lee, Defendant-appellant, United States Court of Appeals, Ninth Circuit. - 472 F.3d 638, Argued and Submitted November 13, 2006 Filed December 27, 2006, http://law.justia.com/cases/federal/appellate-courts/F3/472/638/473342/.

96. Supra note 1.

97. Butler 2004, p. 22.

98. Vic Lee, "Victim of 'Blessing Scam' Helps SF Police Arrest Suspects," ABC KGO-TV (San Francisco), May 29, 2013, accessed June 1, 2015, http://abclocal.go.com/kgo/story?section=news/local/san_francisco&id=9120487.

99. Gordon 1997, p. 22.

Chapter 2

1. California Proposition 35, Ban on Human Trafficking and Sex Slavery, *Ballotpedia*, 2012, accessed 20, 2018, https://ballotpedia.org/California_Proposition_35,_Ban_on_Human_Trafficking_and_Sex_Slavery_(2012).

2. Ibid.

3. Jans Erik Gould, "California's Prop 35: Why Some Oppose an Anti-Sex Trafficking Initiative," *Time*, November 5, 2012, http://nation.time.com/2012/11/05/californias-prop-35-why-some-oppose-an-anti-sex-trafficking-initiative/

4. Schaefer-Gabriel 2011, p. 104.

5. Obokata 2005.

6. See Ewing 1987 and Stryker 2003.

7. Foucault 1994, p. 2–3.

8. Georges Gurvitch's definition of sociology of the law is useful: (1) the study of the manifestation of law as a function of forms of sociality and social reality, (2) studying the manifestation of law as a function of real collective units, and (3) studying the regularities as tendencies and factors of the change, development, and decay of the law within a particular type of society. Gurvitch 1973, pp. 48–49.

9. "Servile" is when a person is a "subject as a slave or serf to a master or owner; living in servitude. Of a class, etc.: composed of slaves or serfs." *Oxford English Dictionary*, "Servile," adjective, accessed June 1, 2012, http://www.oed.com/view/Entry/176697?redirectedFrom=servile#eid. First citation appears by Thomas Cooper, *Thesaurus Linguae Romanae & Britannicae*, 1st ed., 1564 (vol. 1): STC 5686. Edward Gibbons's definition draws a distinction between "free" and "servile." Edward Gibbon, *The History of the Decline and Fall of the Roman Empire*, 1st ed., 1776–88 (6 vols.). For a legal explanation of servitude, see Appendix C.

10. Welch 2009.

11. Anne T. Gallagher cites P. Van Djick and G. J. H. van Hoof. Gallagher 2010, p. 182.

12. Patterson 1982, p. 105.

13. Ibid., p. 13.

14. "What Is Human Trafficking?" Homeland Security Initiative, Blue Campaign, https://www.dhs.gov/blue-campaign/what-human-trafficking.

15. "What Is Modern Slavery?" U.S. Department of State, https://www.state.gov/j /tip/what/.

16. Council on Hemispheric Affairs, "Modern Day Slavery in Mexico and the United States," December 21, 2009, accessed August 13, 2018, http://www.coha.org /modern-day-slavery-in-mexico-and-the-united-states/.

17. Quijano and Wallerstein 1992, p. 556.

18. See Quirk 2011.

19. See Bales 1999.

20. "Executive Summary," Global Slavery Index, 2018, accessed August 13, 2018, https://www.globalslaveryindex.org/2018/findings/executive-summary/.

21. Bales 1999.

22. Batstone 2007, p. 3.

23. Gordon-Reed 2008.

24. Oriola 2016.

25. There are debates as to what is "modern-day slavery." Some argue that human trafficking is a different phenomenon than human slavery. Nimako and Small (2012) refer to the responses to "modern day slavery" as the "new anti-slavery movement."

26. Kempadoo, Sanghera, and Pattanaik 2005.

27. Kara 2009.

28. Merry 2000, p. 258.

29. The founders of the *American Journal of International Law* (*AJIL*) established international law and they embraced the belief that international law would diminish the prominence of power and coercion in global affairs; this is what Richard H. Steinberg and Jonathan M. Zasloff refer to as the "classicist" view of international law. There is a need to establish the multiple scales of laws that impact a single issue. International law may be traced to the establishment of *AJIL* in 1906. Steinberg and Zasloff 2006, p. 64.

30. Ibid., p. 68.

31. Ibid., pp. 70–71.

32. Steinberg and Zasloff summarize realist views as follows: traditional realists see international law as a reflection of both interests of powerful states and the norms held across states; structural realists explain international law through knowing the interests of the powerful states; and realist institutionalist hybrids further the belief that the relative power of states shapes law. Ibid., pp. 74–76.

33. Gallagher 2010.

34. Palermo Protocol, Preamble.

35. Protocol to Prevent, Suppress and Punish Trafficking in Persons, Especially Women and Children, supplementing the United Nations Convention Against Transnational Organized Crime, *United Nations,* November 15, 2000, Art. 2.

36. Preamble. Adopted and Opened for Signature, Ratification and Accession by General Assembly Resolution 55/25, November 15, 2000, accessed January 15, 2008, http://www2.ohchr.org/english/law/protocoltraffic.htm.

37. Warren 2007, p. 243.

38. Ibid., p. 259.

39. Chuang 2006b.

40. DeStefano 2008.

41. Trafficking Victims Protection Act of 2000, Pub. L. No. 106–386, div. A, 114 Stat. 1466 (codified as amended at 22 U.S.C. §§ 7101–7110 (2000)).

42. See Appendix B.

43. Ibid.

44. Ibid.

45. Ibid.

46. Ibid.

47. Ibid.

48. Ibid.

49. Ibid.

50. Ibid.

51. Ibid.

52. Chacón 2006.

53. Kim 2007.

54. United States v. Kozminski, 487 U.S. 931 (1988).

55. See Appendix A for information for certification letter to receive benefits, Appendix B for information about Continued Presence, and Appendix C for information about the T-Visa and U-Visa.

56. See Appendix C.

57. Lee and Lewis 2003–4, pp. 169–95.

58. T-Visa. See Appendix C.

59. The Office on Trafficking in Persons website has a discrepancy. On the webpage it states, "Since 2001, HHS has helped 8,543 victims of human trafficking and their family members." However, in their video campaign, it states 7,346. "Look Beneath the Surface," Office on Trafficking in Persons, an Office on the Administration of Children and Families, May 31, 2018, accessed August 13, 2018, https://www.acf.hhs.gov/otip /partnerships/look-beneath-the-surface.

60. "About Rescue & Restore: Campaign Overview," U.S. Department of Health and Human Services: Administration for Children & Families, August 2010, Campaign

to Rescue & Restore Victims of Human Trafficking, accessed March 10, 2012, http:
//www.acf.hhs.gov/trafficking/rescue_restore/index.html.

61. "Contact Information for Coalitions," U.S. Department of Health and Human
Services: Administration for Children & Families, February 7, 2012, Campaign to Rescue & Restore Victims of Human Trafficking, accessed March 10, 2012, http://www.acf
.hhs.gov/trafficking/about/coalition_list.html.

62. See Appendix D for chart distinguishing between smuggling and human
trafficking.

63. Rescue & Restore Victims of Human Trafficking public awareness campaign,
Look Beneath the Surface, 2011, accessed August 13, 2018, https://www.youtube.com
/watch?v=bqyzW84I3Dc.

64. Barthes 1982, p. 82.

65. Aradau 2004, p. 259.

66. People categorized as human trafficked are dependent on a "perfect victim" status. Srikantiah 2007. And the non-contradictory infallible, or the *perfect victim*, is a
stereotype and a myth that is perpetuated by images both in text and visual that
constitute who a trafficked person is in the twenty-first-century anti-trafficking movement. Srikantiah 2007. See Srikantiah's chapter 6 for more information about the language of "victim" and human trafficking.

67. Tyldum and Brunovskis 2005.

68. Salari 2015.

69. Eng 2010, pp. 23–57.

70. Mitchell, Agle, and Wood (1997) begin with R. E. Freeman's broad definition
of a stakeholder as being "any group or individual who can affect or is affected by the
achievement of the organization's objectives." They affirm that a stakeholder is identified by an organization or what they call a "firm": "by their possession or attributed
possession of one, two, or all three of the following attributes: (1) the stakeholder's power
to influence the firm, (2) the legitimacy of the stakeholder's relationship with the firm,
and (3) the urgency of the stakeholder's claim on the firm." Mitchell, Agle, and Wood
1997, p. 854.

71. *Oxford Dictionary*, "Freedom," Oxford University Press, accessed March 1, 2012,
http://oxforddictionaries.com/definition/freedom?q=freedom.

72. The intertwining of freedom and slavery may be historically traced to the prin-
cipal author of the Declaration of Independence, Thomas Jefferson. The rise of liberties and equality for white men in the United States was accompanied by the rise of
racialized slavery—the two form a central paradox in U.S. history. Freedom, inspired
by Thomas Jefferson's own experiences, was conceived of as constituted by a person
who is economically independent from another, and therefore an economically dependent person is unfree. And the ability for a person to be free of debt and for that reason
free, is also tied to notions that such individuals should also be economically free to
own land. This solidified the relationship between slaves and freedmen. Morgan 2003.

73. Hume 1900.

74. See Allison 1995.

75. Foner 2012, p. 441.

76. Davis 1981, p. 98.

77. Mahmood (2005) discusses this in the context of freedom, feminism, and Islam.

78. The abolition of slavery meant the freeing of slaves. The language of the Thirteenth Amendment is as follows: "Section 1. Neither slavery nor involuntary servitude, except as a punishment for crime whereof the party shall have been duly convicted, shall exist within the United States, or any place subject to their jurisdiction. Section 2. Congress shall have power to enforce this article by appropriate legislation." Thirteenth Amendment, passed by the United States Congress January 31, 1865, ratified on December 6, 1865, National Archives Records Administration, accessed February 15, 2007, http://www.ourdocuments.gov/doc.php?doc=40.

79. McConnell 1991–92, p. 208.

80. Ibid., p. 207.

81. Fourth World Conference on Women, September 4–15, 1995, http://beijing20 .unwomen.org/~/media/headquarters/attachments/sections/csw/pfa_e_final_web .pdf.

82. Woods 2013, p. 123.

83. Foner 1999, p. 106.

84. As conveyed in the Afro-Asian comparative work of Edlie L. Wong, "race is a relational concept, and immigration law . . . fundamentally shaped by the boundaries of race in the U.S." Wong 2015, p. 18.

85. Lowe 1996, p. 6.

86. Ngai 2007, p. 2521.

87. Although Latinx encompasses gender binaries and gender fluidity, the use of Latina/o/x emphasizes the cisgender normative and queer possibilities. Where referencing Latina/o/x, one may account for cisgender and gender nonconforming/trans bodies.

88. Ngai 2007, p. 2521.

89. Marx 1847, p. 94–95.

90. Ibid., p. 54.

91. Ken Lawrence's summary of Marx's capitalist slavery is as follows: (1) the price of a slave is the anticipated profit "to be ground out of him"; (2) the land owner and the exploiter of labor are the same person; (3) a slave has value, exchange value and a free wage-worker has no value, only the power to dispose of his labor; (4) all of the slave's labor appears to be unpaid; and (5) all of the free worker's labor appears to be paid; the money-relation conceals the labor of the worker for the capitalist—the surplus labor. Lawrence 1976, p. 12.

92. Ediberto Román describes anti-immigrant sentiment as likened to hysteria, where it appears in the media and in every day relations through nativist discourse and practice, even having policy implications. Román 2013.

93. California media coverage in 2007 described a major crackdown on human smuggling that spanned a two-month period from February to April of that year. In this crackdown, law enforcement efforts targeted human-smuggling rings that led to five thousand arrests of illegal border crossers, "among them more than 100 people with criminal records." The emphasis on criminal records is an example of the bias. L. Berestein, "Crackdown on Smuggling Results in 5,000 Arrests," *San Diego Union-Tribune* (local), April 25, 2007, B5.

94. Aronowitz 2001, p. 172.

95. Myung Oak Kim, "2 Held in Jeffco in Human Smuggling Case," *Rocky Mountain News* (Denver, CO), September 26, 2007, accessed September 15, 2012, http://m .rockymountainnews.com/news/2007/Sep/26/2-held-in-jeffco-in-human-smuggling -case/.

96. Massey, Durand, and Malone 2002, p. 25.

97. See Bonacich and Appelbaum 2000. See also Bonacich and Light 1988; Chinchilla and Hamilton 2001; Choy 2003; Constable 2007; Glenn 2011; Glenn 2002; Glenn 1986; Ehrenreich and Hochschild 2002; Hondagneu-Sotelo 2001; Romero 1992.

98. Peggy Levitt analyzes transnational connectivities that have developed between the Dominican Republic and Massachusetts, United States. Levitt 2001, p. 25.

99. Ibid., p. 8.

100. International Organization of Migration 2006.

101. "The Rise of Asian Americans," PEW Research Center, June 19, 2012, accessed June 19, 2012, http://www.pewsocialtrends.org/2012/06/19/the-rise-of-asian -americans/.

102. Ehrenreich and Hochschild 2002.

103. Sassen 2001.

104. Heyzer 2002.

105. Parreñas 2001b, pp. 31–33.

106. Curran and Rivero-Fuentes 2003, p. 289.

107. By the end of 2005, they estimated that 8.7 million refugees existed, with the highest concentration of refugees in Asia (40%), followed by Africa (32%), Europe (20%), North America (6%), Oceania (1%), and Latin America and the Caribbean (0.4%). New source countries for mass refugee outflows during 2005 included Togo (39,000), Sudan (34,000), the Democratic Republic of Congo (16,000), Somalia (14,000), Central African Republic (11,000), and Iraq (11,000). Adamson 2006.

108. Ibid., p. 171.

109. Hu-Dehart 2005, pp. 78–111.

110. Takaki 1989, p. 36.

111. Jung 2006, p. 4.

112. Ibid.

113. Ibid., p. 9.

114. Chang 2000, p. 30.

115. Massey, Durand, and Malone 2003, pp. 36–37.

116. Bickerton 2000–2001, p. 897.

117. Cohen 2011, p. 25.

118. Massey, Durand, and Malone 2003, p. 37.

119. Jordan and Walsh 2008.

120. Romero 1992.

121. Glenn 2011, p. 35.

122. Rollins 1987.

123. The most common profession for Japanese American men in 1900 was domestic and personal servant (40.5%). This number declined by 1940 to 10.9%. Glenn 1986, p. 70.

124. First generation of Japanese to migrate to the United States.

125. Single immigrant men had brides picked for them by their parents or relatives. Through a go-between, the men sent photographs and information about their lives to negotiate a marriage. The only difference between arranged marriages is that bridegrooms were physically absent at wedding ceremonies, but they facilitated the legal process. Ichioka 1980, p. 343.

126. McClain 1994.

127. In 1950, 15.8% of Issei Japanese worked in domestic worker. By 1970, this increased to 24.3%. Glenn 1986, p. 82.

128. Hondagneu-Sotelo 2001, p. 15.

129. Romero 1992, pp. 124–25.

130. Glenn 2011, p. 137.

131. Hua 2011.

132. Here, prostitution is used because it denotes the criminalization of the selling of sex.

133. Stetson traces the debates on pornography, prostitution, and trafficking as a gendered construction that intertwines the debates. Stetson 2004, p. 268.

134. See Doezema 2000. See also Doezema 2002; Connelly 1980; Walkowitz 1980; Limoncelli 2010, pp. 20–21.

135. Sociologist Ronald Weitzer defines moral crusades as "one of the forces responsible for transforming such conditions into 'problems.' These movements define a particular condition as an unqualified evil, and see their mission as a righteous enterprise whose goals are both symbolic (attempting to redraw or bolster normative boundaries and moral standards) and instrumental (providing relief to victims, punishing evildoers). To achieve their aims, activists seek to generate widespread public concern about a problem and lobby political elites to either intensify

punishment of offenders or criminalize acts that were previously legal." Weitzer 2007, p. 448.

136. Ronald Weitzer lists a variety of organizations that he lumps into the moral crusades. On the right, crusade members include Focus on the Family, the National Association of Evangelicals, the Catholic Bishops Conference, the Traditional Values Coalition, Concerned Women for America, the Salvation Army, the International Justice Mission, Shared Hope International, the Religious Freedom Coalition, and numerous others. The premier abolitionist feminist organization in the United States is the Coalition Against Trafficking in Women (CATW). Others include Equality Now, the Protection Project, and Standing Against Global Exploitation (SAGE). Ibid.

137. Hua 2011.

138. Gabbert 2003.

139. Beasley 1918.

140. Arista 2011, pp. 40–41.

141. Greer 2000, pp. 185–202.

142. Ibid.

143. See Takaki 1989. See also Hirata 1979.

144. See Seagraves 1994.

145. The *Friends' Intelligencer* documents "human slavery" of Chinese girls at public auctions in San Francisco as occurring on January 19, 1901. They sold for $1,700 to $2,500 each. "It is contrary to law, of course, but the city officials wink at it." *Friends' Intelligencer,* February 16, 1901, pp. 58, 7.

146. Hirata 1979.

147. Ch. 395, 36 Stat. 825; *codified as amended at* 18 U.S.C. §§ 2421–2424. For the original language of the Mann Act (1910), 36 Stats., Vol. I, 825 (1910).

148. Barry 1984.

149. Roe 1911, p. 187.

150. Lui 2009.

151. Jenness 1990, p. 403.

152. Barry 1984, p. 40.

153. Stark and Whisnant 2004, p. xii.

154. Kempadoo and Doezema 1998, p. 34.

155. Kempadoo, Sanghera, and Pattanaik 2005.

156. Ibid.

157. Schaefer-Gabriel 2011.

Chapter 3

1. Human Trafficking & Domestic Workers infographic, National Domestic Workers Alliance, https://www.domesticworkers.org/beyondsurvival/infographic.

2. Original description on the HTLP website, "Human Trafficking Law Project Database," Michigan Law, University of Michigan, 2011, accessed January 1, 2014, https://www.law.umich.edu/clinical/HuTrafficCases/Pages/searchdatabase.aspx.

3. Sassen 2002.

4. See Hondagneu-Sotelo 2001. See also Romero 1992.

5. Dignan 2005, p. 15.

6. The pathetic victim in general is innocent of any wrongdoing, is helpless, and experiences unspeakable suffering, paralleling the image of the ideal victim. Meyers 2011, p. 265. Heroic victims represent such a high moral standard that most of us can only dream of living up to it. Ibid, p. 267.

7. Srikantiah draws upon Nils Christie to suggest that the perfect victim is the ideal victim whose suffering is not due to their own fault. Srikantiah 2007, p. 211. Also described by sociologist Sandra Walklate (2006, pp. 273–85).

8. The ideal victim: "A person or a category of individual who—when hit by crime—most readily [is] given the complete and legitimate status of being a victim." Christie 1986, p. 18.

9. Walklate 2007.

10. Srikantiah 2007.

11. Barthes 1957, p. 115.

12. The human trafficking power-and-control wheel diagrams the forms of abuse that trafficking victims experience that are similar to domestic violence victims: intimidation, emotional abuse, isolation, minimizing, denying, blaming, sexual abuse, use of privilege, economic abuse, coercion, and threats. The original power-and-control wheel was developed by Ellen Pence at the Domestic Abuse Intervention Project, in the 1980s. Pence describes the making of the domestic violence wheel, "Ellen Pence, Battered Women's Movement Leader," YouTube video, 5:37, posted December 6, 2009, accessed December 26, 2009, http://www.youtube.com/watch?v=r9dZOgr78eE.

13. Human trafficking at the China-Vietnam border dates to before the establishment of Indo-China in 1885. Lessard 2009, p. 3.

14. Aiko 2002, pp. 31–52.

15. Agustín 2007, pp. 17–18.

16. Scholars such as Nevins, Ngai, Inda, and Luibhéid have unpacked how "illegal" migration is defined by the nation-state. See Nevins 2002; Ngai 2004; Inda 2006; Luibhéid 2002.

17. See Fragomen 1997.

18. Johnston 2000–2001, p. 2596.

19. Constable 2009, p. 49.

20. Parreñas (2001b) adds that labor develops the human capabilities of the recipient. I would like to argue that it may also develop the inhuman capabilities of the recipient.

21. The works of scholars such as Catherine Ceniza Choy (2003) and Rhacel Salazar Parreñas (2008) provides historical analysis of how immigration and labor arc intrinsically tied to global economies.

22. Sassen 2001, p. 35.

23. Slack 2009.

24. Cesairé 1972, p. 6.

25. Parreñas 2008, pp. 893–94.

26. Another estimate for 2010 is that Filipinos number 2.3 million. This would be a 2,093 percent increase from 1960. "The Rise of Asian Americans," PEW Research Center, June 19, 2012, accessed June 19, 2012, http://www.pewsocialtrends.org/2012/06/19/the-rise-of-asian-americans, p. 42.

27. The figure of 43 percent was reported in "California," Profile of General Population and Housing Characteristics: 2010, United States Census Bureau, 2010, accessed 7 December 2014. In 2010, they reported 46%. This number slightly declined to 43 percent in 2014. A. Terrazas and J. Batalova, "Filipino Migrants in the United States," Migration Policy Institute, U.S. in Focus, April 2010, accessed September 29, 2011, http://www.migrationinformation.org/usfocus/display.cfm?ID=777.

28. Hochschild 2000, pp. 130–31.

29. *Maid in Manhattan* (movie), dir. Wayne Wang, Revolution Studios, 2002.

30. *Mad Men* (television series), AMC, 2007; *The Brady Bunch* (television series), Paramount Television, 1969; and *The Jeffersons* (television series), 1975.

31. *The Jetsons* (television series), Hannah-Barbera Productions, 1962.

32. Christopher Dickey and John Solomon, "The Maid's Tale," *Newsweek*, August 8, 2011, retrieved from Nexis Uni.

33. Time Lemke, "Kobe's Sitting Pretty: Five Years After Rape Charges, Bryant Again Becomes an Appealing Endorser," *Washington Times*, May 13, 2008, C01.

34. "Mildred Baena, Arnold Schwarzenegger's Mistress Breaks Silence," CBS/Associated Press, June 14, 2011, accessed September 28, 2011, http://www.cbsnews.com/8301-31749_162-20071135-10391698.html.

35. Tadiar 1998, p. 927.

36. A survey done by women's research institution estimated that fifty-five thousand women were in prostitution in Angeles and Olongapo alone. Sturdevant and Stoltzfus 1992.

37. Neferti Tadiar defines the prostituted woman as "the figure for the sacrifice of one's moral integrity, conceived as feminine sexuality, and the trammeling of one's sov-

ereignty, conceived as masculine authority—losses which the culture, as a result of its state-keepers betrayal, now suffers." Tadiar 1998, p. 928.

38. Trask (1993) 1999, pp. 136–38.

39. See Regis 2013.

40. San Juan Jr. 2009, p. 99.

41. "World March of Women," Coalition Against Trafficking in Women Asia Pacific, March 8, 2011, accessed September 29, 2011, http://catwap.wordpress.com/.

42. See Fukushima and Liou 2012.

43. U.S. Department of State, Office to Monitor and Combat Trafficking in Persons, "Moving Toward a Decade of Delivery: Prevention," *Trafficking in Persons Report 2011*, http://www.state.gov/g/tip/rls/tiprpt/2011/166768.htm.

44. Tier 1: Countries whose governments fully comply with the TVPA's minimum standards. Tier 2: Countries whose governments do not fully comply with the TVPA's minimum standards but are making significant efforts to bring themselves into compliance with those standards. Tier 2 Watchlist: Countries whose governments do not fully comply with the TVPA's minimum standards but are making significant efforts to bring themselves into compliance with those standards AND (a) the absolute number of victims of severe forms of trafficking is very significant or is significantly increasing; (b) there is a failure to provide evidence of increasing efforts to combat severe forms of trafficking in persons from the previous year; or (c) the determination that a country is making significant efforts to bring itself into compliance with minimum standards was based on commitments by the country to take additional future steps over the next year. Tier 3: Countries whose governments do not fully comply with the minimum standards and are not making significant efforts to do so. http://www.state .gov/j/tip/rls/tiprpt/2011/164228.htm.

45. U.S. Department of State, Office to Monitor and Combat Trafficking in Persons, "Tiers: Placement, Guide, and Penalties for Tier 3 Countries," *Trafficking in Persons Report 2011*, accessed September 29, 2011, http://www.state.gov/g/tip/rls/tiprpt/2011/164221.htm.

46. The top countries of origin for foreign victims in FY 2010 were Thailand, India, Mexico, Philippines, Haiti, Honduras, El Salvador, and the Dominican Republic. U.S. Department of State, Office to Monitor and Combat Trafficking in Persons, "Country Narratives: Countries Through Z—United States," *Trafficking in Persons Report 2011*, accessed September 29, 2011, http://www.state.gov/g/tip/rls/tiprpt/2011 /164233.htm.

47. "Tier 1 in Human Trafficking," *Philippine Star*, June 29, 2017, accessed June 29, 2017, http://www.philstar.com/opinion/2017/06/29/1714560/editorial-tier-1-human -trafficking.

48. M. Bueza, "In Numbers: The Philippines' "War on Drugs," January 6, 2017, accessed January 6, 2017, http://networkagainstkillings.org/wp-content/uploads/2017/01 /010617-IN-NUMBERS_The-Philippines-War-on-Drugs_Rappler.pdf.

49. Nena's case received a wide range of media coverage that revealed her name. Eventually in 2018, she would publish her own story. Tess's nicknames (two separate nicknames, one identified from law enforcement and lawyers and the other from her traffickers) appeared in court documents. While original versions of this chapter illustrate my not using Nena's real name, due to her having published her own story publicly, I am now able to use her real name. However, I have chosen not to use Tess's real name as she has not authored her own story. Rather than reproduce the public exposure of the survivor, I draw attention to the lessons learned from their narratives.

50. ICE, "Human Trafficking and Smuggling," January 16, 2013, accessed August 14, 2018, https://www.ice.gov/factsheets/human-trafficking. See also Appendix D.

51. Gotanda 1998, p. 66.

52. Anderson Cooper, "The World's Largest Employment Category for Children Under 16 Is Domestic Work in the Homes of Others" (transcripts), *Anderson Cooper 360*, CNN, January 24, 2007.

53. Ibid.

54. Ibid.

55. Yong B. Chavez, "Pinay's Former Bosses Plead Guilty to Human Trafficking," *Filipino Online,* August 22, 2007, http://filipinonline.blogspot.com/2007/08/pinays -former-bosses-pleads-guilty-to.html.

56. Andrew Gumbel, "Hollywood Executive Treated His Filipina Maid Like a Slave," *Independent on Sunday,* 1st ed., foreign news, September 12, 2004, p. 21.

57. Supra note 52.

58. Hondagneu-Sotelo and Avila 1997.

59. Janet Napales, "Hollywood Lawyer, Pinay Wife in Slavery Conviction File Bankruptcy," GMA News, February 6, 2008, accessed February 6 2008, http://www .gmanetwork.com/news/story/79553/pinoyabroad/hollywood-lawyer-pinay-wife-in -slavery-conviction-file-bankruptcy.

60. Nena Ruiz, "I Am a Survivor of Human Trafficking: Nena's Story," *The Atlantic,* March 12, 2018, https://www.theatlantic.com/business/archive/2018/03/human -trafficking-nena/554846/.

61. Ibid.

62. Ibid.

63. Geneva Whitmarsh, "'Slave' Case Rests in the Hands of Jury," *Santa Monica Daily Press,* vol. 3, issue 24, August 25, 2004.

64. Associated Press, "Couple Sentenced in Maid Abuse Case," *USA Today,* January 29, 2008, accessed September 28, 2011, http://www.usatoday.com/news/nation/2008 -01-29-2013858599_x.htm.

65. Ibid.

66. Ibid.

67. Cynthia de Castro, "Couple Sentenced for Slavery of Pinay," *The Asian Journal Blog*, January 29, 2008, accessed September 29, 2011, https://asianjournal.wordpress .com/2008/01/29/.

68. Laura Wides, "Maid Who Won Suit Against Sony Executive Decries Slavery," *Sacramento Bee*, September 3, 2004, accessed September 28, 2011, http://www.genderberg .com/phpNuke/modules.php?name=News&file=article&sid=9.

69. Supra note 64.

70. Supra note 56.

71. Supra note 68. Supra note 64.

72. Supra note 64.

73. "Former California Couple Pleads Guilty to Human Trafficking Charges," Department of Justice, Case # 07-637.

74. "Tacoma Woman Sentenced for Holding Domestic Servant in Forced Labor," Department of Justice, January 28, 2008, Case # 08-072.

75. Supra note 60.

76. Supra note 68.

77. Supra note 60.

78. K. Connie Kang, "Filipina Who Says She Was a Slave Wants Family Here," *Los Angeles Times*, September 6, 2004, accessed September 28, 2011.

79. Supra note 68.

80. Rodriguez 2010.

81. Center for Migrant Advocacy and Friedrich Ebert Stiftung 2009.

82. Supra note 64.

83. Ibid.

84. Brennan 2014, p. 174.

85. Harold 2006–7.

86. Supra note 56.

87. Fresnoza-Flot 2009.

88. Menjivar and Abrego 2012.

89. Supra note 58.

90. Ibid.

91. Brennan 2014, p. 20.

92. USA v. the Lundbergs, November 18, 2009, Case4:09-cr-00661-CW.

93. Ibid.

94. Although the courts describe the Lundbergs' sexual lifestyle as a "sexually extroverted lifestyle," they do not describe the sex tours.

95. See Appendix C.

96. Supra note 43.

97. In the case of Maria, photos were taken to document "one of her eyes bloodied and infected and thick welt and scars on her skin where the chains had cut into her. She had not eaten in four days." Bales and Soodalter 2009, p. 4.

98. Court hearing of Lilliana during Dann v. USA (2010).

99. 18 U.S.C. § 1324(a)(1)(A)(iii) and (B)(1).

100. Farrell et al. 2012.

101. Ibid., pp. 225–28.

102. United States v. the Lundbergs, No. CR 09-00661, United States' Sentencing Memorandum, November 18, 2009, United States District Court of California, Oakland Division.

103. Ibid.

104. "Minimum Wage Laws in the States," Wage and Hour Division, Department of Labor, January 1, 2011, accessed September 29, 2011, http://www.dol.gov/whd/minwage/america.htm.

105. Evan Sernoffsky, "New SF Policies Bar Arrest of Sex Workers Who Come Forward to Report Violence," SF Gate, January 11, 2018, https://www.sfgate.com/crime/article/New-SF-policies-bar-arrest-of-sex-workers-who-12492173.php.

106. Sherman et al. 2015.

107. Supra note 93.

108. "Last Name: Lundberg," http://www.surnamedb.com/Surname/Lundberg.

109. Sadruddin, Walter, and Hidalgo 2005.

110. Haines 2007.

111. The range in numbers comes from Silliman and Bhattacharjee (2002).

112. Daguno 1998, pp. 1–16.

113. U.S. Department of State, Office to Monitor and Combat Trafficking in Persons, "Philippines," 2015 Trafficking in Persons Report, accessed September 31, 2016, http://www.state.gov/j/tip/rls/tiprpt/countries/2015/243514.htm.

114. The demand for sex in the Philippines is a transnational phenomenon that is historically constituted by U.S. militarisms and colonization of the Philippines.

115. "Two Swedes Jailed for Life over Philippine Cybersex Den," BBC News, May 11, 2011, http://www.bbc.co.uk/news/world-asia-pacific-13356721.

116. Jyrkinen 2012.

117. See Sturdevant and Stoltzfus 1992. See also Enloe 2007; Enloe 2014.

118. Srikantiah 2007, p. 160.

119. United States v. Eric Gwynn Lundberg and Susan Randall Lundberg, No. CR 09-00661, United States' Sentencing Memorandum, November 18, 2009, United States District Court of California, Oakland Division.

120. Ibid.

121. Cotton, Farley, and Baron 2002, p. 1791.

122. Melissa Farley and Vanessa Kelly provide an example of this bias through a case where a California judge overturned a jury's decision to charge a customer with rape, saying that "a woman who goes out on the street and makes a whore out of herself opens herself up to anybody." Summarizing news media reports, they conveyed that "one juror interpreted the judge's decision as a refusal to give rights to prostitutes. Because of the

difficulty in obtaining testimony from those who are addicted or homeless, and because of bias against those in prostitution, district attorneys and police are summarized as placing a low priority on prosecution of those who rape prostitutes" (Farley and Kelly 2000, p. 43).

123. Chuang 2006a.

124. Panethnicity is a political-cultural group made up of peoples of several distinct tribal or national origins. Espiritu 1992.

125. Filipino Advocates for Justice and Pilipino Workers Center.

126. Coalition for Human Immigrant Rights of Los Angeles, Mujeres Unidas y Activas, and Women's Collective of La Raza Centro Legal.

127. Graton Day Labor Center, People Organized to Win Employment Rights.

128. See Sturdevant and Stoltzfus 1992.

Chapter 4

1. The survivor's name appears in newspapers; however, it is erased from legal records. Therefore, to respect her preferences of being anonymously represented in the law, I also use a pseudonym. In legal records she is referred to as ZPC. Liliana is a common female Peruvian name. It has nothing to do with any inspirations or people I personally know.

2. United States District Court for the Northern District of California. Oakland. Case 08- r-00390-CW. Filed 02/04/2009.

3. ICE, "Bay Area Woman Found Guilty of Trafficking Nanny from Peru: Conviction Is First in Human Trafficking Trial in Northern District of California," October 9, 2009, accessed October 9, 2009, https://ice.gov/pi/nr/0910/0910090akland.htm.

4. TVPA 2000, 22 USC 7101 Sec 103 (8) defines severe forms of human trafficking as: (A) sex trafficking in which a commercial sex act is induced by force, fraud, or coercion, or in which the person induced to perform such act has not attained 18 years of age; or (B) the recruitment, harboring, transportation, provision, or obtaining of a person for labor or services, through the use of force, fraud, or coercion for the purpose of subjection to involuntary servitude, peonage, debt bondage, or slavery. The various definitions are also traced by Parreñas, Hwang, and Lee (2012), in which they ascertain that the study of human trafficking is fragmented, although defined by specific categories: international law, contemporary issues, and labor.

5. "Peruvian Nanny Exploited in Shocking ICE Case," KTVU, November 18, 2008, accessed November 10, 2010, http://www.ktvu.com/news/18012707/detail.html.

6. Henry K. Lee, "Walnut Creek Woman Convicted of Enslaving Nanny," *San Francisco Chronicle*, October 10, 2009, accessed November 10, 2010, http://www.sfgate.com/crime/article/Walnut-Creek-woman-convicted-of-enslaving-nanny-3284170.php.

7. "Coco Real Estate Agent Convicted of Forced Labor," CBS 5 Crime watch, October 5, 2009.

8. See Doezema 2010. See also Parreñas, Hwang, and Lee 2012.

9. See Chacón 2006. See also Chuang 2006a; Scarpa 2008.

10. See Limoncelli 2010. See also Srikantiah 2007.

11. Hua 2011.

12. See Bales 2007. See also Bales and Trodd 2008; Brysk and Choi-Fitzpatrick 2012; Kara 2009.

13. See Agustín 2007. See also Aronowitz 2009; Chapkis 2003; Chuang 2006a.

14. Barry 1984.

15. See Kempadoo, Sanghera, and Pattanaik 2005. See also MacKinnon 2006; Brysk and Choi-Fitzpatrick 2012.

16. Wadhia 2015.

17. 22 USC § 7102 (6) Involuntary servitude: The term "involuntary servitude" includes a condition of servitude induced by means of—(A) any scheme, plan, or pattern intended to cause a person to believe that, if the person did not enter into or continue in such condition, that person or another person would suffer serious harm or physical restraint; or (B) the abuse or threatened abuse of the legal process.

18. Glenn 1992.

19. Mary Romero argues that examining "sisterhood" enables an understanding of the home as a site of class struggle. Romero 1992, p. 45. See also Rollins 1987.

20. Parreñas 2001b.

21. Hondagneu-Sotelo 2001, p. 13.

22. Cultures of servitude are described as "normalized so that it is virtually impossible to imagine a life without it and practices, and thoughts and feelings about practices are patterned on it . . . [cultures of servitude are] social relations of domination/subordination, dependency, and inequality are normalized and permeate both the domestic and public spheres." Ray and Qayum 2009, p. 3.

23. For example, in the United States, domestic service industries and attitudes to servitude are defined by labor and anti-trafficking movements: movements respond to denial of overtime and minimum wage pay and are also imbricated in a discourse of rights, rescue, and human trafficking. A wide range of scholars examine rescue discourse and human trafficking. See, e.g., Agustín 2007 and Hua 2011.

24. Domestic work is not covered by the FLSA. See Glenn 2011.

25. Deleuze and Guattari 1987.

26. As conveyed by Gayatri Spivak, "It is through the significance of my body and others' bodies that culture become gendered, economic-political, selved and substantive." Spivak 1988, pp. 124–56.

27. Parreñas, Hwang, and Lee (2012, pp. 1015–29) describe the challenges of defining "exploitation."

28. The Standing Against Global Exploitation Project, Inc.

29. Z.P.C. testimony, Joshua Hill, Assistant United States Attorney, Joseph P. Russoniello, Esq., United States Attorney, Vol. 4, United States v. Dann. Before the

Honorable Judge Claudia Wilken. Vol. 7, No. CR 08-00390 CW, United States District Court Northern District of California. Oakland, California (October 6, 2009): 353–500.

30. María Lugones's concepts of witnessing—collaborative witnessing and faithful witnessing—are useful for my approach because they lay the groundwork. To witness as a collaborator is to witness on the "side of power." And "to witness faithfully, one must be able to sense resistance, to interpret behavior as resistant even when it is dangerous, when that interpretation places one psychologically against common sense, or when one is moved to act in collision with common sense, with oppression." Lugones 2003, p. 7.

31. Therefore, I draw upon scholarship in art history, that of Andrea Liss in particular, to invoke a kind of witnessing that needs to take place: an (im)possible witnessing. Andrea Liss describes an (im)possible witnessing as difficult and possible witnessing (of Holocaust photographs) mediated through institutional structures for an impossible accuracy that also cannot be discounted. Liss 1998, p. xix.

32. Supra note 3.

33. Judge Nancy Gertner, filed July 22, 2011, opinion, United States v. Dann. Argued and submitted May 9, 2011. *United States Court of Appeals for the Ninth Court.* No. 10-10191. D.C. No. 08-390-CW Opinion: 9723–9766.

34. Ibid.

35. Ibid., p. 160.

36. Fukushima and Liou 2012.

37. Supra note 33.

38. Ibid.

39. Robert Salonga, "Walnut Creek Woman Charged with Holding Peruvian Nanny as Indentured Servant," *San Jose Mercury News*, November 19, 2008.

40. Ibid., p. 165.

41. "The World Fact Book: Peru," *Central Intelligence Agency*, https://www.cia.gov /library/publications/the-world-factbook/geos/pe.html.

42. US-Peru Trade Promotion Agreement (PTPA), entered into force February 1, 2009.

43. Actual number is 10.4%. *International Office of Migration.*

44. Massey, Durand, and Malone 2003, p. 62.

45. Hondagneu-Sotelo 2001, p. 124.

46. Rodriguez 2003, p. 10.

47. Heterogeneity is "the existence of differences and differential relationships within a bounded category," hybridity is "produced by the histories of uneven and unsynthetic power relations," and multiplicity designates "the ways in which subjects located within social relations are determined by several different axes of power." Lowe 1996, p. 67.

48. Berghe and Ochoa 2000, p. 8.

49. Roberts 1996.

50. Castaneda, Manz, and Davenport (2002) define Mexicanization as a survival strategy for non-Mexicans during migration and settlement in the United States that is used to describe the ambiguous relationship Latinas/os have with Mexico and Mexicans, and a dynamic process.

51. Chinchilla and Hamilton 2001.

52. Although Quechua is considered an endangered language, it has a substantial population of eight to twelve million speakers in six Latin American countries, including Peru. Hornberger and Coronel-Molina 2004.

53. Sadowski-Smith 2008, p. 779.

54. Anzaldúa 1989, p. 100. Anzaldúa identifies *una cultura mestiza*, which for her is "with [her] own lumber, [her] own bricks and mortar and [her] own feminist architecture." Ibid., p. 44.

55. Suzanne Bost (2003) presents a mixed-race studies evaluation of the discourse about *mestizo/mestizaje* and *mulatta/o* in African American studies.

56. Saldaña-Portillo 2001.

57. Ibid., p. 318.

58. G. Baumann, "Slavery and Women: Theory of Change," April 2007, www.freetheslaves.net.

59. "Arnold Schwarzenegger Fathered Child with Household Staffer: Report," *Huffington Post*, May 17, 2011, accessed July 16, 2011, http://www.huffingtonpost.com/2011/05/17/arnold-schwarzenegger-fat_n_862866.html.

60. Take, for example, the National Domestic Workers Alliance (www.domesticworkers.org). Members of NDWA have advocated for the passage of a Domestic Workers Bill of Rights at the state level (e.g., California's Domestic Worker Bill of Rights, Seattle Council Bill 119286, and Connecticut SB 393).

61. United States v. Dann, Judge Claudia Wilken, transcript of proceedings, No. CR 08-00390 CW, September 29, 2009.

62. Ibid.

63. Andrew Huang, closing statement, United States v. Dann. Before the Honorable Judge Claudia Wilken. Vol. 7, No. CR 08-00390 CW, United States District Court Northern District of California. Oakland, California (October 6, 2009): 870–995.

64. Ibid.

65. Every year the government issues T-Visas. However, the image of migrants that illegally enter the United States and then trick the system in order to receive immigration relief does not reflect general trafficking visa trends. To date, the collective number of T-Visas issued since 2002 have not reached the cap for a single year. Between 2002 and 2010 the total number of T-Visas applied for was a mere 2,968; with the number capped at 5,000 a year, that means a little over 38,000 visas that could have been issued were wasted; 1,862 were approved and 880 denied (2002–10). Siskin and Wyler,

December 23, 2010, "Trafficking in Persons: US Policy and Issues for Congress. Congressional Research Service Report for Congress.

66. Jerome E. Matthews, closing statement, United States v. Dann. Before the Honorable Judge Claudia Wilken. Vol. 7, No. CR 08-00390 CW, United States District Court Northern District of California. Oakland, California (October 6, 2009): 870–995.

67. Issued on September 8, 2005. Case 4:08-cr-00390-CW, filed 02/04/2009.

68. "B-1 Business Visa Application Guide," US Immigration Support: Your Online Guide to US Visas, Green Cards and Citizenship, https://www.usimmigrationsupport .org/b1-business-visa.html.

69. The only point that Dann's immigration story comes up is during the presentencing hearing. Her public defense corrects the presentencing report and Dann's upbringing in privilege: "Based on my investigation of the case and contact especially Ms. Dann's mother, they did not have a privileged upbringing in Peru. The father was away for a significant period of the time and left the family in some fairly dire financial consequence." Jerome Matthew, Assistant Public Defender, Barry Portman, Federal Public Defender, United States v. Dann. Before the Honorable Judge Claudia Wilken. Vol. 7, No. CR 08-00390 CW, United States District Court Northern District of California. Oakland, California (April 14, 2010): 3.

70. See Gordon (1997, p. 4), who defines complex personhood as "all people remember and forget, are beset by contradiction, and recognize and misrecognize themselves and others."

71. A. Huang, "Prosecuting Federal Cases: Lessons Learned Since the TVPA," presented at A Conference on Human Trafficking: Train the Trainer, Pleasanton, CA, March 15, 2011.

72. Amy Fine Collins, "Sex Trafficking of Americans: The Girls Next Door," *Vanity Fair,* May 24, 2011, accessed May 24, 2011, https://www.vanityfair.com/news/2011 /05/sex-trafficking-201105.

73. In a Houston trafficking case, undocumented Mexican girls were referred to as "fresh meat." Susan Carroll, "Feds Say Human-Trafficking Ring Prostituted Young Girls," *Houston Chronicle,* October 11, 2013, https://www.houstonchronicle.com/news /houston-texas/houston/article/Feds-say-human-trafficking-ring-prostituted-young -4889688.php.

74. Hua 2011, pp. 71–94.

75. A. Kandasamy, "US Visas Aid Trafficking Victims, at Their Peril," *SF Public Press,* February 22, 2012, accessed February 22, 2012, http://newamericamedia.org /2012/02/us-visas-aid-trafficking-victims-at-their-peril.php.

76. Legal scholar Chacón also examines the centrality of force, fraud, and coercion. Chacón 2006.

77. Chang 2000, pp. 93–121.

78. J. Gillund, "Walnut Creek Woman Charged with Forced Labor of Domestic Servant: Five-Count Indictment Also Alleges Visa Fraud and Immigration Violations," United States Department of Justice, Northern District of California press release (February 9, 2009), www.usdoj.gov/usao/can.

79. Liliana's workday is described as beginning at six in the morning, when she woke up and made breakfast for Dann and Dann's children. The day closed out for her at ten o'clock at night, after the children had been put to bed and she had tidied up the house. Judge Nancy Gertner, filed July 22, 2011, opinion, United States v Dann. Argued and submitted May 9, 2011. *United States Court of Appeals for the Ninth Court.* No. 10-10191. D.C. No. 08-390-CW Opinion: 9723–9766. For two years, Liliana was not paid for her labor and worked over-time of sixteen-hour workdays. The absence of pay was a labor violation, and the long hours were not; domestic workers are exempt from overtime pay. See Fair Labor Standards Act of 1938, as Amended 2011, § 213. Exemptions (a)(15).

80. Liliana was not allowed to use the phone, and she was told she was not allowed to talk to anyone at the children's school.

81. Dann told Liliana that the government would take the children away if no one cared for them. And therefore, Liliana needed to stay in Dann's services.

82. Supra note 39.

83. Judge Nancy Gertner, filed July 22, 2011, opinion, United States v. Dann. Argued and submitted May 9, 2011. *United States Court of Appeals for the Ninth Court.* No. 10-10191. D.C. No. 08-390-CW Opinion: 9723–9766.

84. It was recommended that Liliana dress in sneakers and wear comfortable casual clothes (personal notes, day of Liliana's testimonial). United States v. Dann. Before the Honorable Judge Claudia Wilken. Vol. 4, No. CR 08-00390 CW, United States District Court Northern District of California. Oakland, California (October 1, 2009): 353–500.

85. Ahmed 2004.

86. Henry K. Lee, "Woman Indicted for Allegedly Exploiting Nanny," *San Francisco Chronicle,* November 20, 2008, accessed April 31, 2009, http://www.sfgate.com /bayarea/article/Woman-indicted-for-allegedly-exploiting-nanny-3184255.php.

87. Barthes 1977, p. 182.

88. Kim 2007, p. 953.

89. "Near universal problems with sleeping/nightmares, anxiety and fear and common problems with loss of appetite and controlling aggression. Many women also talked about experiencing panic attacks, memory problems, self blame . . . flashbacks . . . thoughts of suicide, self-harm and crying constantly. One woman articulately sums this up as feeling like she is 'screaming inside all the time.'" "When Women Are Trafficked: Quantifying the Gendered Experience of Trafficking in the UK," Poppy Project, April 2004, accessed August 1, 2005, http://i4.cmsfiles.com/eaves/2012/04/When -Women-are-Trafficked,-April-2004-30380e.pdf.

90. Andrew Huang, opening statement, United States v. Dann. Before the Honorable Judge Claudia Wilken. Vol. 2, No. CR 08-00390 CW, United States District Court Northern District of California. Oakland, California (September 29, 2009): 1–207.

91. Supra note 5.

92. Personal notes, April 15, 2009.

93. Benjamin 1969, pp. 69–82.

94. Spivak 1993.

95. The *testimonio* is described by John Beverly as a document that is printed, told in the form of a first-person narrator, who is the witness of the events he or she recounts, "whose unit of narration is usually a 'life' or significant life experience." Beverly 2004.

96. Laub 1995, p. 71.

97. Dori Laub's research of testimonies and *truth* with holocaust survivor stories says: "Yet no amount of telling seems to ever to do justice to this inner compulsion. There are never enough words or the right words, there is never enough time or the right time, and never enough listening or the right listening to articulate the story that can not be fully captured in *thought, memory,* and *speech.*" Ibid., p. 78.

98. Young 2003.

99. Instructions from the court, United States v. Dann. Before the Honorable Judge Claudia Wilken. Vol. 7, No. CR 08-00390 CW, United States District Court Northern District of California. Oakland, California (October 6, 2009): 870–995.

100. Supra note 2.

101. It included cleaning, but also specific details such as being required to inspect Dann's son's school bag on a regular basis.

102. Dann's son told her that he saw Liliana speaking to his schoolteacher, and soon after Liliana described experiencing verbal abuse.

103. The difference is "the translator knows that his performance may be the only one." Wechsler 1998, p. 241.

104. Jennifer Adelrete, Avantika Rao, and Andrew Huang, "The TVPA Decade: Progress and Promise," presented at the National Conference on Human Trafficking, Department of Justice, Washington, DC, May 3–5, 2010.

105. Supra note 5.

106. Liliana's testimonial summarized this. Although she was captured in an interview, the focus was on Liliana's immigration attorney, not on Liliana herself.

107. Restitution amounted to $618,812.82 from defendant Dann for unpaid wages, emotional distress damages, and punitive damages. Defendant Vittet de la Rosa was jointly and severally liable for $22,858.65 of that amount for unpaid wages. No. 09-03366 CW. Order Granting Plaintiff's Motion to Amend Default Judgment for Attorney's Fees.

Chapter 5

1. Steven Borowiec and Faras Ghani, "South Korea: Sex Workers Hit Hard by Government's Crackdown," *Al Jazeera* (Asia Pacific), March 18, 2018, accessed March 18, 2018, https://www.aljazeera.com/indepth/features/south-korea-sex-workers-hit-hard-government-crackdown-180311092215650.html.

2. Jones 2013, p. 526.

3. "Newsletter # 3," Rainbow Center, Flushing, New York, January, 1994, 8.

4. "GI Flashbacks: The 1992 Private Kenneth Markle Murder Case," *ROK Drop: Korea from North to South,* August 3, 2015, http://www.rokdrop.net/2015/08/gi-flashbacks-the-1992-private-kenneth-markle-murder-case/.

5. Cho 2008, p. 116.

6. Hughes, Chon, and Ellerman, 2004. See also Argibay 2003.

7. House Resolution 121, 110th Congress (2007–8), https://www.congress.gov/bill/110th-congress/house-resolution/121.

8. Priest 2010, p. 4.

9. Ibid., p. 6.

10. Soh 2008, p. 1.

11. Ibid., p. 39.

12. Prepared Statement of Ms. Koon Ja Kim, Surviving Comfort Woman, National Korean American Service and Education Consortium, hearing before the Subcommittee on Asia, the Pacific, and the Global Environment of the Committee on Foreign Affairs House of Representatives, 110th Cong., 1st Sess., February 15, 2007, serial no. 110–16, http://www.foreignaffairs.house.gov.

13. "Honda Testifies in Support of Comfort Women," Congressman Mike Honda press release (February 15, 2007), http://honda.house.gov/news/press-releases/honda-testifies-in-support-of-comfort-women.

14. Here I am drawing upon Orlando Patterson, who conveys that the Egyptian word for *captive* translates into "living dead." Patterson 1982, p. 42.

15. *Wianbu* means "fallen woman." Patterson also illustrates how in Korea, slaves were seen as people who had "fallen" into their slave status (Patterson 1982, p. 39).

16. Kaplan 2007.

17. Davis 1988.

18. Brooks 2014.

19. Horlyck and Pettid 2014.

20. Priest cites what Barbara Christian called a "fixing methodology." Priest 2010, p. 15.

21. Kirk Simple, "In New Jersey, Memorial for 'Comfort Women' Deepens Old Animosity," *New York Times,* May 18, 2012, accessed May 18, 2012, http://www.nytimes.com/2012/05/19/nyregion/monument-in-palisades-park-nj-irritates-japanese-officials.html?_r=0.

22. In 2014, a comfort woman memorial was erected behind government buildings adjacent to a 9-11 memorial in Fairfax, Virginia: a boulder with two butterflies as benches. The memorialization of the comfort women and the community discussions illuminated the links between their dying status and the historic event of militarized sexual violence during World War II. As historian Jung-Shil Lee states, "The comfort women issue is one of the earlier examples of mass performed human trafficking organized by a military and government." Christine Ahn, "Seeking Justice—Or at Least the Truth—for 'Comfort Women,'" *Huffington Post*, August 25, 2014, https://www.huffingtonpost.com/christine-ahn/seeking-justiceor-at-comfort-women_b_5526919.html.

23. "Comfort Women Memorial – by Steven Whyte, Sculptor," San Francisco Arts Commission, 2017, https://sfgov.org/arts/sites/default/files/7182018_Comfort%20Women_ALL.pdf.

24. "By the Numbers: Today's Military," NPR, July 3, 2011, http://www.npr.org/2011/07/03/137536111/by-the-numbers-todays-military.

25. Mbembe defines necropolitics as "contemporary forms of subjugation of life to the power of death . . . in which, in our contemporary world, weapons are deployed in the interest of maximum destruction of persons and the creation of *death-worlds*, new and unique forms of social existence in which vast populations are subjected to conditions of life conferring upon them the status of *living dead*." Mbembe 2003, p. 39. Who are these living dead subjects that exist in the contemporary world? For me, furthering Mbembe's analysis of necropolitics, biopower and necropolitcs not only shape the living and the dead through weaponry but also through other mediums that maintain the destruction of persons and the creation of deathworlds.

26. Ibid., p. 40.

27. Cacho 2012, p. 6, citing Holland 2000.

28. Cho 2008, p. 33.

29. Also known as a *mamasan,* a woman who runs a brothel.

30. Patterson 1982, p. 44.

31. Yoshiaki 2000, p. 48.

32. Oh and Stetz 2001, p. 14.

33. Soh 2008, p. 79.

34. Oh and Stetz 2001, p. 3.

35. Yoshiaki 2000, p. 10.

36. Soh 2008, p. 22.

37. The nineteen testimonials, translated into English, were published in 2000 in Sangmie Choi Schellstede, ed., *Comfort Women Speak: Testimony by Sex Slaves of the Japanese Military.*

38. Soh 2008, p. 80.

39. Henson 1996, p. xviii.

40. Ibid., p. 87.

41. Keller 1998, p. 196.

42. Duncan 2009, p. 182.

43. Ibid., p. 183.

44. Tim Wyatt, "Madam's Fall Offers Look at Lucrative Sex Trade," *Dallas Morning News*, May 10, 2006, accessed May 10, 2006, http://www.dallasnews.com/sharedcontent /dws/news/localnews/ stories/DN-sexdallas_08 met.State.Edition l.ceod677.htm.

45. Ibid.

46. "Brothel Owner Sentenced to 10 Years for Coercing Korean Aliens into Prostitution," Department of Justice Press Release (Washington DC, July 18, 2006). See also Cianciarulo 2008.

47. "Flower Mound Police Department Receives Forfeited Proceeds," Internal Revenue Service: Criminal Investigation, Dallas Field Officer press release (Dallas, TX, August 9, 2007).

48. In the Korean/American community, her narrative of being a military bride reinforces secrecy and attached to a social stigma. Historian Ji-Yeon Yuh's interviews with Korean migrants provide insights into the stereotype of the Korean "military bride" whose identity is enmeshed in questions of how she met her husband. It is commonly assumed that military brides met their husbands in a camp town while working in Korea's sex industry. Yuh 2002, p. 21.

49. Supra note 44.

50. Ibid.

51. Ibid.

52. See Sudbury for further explanation of the prison industrial complex as a system that the "government provides a steady flow of imprisonable bodies as fuel for the transnational prison-industrial complex." Sudbury 2005, p. xxiii.

53. Priest 2010, p. 6.

54. Lynes 2011.

55. Bob represents the very structural and hidden ways that human trafficking operates—as a marshal he represents the complicity in U.S. structures, where he also runs a brothel in the desert of Nevada.

56. Stephen Holden, "True Story Inspires Tale of Sex Trade; in a Twist, a U.S. Marshal is the Bad Guy," *New York Times*, March 20, 2013, http://www.nytimes.com/2013 /03/20/movies/eden-depicts-sex-trafficking-in-the-united-states.html?_r=0.

57. Ibid.

58. Drew Taylor, "Review: 'Eden' Is a Gripping Sex Slaver Drama That Isn't As Dour As It Sounds," *IndieWire*, March 21, 2013, http://blogs.indiewire.com/theplaylist /review-eden-is-a-gripping-sex-slavery-drama-that-isnt-as-dour-as-it-sounds -20130321.

59. Cisneros 2008.

60. Lee 2007.

61. Ono and Pham 2009.

62. Ibid., pp. 45–47.

63. Michelle Raheja describes how Native Americans participated in red-facing. Likewise, Asian Americans also participate in yellow-facing when they cross over or play roles of other Asians (e.g., in *Memoirs of a Geisha*, Chinese actors performed as Japanese actors). Raheja 2010.

64. Jones 2013, p. 527.

65. Laura Bates, "The Trouble with Sex Robots," *New York Times,* July 17, 2017, accessed April 26, 2018, https://www.nytimes.com/2017/07/17/opinion/sex-robots-consent .html.

66. Chen 2012.

67. Byrd 2011, p. 269.

68. Hartman and Best 2005, p. 2.

Conclusion

1. "Executive Order Protecting the Nation from Foreign Terrorist Entry into the United States," The White House Office of the Press Secretary press release (March 6, 2017), https://www.whitehouse.gov/the-press-office/2017/03/06/executive-order-protect ing-nation-foreign-terrorist-entry-united-states.

2. Sara Murray and Dan Merica, "Trump Backs Plan That Would Curb Legal Immigration," CNN, August 3, 2017, accessed August 15, 2018, http://www.cnn.com/2017 /08/02/politics/trump-skills-immigration-plan-cotton-perdue/index.html.

3. New directives under the Trump administration mean that even a person convicted of a minor crime may be deported, regardless of their legal record. Nicholas Kulish, Vivian Yee, Caitlin Dickerson, Liz Robbins, Fernanda Santos, and Jennifer Medina, "Trump's Immigration Policies Explained," *New York Times*, February 22, 2017, accessed August 15, 2018, https://www.nytimes.com/2017/02/21/us/trump-immigration -policies-deportation.html.

4. "The Freedom Network's Response to the Current Influx of Unaccompanied Children at the US-Mexico Border," Freedom Network USA, August 2014, accessed September 15, 2018, http://freedomnetworkusa.org/wp-content/uploads/2012/05/FN -Statement-on-UACs.pdf.

5. United States Department of Agriculture, "Imports," April 5, 2017, accessed August 21, 2017, https://www.ers.usda.gov/topics/international-markets-trade/us -agricultural-trade/imports/.

6. National Archives and Records Administration, "Transnational Organized Crime: A Growing Threat to National and International Security," accessed August 15, 2018, https://obamawhitehouse.archives.gov/administration/eop/nsc/transnational -crime/threat.

7. Ezra Klein, "READ: President Obama's Speech on the Future of the War on Terror," *Washington Post,* May 23, 2013, accessed August 15, 2018, https://www.washingtonpost.com/news/wonk/wp/2013/05/23/read-president-obamas-speech-on-the-future-of-the-war-on-terror/?utm_term=.b78e2d979071.

8. Mahdavi 2014.

9. "Prostitutes" was how they were legally defined.

10. Young Jun Kang (Jimmy), Kesheng Zhu (Michael), Rujing Jiang (Do Do), Zhenhua Liu (Jo Jo), Liancheng Ning (Lao Li), Pengquan Xie (Lee), Zheng Qu (John), and Thongyot Liamurai (Laura). United States District Court Western District of Washington at Seattle, Judgment: February 23, 2007, case number CR06-00298JCC.

11. Law enforcement initiatives regarding sexual economies are not new; prostitution is a crime in all states, but Nevada counties. Technology, used to ensure security and safety of the nation, creates an all-seeing eye for acts considered criminal or threatening to the state. While much research has focused on this discourse in a military context, I bring it back to the domestic in sites that are seemingly innocuous and may even considered, in some human rights endeavors, a necessity.

12. (1) technologies of production, which permit us to produce, transform, or manipulate things; (2) technologies of sign systems, which permit us to use signs, meanings, symbols, or signification; (3) technologies of power, which determine the conduct of individuals and submit them to certain ends or domination, an objectivizing of the subject; (4) technologies of the self, which permit individuals to effect by their own means or with the help of others a certain number of operations on their own bodies and souls, thoughts, conduct, and way of being, so as to transform I themselves in order to attain a certain state of happiness, purity, wisdom, perfection, or immortality. Foucault et al. 1988, p. 14.

13. Anne Balsamo's concept of *technocultures* illuminates how culture shapes technology and vice versa, where the two are not in opposition (2011).

14. Schaeffer 2012.

15. Gaytán 2011.

16. "Leaders of Conspiracy to Transport Women for Prostitution Sentenced to Prison: Seattle Area Residents Ran Brothels or Escort Services Using Undocumented Asian Women," United States Attorney's Office, Western District of Washington press release (February 23, 2007), https://www.justice.gov/archive/usao/waw/press/2007/feb/kang.html.

17. Jeff Stone, "What Is Memex? How DARPA's Secret Search Engine Trawls the Dark Web for Sex Trafficking," *International Business Times,* February 11, 2015.

18. Martina Vandenberg, email message to author, July 8, 2016.

19. Aradau 2004, p. 254.

20. Ibid., p. 265.

21. Global Slavery Index, http://www.globalslaveryindex.org/findings/.

198 NOTES TO CONCLUSION

22. 18 U.S.C. 371. See also L. Jones 2010.

23. Doyle 2016.

24. Goodnight and Poulakos 1981.

25. Mahdavi 2014, p. 14.

26. I am inspired by Hokulani Aikau, who speaks to indigenous ontologies and calls for a trans-indigenous and settler futurity that excludes state governmentality. See Aikau 2015.

BIBLIOGRAPHY

Published Works

Abrego, Leisy, Mat Coleman, Daniel E. Martínez, Cecilia Menjívar, and Jeremy Slack. 2017. "Making Immigrants into Criminals: Legal Processes of Criminalization in the Post-IIRIRA Era." *Journal on Migration and Human Security* 5 (3): 694–715. doi:10.14240/jmhs.v5i3.105.

Adamson, Fiona. 2006. "Crossing Borders: International Migration and National Security." *International Security* 31 (1): 165–99.

Agustín, Laura María. 2007. *Sex on the Margins: Migration, Labour Markets and the Rescue Industry.* New York: Zed Books.

Ahmed, Sara. 2004. "Affective Economies." *Social Text* 22 (2): 117–39.

Aikau, Hōkūlani K. 2015. "Indigenous Futurity Without the State (United States or Otherwise)." *American Quarterly* 67 (3): 653–61.

Aiko, Joshi. 2002. "The Face of Human Trafficking." *Hastings Women's Law Journal* 13: 31–52.

Alarcon, Norma, Caren Kaplan, and Minoo Moallem, eds. 1999. *Between Woman and Nation: Nationalisms, Transnational Feminisms, and the State.* Durham, NC: Duke University Press.

Alcoff, Linda Martin. 2006. *Visible Identities: Race, Gender and the Self.* Oxford: Oxford University Press.

Alexander, Jacqui M. 2005. *Pedagogies of Crossing: Mediations of Feminism, Sexual Politics, Memory, and the Sacred.* Durham, NC: Duke University Press.

Alexander, Jacqui M., and Chandra Tapalde Mohanty, eds. 1997. *Feminist Genealogies, Colonial Legacies, Democratic Futures.* New York: Routledge.

Allison, Robert J., ed. 1995. *The Interesting Narrative of the Life of Olaudah Equiano: Written by Himself.* Boston: Bedford Books.

Althusser, Louis. 2001. *Lenin and Philosophy and Other Essays.* New York: Monthly Review Press.

Anderson, Benedict. 1983. *Imagined Communities: Reflections on the Origin and Spread of Nationalism.* London: Verso.

Anderson, Bridget, and Rutvica Andrijasevic. 2008. "Sex, Slaves and Citizens: The Politics of Anti-trafficking." *Soundings* 40: 135–45.

Anderson, Wanni W., and Robert G. Lee, eds. 2005. *Displacements and Diasporas: Asians in the Americas.* New Brunswick, NJ: Rutgers University Press.

Andrijasevic, Rutvica. 2007. "Beautiful Dead Bodies: Gender, Migration and Representation in Anti-Trafficking Campaigns." *Feminist Review* 86: 24–44.

Anzaldúa, Gloria. 1989. *Borderlands/La Frontera: The New Mestiza.* Second edition. San Francisco: Aunt Lute Books, 1989.

Anzaldúa, Gloria, and Cherrie Moraga, eds. (1981) 1983. *This Bridge Called My Back: Writings by Radical Women of Color.* Second edition. New York: Kitchen Table: Women of Color Press.

Appadurai, Arjun. 1996. *Modernity at Large: Cultural Dimensions of Globalization.* Minneapolis: University of Minnesota Press.

Aradau, Claudia. 2004. "The Perverse Politics of Four-Letter Words: Risk and Pity in the Securitisation of Human Trafficking." *Millennium: Journal of International Studies* 33 (2): 251–78.

Argibay, Carmen M. 2003. "Sexual Slavery and the Comfort Women of World War II." *Berkeley Journal of International Law* 21 (2): 375–89.

Arista, Noelani. 2011. "Captive Women in Paradise 1796–1826: The *Kapu* on Prostitution in Hawaiian Historical Legal Context." *American Indian Culture and Research Journal* 35 (4): 39–55.

Aronowitz, Alexis A. 2001. "Smuggling and Trafficking in Human Beings: The Phenomenon, the Markets That Drive It and the Organisations That Promote It." *European Journal on Criminal Policy and Research* 9: 163–95.

Aronowitz, Alexis A. 2009. *Human Trafficking, Human Misery: The Global Trade in Human Beings.* Westport, CT: Praeger.

Armaline, William T., Davita Silfen Glasberg, and Bandana Purkayastha. 2011. *Human Rights in Our Own Backyard: Injustice and Resistance in the United States.* Philadelphia: University of Pennsylvania Press.

Arvin, Maile, Eve Tuck, and Angie Morrill. 2013. "Decolonizing Feminism: Challenging Connections Between Settler Colonialism and Heteropatriarchy." *Feminist Formations* 25 (1): 8–34.

Bakhtin, Mikhail. 1981. *The Dialogic Imagination: Four Essays.* Edited by Michael Holquist. Translated by Caryl Emerson and Michael Holquist. Austin: University of Texas Press.

Bal, Mieke. 2009. *Narratology: Introduction to the Theory of Narrative.* Third edition. Toronto, Canada: University of Toronto Press.

Bales, Kevin. 1999. *Disposable People: New Slavery in the Global Economy*. Berkeley: University of California Press.

Bales, Kevin. 2005. *Understanding Global Slavery. A Reader*. Berkeley: University of California Press.

Bales, Kevin. 2007. *Ending Slavery: How to Free Today's Slaves*. Berkeley: University of California Press.

Bales, Kevin, and Ron Soodalter. 2009. *The Slave Next Door: Human Trafficking and Slavery in America Today*. Berkeley: University of California Press.

Bales, Kevin, and Zoe Trodd, eds. 2008. *To Plead Our Own Cause: Personal Stories by Today's Slaves*. Ithaca, NY: Cornell University Press.

Balsamo, Anne. 2011. *Designing Culture: The Technological Imagination at Work*. Durham, NC: Duke University Press.

Barry, Kathleen. 1984. *Female Sexual Slavery*. New York: New York University Press.

Barry, Kathleen. 1995. *The Prostitution of Sexuality: The Global Exploitation of Women*. New York: New York University Press.

Barry, Kathleen, Charlotte Bunch, and Shirley Castley. 1984. *International Feminism: Networking against Female Sexual Slavery*. New York: International Women's Tribune Centre.

Barstow, Anne Llewellyn, ed. 2000. *War's Dirty Secret: Rape, Prostitution, and Other Crimes Against Women*. Cleveland, OH: Pilgrim Press.

Barthes, Roland. 1957. *Mythologies*. Translated by Annette Lavers. Paris: Editions du Seuil.

Barthes, Roland. 1977. *Image, Music, Text*. Edited and translated by Stephen Heath. New York: Hill and Wang.

Barthes, Roland. 1982. *Camera Lucida: Reflections on Photography*. Translated by Richard Howard. New York: Hill and Wang.

Barthes, Roland. 1997. *A Lover's Discourse: Fragments*. New York: Hill and Wang.

Batstone, David. 2007. *Not for Sale: The Return of the Global Slave Trade and How We Can Fight It*. New York: HarperCollins.

Beasley, Delilah L. 1918. "Slavery in California." *Journal of Negro History* 3 (1): 33–44.

Bederman, Gail. 1995. *Manliness & Civilization: A Cultural History of Gender and Race in the United States, 1880–1917*. Chicago: University of Chicago Press.

Beck, Ulrich. 2002. "The Terrorist Threat: World Risk Society Revisited." *Theory, Culture & Society* 19 (4): 39–55.

Beeks, Karen, and Delila Amir, eds. 2006. *Trafficking and the Global Sex Industry*. UK: Rowman and Littlefield Publishers.

Benjamin, Walter. 1969. *Illuminations: Essays & Reflections*. Edited by Hannah Arendt. New York: Schocken.

Berger, D. 2016. "Subjugated Knowledges: Activism, Scholarship, and Ethnic Studies Ways of Knowing." In *Critical Ethnic Studies: A Reader*, edited by N. Elia, D.M. Hernanez,

J. Kim, S.L. Redmond, D. Rodriguez, and S.E. See, 215–28. Durham, NC: Duke University Press.

Berghe, Pierre L. van Den, and Jorge Flores Ochoa. 2000. "Tourism and Nativistic Ideology in Cuzco, Peru." *Annals of Tourism Research* 27 (1): 7–26.

Berkhoffer, Robert F. Jr. 1995. *Beyond the Great Story: History as Text and Discourse.* Cambridge, MA: Harvard University Press.

Berlant, Lauren. 1999. "The Subject of True Feeling: Pain, Privacy, and Politics." In *Cultural Pluralism, Identity Politics, and the Law,* edited by Austin Sarat and Thomas R. Kearns, 49–84. Ann Arbor: University of Michigan Press.

Bernard, H. Russell. 1999. "Languages and Scripts in Contact: Historical Perspectives." In *Literacy: An International Handbook,* edited by Daniel A. Wagner, Richard L. Venezky, and Brian Street, 22–28. Boulder, CO: Westview Press.

Bernstein, Elizabeth. 2010. "Militarized Humanitarianism Meets Carceral Feminism: The Politics of Sex, Rights, and Freedom in Contemporary Antitrafficking Campaigns." *Signs: Journal of Women in Culture and Society* 36 (1): 45–71.

Beverly, John. 2004. *Testimonio: On the Politics of Truth.* Minneapolis: University of Minnesota Press.

Beynon, John, and David Dunkerly, eds. 2000. *Globalization: The Reader.* New York: Routledge.

Bickerton, Maria Elena. 2000–2001. "Prospects for a Bilateral Immigration Agreement with Mexico: Lessons from the Bracero Program." *Texas Law Review* 79: 895–920.

Billings, Warren M. 1991. "The Law of Servants and Slaves in Seventeenth-Century Virginia." *Virginia Magazine of History and Biography* 99 (1): 45–62.

Bindman, Jo. 1998. "An International Perspective on Slavery in the Sex Industry." In *Global Sex Workers: Rights, Resistance, and Redefinition,* edited by Kamala Kempadoo and Jo Doezzema, 65–68. New York: Routledge.

Bishop, Ryan, and Lillian S. Robinson. 2000. *Night Market: Sexual Cultures and the Thai Economic Miracle.* New York: Routledge.

Bohrman, Rebecca, and Naomi Murkawa. 2005. "Remaking Big Government: Immigration and Crime Control in the United States." In *Global Lockdown: Race, Gender, and the Prison-Industrial Complex,* edited by Julia Sudbury, 109–26. New York: Routledge.

Bonacich, Edna, and Richard P. Appelbaum, eds. 2000. *Behind the Label: Inequality in the Los Angeles Apparel Industry.* Berkeley: University of California Press.

Bonacich, Edna, and Ivan Light. 1998. *Immigrant Entrepreneurs: Koreans in Los Angeles, 1965–1982.* Berkeley: University of California Press.

Bost, Suzanne. 2003. *Mulattas and Mestizas: Representing Mixed Identities in the Americas, 1850–2000.* Athens: University of Georgia Press.

Bouche, Vanessa. 2011. "Sex Trafficking: Inside the Business of Modern Day Slavery (Review)." *Human Rights Quarterly* 33 (3): 899–906.

Breckenridge, Karen D. 2004. "Justice Beyond Borders: A Comparison of Australian and U.S. Child-Sex Tourism Laws." *Pacific Rim Law & Policy Journal Association* 13 (2): 405–38.

Brennan, Denise. 2014. *Life Interrupted: Trafficking into Forced Labor in the United States*. Durham, NC: Duke University Press.

Brenner, Rachel Feldhay. 1996. "Writing Herself Against History: Anne Frank's Self Portrait as a Young Artist." *Modern Judaism* 16 (2): 105–34.

Brooks, Kinitra D. 2014. "The Importance of Neglected Intersections: Race and Gender in Contemporary Zombie Texts and Theories." *African American Review* 47 (4): 461–75.

Brown, Louise. 2000. *Sex Slaves: The Trafficking of Women in Asia*. London: Virago Press.

Brown, Michael K, Martin Carnoy, Elliott Currie, Troy Duster, Daivd B. Oppenheimer, Marjorie M. Shultz, and David Wellman. 2003. *White-Washing Race: The Myth of a Color Blind Society*. Berkeley: University of California Press.

Brownmiller, Susan. 1975. *Against Our Will: Men, Women, and Rape*. New York: Fawcett Books.

Brysk, Alison, and Austin Choi-Fitzpatrick. 2012. *From Human Trafficking to Human Rights: Reframing Contemporary Slavery*. Philadelphia: University of Pennsylvania Press.

Bulosan, Carlos. 1973. *America Is in the Heart: A Personal History*. Seattle: University of Washington Press.

Busza, Joanna. 2004. "Sex Work and Migration: The Dangers of Oversimplification: A Case Study of Vietnam and Cambodia." *Health and Human Rights* 7 (2): 231–49.

Butler, Jennifer S. 2000. "Militarized Prostitution: The Untold Story (USA)." In *War's Dirty Secret: Rape, Prostitution, and Other Crimes Against Women*, edited by Anne Llewellyn Barstow, 167–203. Cleveland, OH: Pilgrim Press.

Butler, Judith. 1993. *Bodies That Matter: On the Discursive Limits of "Sex."* New York: Routledge.

Butler, Judith. 2004. *Precarious Life: The Powers of Mourning and Violence*. London: Verso.

Byrd, Jodi A. 2011. *Transit of Empire: Indigenous Critiques of Colonialism*. Minneapolis: University of Minnesota Press.

Cacho, Lisa Marie. 2012. *Social Death: Racialized Rightlessness and the Criminalization of the Unprotected*. New York: New York University Press.

Cadena, Marisol de la. 2000. *Indigenous Mestizos: The Politics of Race and Culture in Cuzco, Peru, 1919–1991*. Durham, NC: Duke University Press.

Campt, Tina, and Deborah A. Thomas. 2008. "Gendering Diaspora: Transnational Feminism, Diaspora and Its Hegemonies." *Feminist Review* 90 (1): 1–8. doi:10.1057/fr.2008.41.

Caraway, Nancie. 2005–6. "Human Rights and Existing Contradictions in Asia-Pacific Human Trafficking Politics and Discourse." *Tulane Journal of International and Comparative Law* 14: 295–316.

Caruth, Cathy. 2002. "The Claims of the Dead: History, Haunted Property, and the Law." *Critical Inquiry* 28: 419–41.

Castaneda, Xochitl, Beatriz Manz, and Allison Davenport. 2002. "Mexicanization: A Survival Strategy for Guatemalan Mayans in the San Francisco Bay Area." *International Migration* 1 (3): 102–23.

Castells, Manuel. 2000. *The Rise of the Network Society: The Information Age: Economy, Society and Culture Vol. 1.* Malden, MA: Blackwell Publishers.

Center for Migrant Advocacy and Friedrich Ebert Stiftung. 2009. *The Philippines: A Global Model on Labor Migration?* Manila: Center for Migrant Advocacy and Friedrich Ebert Stiftung.

Cesairé, Aimé. 1972. *Discourse on Colonialism.* Translated by Joan Pinkham. New York: Monthly Review Press.

Chacón, Jennifer M. 2006. "Misery and Myopia: Understanding the Failures of U.S. Efforts to Stop Human Trafficking." *Fordham Law Review* 74: 2977–3012.

Chacón, Jennifer M. 2010. "Tensions and Trade-Offs: Protecting Trafficking Victims in the Era of Immigration Enforcement." *University of Pennsylvania Law Review* 158 (6): 1609–53.

Chai, Alice Yun. 1993. "Asian-Pacific Feminist Coalitions Politics: The Chonghindae/Jugunianfu ('Comfort Women') Movement." *Korean Studies* 17: 67–91.

Chan, Cheris Shun-Ching. 2004. "The Falun Gong in China: A Sociological Perspective." *China Quarterly* 179: 665–83.

Chang, Grace. 2000. *Disposable Domestics: Immigrant Women Workers in the Global Economy.* Cambridge, MA: South End Press.

Chang, Grace, and Kathleen Kim. 2007. "Reconceptualizing Approaches to Human Trafficking: New Directions and Perspectives from the Field(s)." *Stanford Journal of Civil Rights & Civil Liberties* 3 (2): 317–44.

Chang, Iris. 1997. *The Rape of Nanking: The Forgotten Holocaust of World War II.* New York: Penguin.

Chang, Jason Oliver. 2017. *Chino: Anti-Chinese Racism in Mexico, 1880–1940 (Asian American Experience).* Champaign: University of Illinois Press.

Chapkis, Wendy. 2003. "Trafficking, Migration, and the Law: Protecting Innocents, Punishing Immigrants." *Gender & Society* 17: 923–37.

Chen, Edith Wen-Chu, and Grace J. Yoo, eds. 2010. *Encyclopedia of Asian American Issues Today.* 2 volumes. Santa Barbara, CA: Greenwood Press.

Chen, Mel. 2012. *Animacies: Biopolitics, Racial Mattering, and Queer Affect*. Durham, NC: Duke University Press.

Cheng, Sealing. 2010. *On the Move for Love: Migrant Entertainers and the U.S. Military in South Korea*. Philadelphia: University of Pennsylvania Press.

Cheng, Sealing. 2011. "The Paradox of Vernacularization: Women's Human Rights and the Gendering of Nationhood." *Anthropological Quarterly* 84 (2): 475–506.

Cheng, Sealing. and Eunjung Kim. 2014. "The Paradoxes of Neoliberalism: Migrant Korean Sex Workers in the United States and 'Sex Trafficking.'" *Social Politics: International Studies in Gender, State and Society* 21 (3): 355–81.

Chernin, Ted. 2000. "My Experiences in the Honolulu Chinatown Red-Light District." *Hawaiian Journal of History* 34: 203–17.

Chesney-Lind, Meda, and Lisa Pasko. 2004. *Offender: Girls, Women, and Crime*. Second edition. Thousand Oaks, CA: Sage.

Chew, Lin. 1999. "Global Trafficking in Women: Some Issues and Strategies." *Women's Studies Quarterly* 27 (1–2): 11–18.

Chin, Gabriel J. 2013. "'A Chinaman's Chance' in Court Asian Pacific Americans and Racial Rules of Evidence." *University of California Law Review* 3: 965–90.

Chin, Kevin, and Kristi Rudelius-Palmer. 2010. "Storytelling as a Relational and Instrumental Tool for Addressing Racial Justice." *Race/Ethnicity: Multidisciplinary Global Contexts* 3 (2): 265–81.

Chin, Ko Lin. 1999. *Smuggled Chinese: Clandestine Immigration to the United States*. Philadelphia, PA: Temple University Press.

Chin, Ko-lin, and James O. Finckenauer. 2012. *Selling Sex Overseas: Chinese Women and the Realities of Prostitution and Global Sex Trafficking*. New York: New York University Press.

Chinchilla, Norma Stoltz, and Nora Hamilton. 2001. *Seeking Community in a Global City: Guatemalans and Salvadorans in Los Angeles*. Philadelphia, PA: Temple University Press.

Cho, Grace M. 2008. *Haunting the Korean Diaspora: Shame, Secrecy, and the Forgotten War*. Minneapolis: University of Minnesota Press.

Chon, Katherine, and Derek Ellerman. 2004. "Modern-Day Comfort Women: The U.S. Military, Transnational Crime, and the Trafficking of Women." *Violence Against Women* 13 (9): 901–22.

Chouliaraki, Lilie. 2006. *The Spectatorship of Suffering*. London: Sage.

Chouliaraki, Lilie. 2009. "Witnessing War: Economies of Regulation in Reporting War and Conflict." *Communication Review* 12 (3): 215–26.

Choy, Catherine Ceniza. 2003. *Empire of Care: Nursing and Migration in Filipino American History*. Durham, NC: Duke University Press.

Christie, Nils. 1986. *From Crime Policy to Victim Policy: Reorienting the Justice System*. London: Macmillan.

Chuang, Janie. 2006a. "Beyond a Snapshot: Preventing Human Trafficking in the Global Economy." *Indiana Journal of Global Legal Studies* 13 (1): 137–63.

Chuang, Janie. 2006b. "The United States as Global Sheriff: Using Unilateral Sanctions to Combat Human Trafficking." *Michigan Journal of International Law* 27: 437–94.

Chuang, Janie A. 2010. "Rescuing Trafficking from Ideological Capture: Prostitution Reform and Anti-Trafficking Law and Policy." *University of Pennsylvania Law Review* 158 (6): 1655–728.

Chuang, Janie A. 2014. "Exploitation Creep and the Unmaking of Human Trafficking Law." *American Journal of International Law* 108 (4): 609–49.

Chuh, Kandice. 2003. *Imagine Otherwise: On Asian Americanist Critique.* Durham, NC: Duke University Press.

Chung, Hyun-Kyung. 2000. "'Your Comfort versus My Death': Korean Comfort Women." In *War's Dirty Secret: Rape, Prostitution, and Other Crimes Against Women,* edited by Anne Llewellyn Barstow, 13–25. Cleveland, OH: Pilgrim Press.

Cianciarulo, Marisa Silenzi. 2008. "The Trafficking and Exploitation Victims Assistance Program: A Proposed Early Response Plan for Victims of International Trafficking in the United States." *New Mexico Law Review* 38: 373–408.

Cisneros, J. David. 2008. "Contaminated Communities: The Metaphor of "Immigrant as Pollutant" in Media Representations of Immigration." *Rhetoric & Public Affairs* 11 (4): 569–601. doi:10.1353/rap.0.0068.

Clawson, Heather J., Nicole Dutch, Amy Solomon, and Lisa Goldblatt Grace. August 2009. "Human Trafficking into and Within the United States: A Review of the Literature." U.S. Department of Health and Human Services. Office of the Assistant Secretary for Planning and Evaluation. http://aspe.hhs.gov/hsp/07/humantrafficking/LitRev/index.pdf.

Cohen, Deborah. 2011. *Braceros: Migrant Citizens and Transnational Subjects in the Postwar United States and Mexico.* Chapel Hill: University of North Carolina Press.

Collins, Patricia Hill. 2000. *Black Feminist Thought: Knowledge, Consciousness, and the Politics of Empowerment.* Second Edition. New York: Routledge.

Combahee River Collective. 1986. *The Combahee River Collective Statement: Black Feminist Organizing in the Seventies and Eighties.* New York: Kitchen Table: Women of Color Press.

Connelly, Mark Thomas. 1980. *The Response to Prostitution in the Progressive Era.* Chapel Hill: University of North Carolina Press.

Constable, Nicole. 2007. *Maid to Order in Hong Kong: Stories of Migrant Workers.* Ithaca, NY: Cornell University Press.

Constable, Nicole. 2009. "The Commodification of Intimacy: Marriage, Sex, and Reproductive Labor." *Annual Review of Anthropology* 38: 44–64.

Constable, Nicole. 2012. "International Marriage Brokers, Cross-border Marriages and the US Anti-trafficking Campaign." *Journal of Ethnic and Migration Studies* 38 (7): 1136–54. doi:10.1080/1369183X.2012.681457.

Cotton, Ann, Melissa Farley, and Robert Baron. 2002. "Attitudes Toward Prostitution and Acceptance of Rape Myths." *Journal of Applied Social Psychology* 32 (9): 1790–96.

Crenshaw, Kimberle. 1991. "Mapping the Margins: Intersectionality, Identity Politics, and Violence Against Women of Color." *Stanford Law Review* 43 (6): 1241–99.

Curran, Sara R., and Estela Rivero-Fuentes. 2003. "Engendering Migrant Networks: The Case of Mexican Migration." *Demography* 40 (2): 289–307.

Curtis, James R., and Daniel D. Arreola. 1991. "Zonas de Tolerancia on the Northern Mexican Border." *Geographical Review* 81 (3): 333–46.

Cruz, Cindy. 2001. "Toward an epistemology of a Brown Body." *International Journal of Qualitative Studies in Education* 14 (5): 657–69.

Daguno, Irene. 1998. "Migration and Trafficking of Filipino Women for Prostitution." In *Halfway Through the Circle: The Lives of Eight Filipino Women Survivors of Prostitution and Trafficking*, edited by Doreen Jose and Marilyn T. Erpelo, 1–16. Manila: Women's Education, Development, Productivity and Research Organization.

Daniels, Roger. 2004. *Guarding the Golden Door: American Immigration Policy and Immigrants Since 1882*. New York: Hill and Wang.

Davidson, Julia O'Connell. 1999. *Prostitution, Power and Freedom*. Cambridge, UK: Polity Press.

Davidson, Julia O'Connell. 2005. *Children in the Global Sex Trade*. Cambridge, UK: Polity Press.

Davis, Angela. 1981. *Women, Race & Class*. New York: Vintage Books.

Davis, Wade. 1988. *Passage of Darkness: The Ethnobiology of the Haitian Zombie*. Durham: University of North Carolina Press.

Deer, Sarah. 2009. "Relocation Revisited: Sex Trafficking of Native Women in the United States." *William Mitchel Law Review* 36 (2): 621–83.

Degenova, Nicholas. 2002. "Migrant 'Illegality' and Deportability in Everyday Life." *Annual Review of Anthropology* 31: 419–47.

Degenova, Nicholas, and Nathalie Peutz. 2010. *The Deportation Regime: Sovereignty, Space, and the Freedom of Movement*. Durham, NC: Duke University Press.

Deleuze, Gilles, and Felix Guattari. 1987. *A Thousand Plateaus: Capitalism and Schizophrenia*. Minneapolis: University of Minnesota Press.

Demleitner, Nora V. 2001. "The Law at the Crossroads: The Construction of Migrant Women Trafficked into Prostitution." In *Global Human Smuggling: Comparative Perspectives*, edited by David Kyle and Rey Koslowski, 257–93. Baltimore, MD: Johns Hopkins University Press.

DeStefano, Anthony. 2008. *The War on Human Trafficking: U.S. Policy Assessed*. New Brunswick, NJ: Rutgers University Press.

Diaz, Rafael M. 2000. "Cultural Regulation, Self-Regulation, and Sexuality: A Psycho-Cultural Model of HIV Risk in Latino Gay Men." In *Framing the Sexual Subject: The Politics of Gender, Sexuality, and Power*, edited by Richard Parker, Regina Maria Barbosa, and Peter Aggleton, 165–90. Berkeley: University of California Press.

Dignan, James. 2005. *Understanding Victims & Restorative Justice*. New York: Open University Press.

Doezema, Jo. 1998. "Forced to Choose: Beyond the Voluntary v. Forced Prostitution Dichotomy." In *Global Sex Workers: Rights, Resistance, and Redefinition*, edited by Kamala Kempadoo and Jo Doezema, 34–50. New York: Routledge.

Doezema, Jo. 2000. "Loose Women or Lost Women? The Re-emergence of the Myth of White Slavery in Contemporary Discourses of Trafficking in Women." *Gender Issues* 18 (1): 23–50.

Doezema, Jo. 2002. "Who Gets to Choose? Coercion Consent, and the UN Trafficking Protocol." In *Gender, Trafficking and Slavery*, edited by Rachel Masika, 20–37. Oxford: Oxfam Publishing.

Doezema, Jo. 2010. *Sex Slaves and Discourse Masters: The Construction of Trafficking*. London: Zed Books.

Dougherty Delano, Page. 2000. "Making Up for War: Sexuality and Citizenship in Wartime Culture." *Feminist Studies* 26 (1): 33–68.

Douglass, Ana, and Thomas A. Vogler. 2003. *Witness & Memory: The Discourse of Trauma*. New York: Routledge.

Doyle, Charles. 2016. *Federal Conspiracy Law: A Brief Overview*. Congressional Research Service. https://fas.org/sgp/crs/misc/R41223.pdf.

Dragiewicz, Molly. 2008. "Teaching About Trafficking: Opportunities and Challenges for Critical Engagement." *Feminist Teacher* 18 (3): 185–201.

Duggan, Lisa. 2002. "The New Homonormativity: The Sexual Politics of Neoliberalism." In *Materializing Democracy: Toward a Revitalized Cultural Politics*, edited by Russ Castronovo and Dana D. Nelson, 175–94. Durham, NC: Duke University Press.

Duncan, Patti. 2009. *Tell This Silence: Asian American Women Writers and the Politics of Speech*. Iowa City: University of Iowa Press.

Ehrenreich, Barbara, and Arlie Russell Hochschild. 2002. *Global Woman: Nannies, Maids, and Sex Workers in the New Economy*. New York: Henry Holt.

Ehrenreich, John H. 1985. *The Altruistic Imagination: A History of Social Work and Social Policy in the United States*. Ithaca, NY: Cornell University Press.

Emmers, Ralf, Beth Greener-Barcham, and Thomas Nicholas. 2006. "Institutional Arrangements to Counter Human Trafficking in the Asia Pacific." *Contemporary Southeast Asia: A Journal of International and Strategic Affairs* 28 (3): 490–511.

Eng, David L. 2010. *The Feeling of Kinship: Queer Liberalism and the Racialization of Intimacy.* Durham, NC: Duke University Press.

Enloe, Cynthia. 2007. *Globalization and Militarism: Feminists Make the Link.* Lanham, MD: Rowman & Littlefield.

Enloe, Cynthia. 2014. *Bananas, Beaches and Bases: Making Feminist Sense of International Politics.* Second edition. Berkeley: University of California Press.

Enrile, Annalisa. 2017. *Ending Human Trafficking and Modern-Day Slavery: Freedom's Journey.* Thousand Oaks, CA: Sage.

Espiritu, Yen. 1992. *Asian American Panethnicity: Bridging Institutions and Identities.* Philadelphia, PA: Temple University Press.

Espritu, Yen Le. 2006. "Toward a Critical Refugee Study: The Vietnamese Refugee Subject in U.S. Scholarship." *Journal of Vietnamese Studies* 1 (1–2): 410–33.

Ewing, Sally. 1987. "Formal Justice and the Spirit of Capitalism: Max Weber's Sociology of Law." *Law & Society Review* 21 (3): 487–512.

Fantone, Laura. 2007. "Precarious Changes: Gender and Generational Politics in Contemporary Italy." *Feminist Review* 87: 5–20.

Farley, Melissa. 2003. *Prostitution, Trafficking, and Traumatic Stress.* Binghamton, NY: Hawthorn Press.

Farley, Melissa. 2007. *Prostitution and Trafficking in Nevada: Making the Connections.* San Francisco: Prostitution Research & Education.

Farley, Melissa, Ann Cotton, Jacqueline Lynne, Sybille Zumbeck, Frida Spiwak, Maria E. Reyes, Dinorah Alvarez, and Ufuk Sezgin. 2004. "Prostitution and Trafficking in Nine Countries: An Update on Violence and Postraumatic Stress Disorder." In *Prostitution, Trafficking, and Traumatic Stress*, edited by Melissa Farley, 33–74. New York: The Haworth Maltreatment & Trauma Press.

Farley, Melissa, and Vanessa Kelly. 2000. "Prostitution: A Critical Review of the Medical and Social Sciences Literature." *Women & Criminal Justice* 11 (4): 29–64.

Farr, Kathryn. 2005. *Sex Trafficking: The Global Market in Women and Children.* New York: Worth Publishers.

Farrell, Amy, Jack McDevitt, Rebecca Pfeffer, Stephanie Fahy, Colleen Owens, Meredith Dank, and William Adams. 2012. *Identifying Challenges to Improve the Investigation and Prosecution of State and Local Human Trafficking Cases.* Urban Institute Justice Policy Center and North Eastern University Institute on Race and Justice School of Criminology and Criminal Justice. http://www.ncdsv .org/images/NEUniv-UrbanInsti_IDingChallengesImproveInvesProsecStateLo calHumanTraffickingCases_4-2012.pdf.

Feingold, David A. 2015. "Human Trafficking." *Foreign Policy* 150: 26–30.

Felman, Shoshana, and Dori Laub. 1992. *Testimony: Crises of Witnessing in Literature, Psychoanalysis, and History.* New York: Routledge.

Ferraro, Kathleen. 2006. *Neither Angels Nor Demons: Women, Crime and Victimization*. Boston, MA: Northeastern University Press.

Fitzgerald, David Scott. 2015. "The Sociology of International Migration." In *Migration Theory: Talking Across Disciplines*, edited by Caroline B. Brettell and James F. Hollifield, 115–47. New York: Routledge.

Fleetwood, Nicole. 2011. *Troubling Vision: Performance, Visuality, and Blackness*. Chicago: University of Chicago Press.

Fojas, Camilla, and Rudy Guevarra. 2012. *Transnational Crossroads: Remapping the Americas and the Pacific*. Lincoln: University of Nebraska Press.

Foner, Eric. 1999. *The Story of American Freedom*. New York: W. W. Norton.

Foner, Eric. 2012. *Give Me Liberty! An American History*. New York: W. W. Norton.

Foucault, Michel. 1972. *Power/Knowledge: Selected Interviews and Other Writings, 1972–1977*. Translated by Colin Gordon, Leo Marshall, John Mepham, and Kate Soper. Edited by Colin Gordon. Brighton, Sussex: Harvester Press.

Foucault, Michel. 1978. *The History of Sexuality*. Vol. 1: *An Introduction*. New York: Vintage Books.

Foucault, Michel. 1982. *The Archaeology of Knowledge & the Discourse on Language*. New York: Vintage Books.

Foucault, Michel. 1994. *Power*. New York: The New Press.

Foucault, Michel, Luther H. Martin, Huck Gutman, and Patrick H. Hutton. 1988. *Technologies of the Self: A Seminar with Michel Foucault*. Amherst: University of Massachusetts Press.

Fragomen, Austin T. Jr. 1997. "The Illegal Immigration Reform and Immigrant Responsibility Act of 1996: An Overview." *International Migration Review* 31 (2): 438–60.

Fraser, Nancy. 2005. "Mapping the Feminist Imagination: From Redistribution to Recognition to Representation." *Constellations: An International Journal of Critical and Democratic Theory* 12 (3): 295–307.

Fraser, Nancy, and Linda Gordon. 1994. "A Genealogy of Dependency: Tracing a Keyword of the U.S. Welfare State." *Signs* 19 (2): 309–36.

Fregoso, Rosalinda, and Cynthia Bejarno, eds. 2010. *Terrorizing Women: Feminicides in the Americas*. Durham, NC: Duke University Press.

Fresnoza-Flot, Asuncion. 2009. "Migration Status and Transnational Mothering: The Case of Filipino Migrants in France." *Global Networks* 9 (2): 252–70.

Fukushima, Annie. 2008. "Coerced Migration." In *Battleground: Immigration*, edited by Judith Warner, 104–17. Westport, CT: Greenwood Press.

Fukushima, Annie. 2012. *Asian and Latina Migrants in the United States and the Invisible/Visible Paradigm of Human Trafficking*. PhD diss., University of California, Berkeley.

Fukushima, Annie Isabel. 2014. "Beyond Supply & Demand: The Limitations of End-Demand Strategies." In *Human Trafficking Reconsidered: Rethinking the Problem,*

Envisioning New Solutions, edited by Kimberly Kay Hoang and Rhacel Salazar Parreñas, 91–101. New York: International Debate Education Association.

Fukushima, Annie Isabel. 2015. "Anti-violence Iconographies of the Cage: Diasporan Crossings and the (Un)Tethering of Subjectivities." *Frontiers: A Journal of Women Studies* 36 (3): 160–92.

Fukushima, Annie Isabel, and Julietta Hua. 2015. "Calling the Consumer Activist, Consuming the Trafficking Subject: *Call + Response* and the Terms of Legibility." In *Documenting Gendered Violence: Representations, Collaborations, and Movements*, edited by Lisa M. Cuklanz and Heather McIntosh, 45–66. London: Bloomsbury.

Fukushima, Annie, and Cindy Liou. 2012. "An Interdisciplinary Approach to Strategic Anti-Trafficking Partnerships and the Fourth 'P' in the Human Trafficking Paradigm." PHR Working Paper, Stanford University Program on Human Rights, Stanford, CA.

Gabbert, Ann R. 2003. "Prostitution and Moral Reform in the Borderlands: El Paso, 1890–1920." *Journal of History of Sexuality* 12 (4): 575–604.

Gallagher, Anne T. 2010. *The International Law of Human Trafficking*. Cambridge, UK: Cambridge University Press.

Gallagher, Anne, and Elaine Pearson. 2009. "The High Cost of Freedom: A Legal and Policy Analysis of Shelter Detention for Victims of Trafficking." *Human Rights Quarterly* 32 (1): 73–114.

Gallagher, Anne T., and Elaine Pearson. 2010. "Policy Analysis of Shelter Detention for Victims of Trafficking." *Human Rights Quarterly* 32: 73–114.

Galusca, Roxana. 2012. "Slave Hunters, Brothel Busters, and Feminist Interventions: Investigative Journalists as Anti-Sex-Trafficking Humanitarians." *Feminist Formations* 24 (2): 1–24.

Garcia, Alma, ed. 1997. *Chicana Feminist Thought: The Basic Historical Writings*. New York: Routledge.

Garcia, Ruben J. 2013. *Marginal Workers: How Legal Fault Lines Divide Workers and Leave Them Without Protection*. New York: New York University Press.

Gaytán, Marie Sarita. 2011. "Tequila Talk: Consumption, Gender and the Transnational Terrain of Cultural Identity." *Latino Studies* 9 (1): 62–86.

Gilory, Paul. 1991. *'There Ain't No Black in the Union Jack': The Cultural Politics of Race and Nation*. Chicago: University of Chicago Press.

Glenn, Evelyn Nakano. 1986. *Issei, Nisei, War Bride: Three Generations of Japanese American Women in Domestic Service*. Philadelphia, PA: Temple University Press.

Glenn, Evelyn Nakano. 1992. "From Servitude to Service Work: Historical Continuities in the Racial Division of Paid Reproductive Labor." *Signs* 18 (1): 1–43.

Glenn, Evelyn Nakano. 2002. *Unequal Freedom: How Race and Gender Shaped American Citizenship and Labor*. Cambridge, MA: Harvard University Press.

Glenn, Evelyn Nakano. 2011. *Forced to Care: Coercion and Caregiving in America*. Cambridge, MA: Harvard University Press.

Goldberg, David Theo. 1993. *Racist Culture: Philosophy and the Politics of Meaning*. Oxford, UK: Blackwell.

Gonzalez, Wendy M. 2002–3. "Human Trafficking: Criminalization of Victims in the Sex Industry." *Buffalo Women's Law Journal* 19: 19–26.

Goodnight, G. Thomas, and John Poulakos. 1981. "Conspiracy Rhetoric: From Pragmatism to Fantasy in Public Discourse." *Western Journal of Speech Communication* 45 (4): 299–316.

Gopinath, Gayatri. 2005. *Impossible Desires: Queer Diasporas and South Asian Public Cultures*. Durham, NC: Duke University Press.

Gordon, Avery F. 1997. *Ghostly Matters: Haunting and the Sociological Imagination*. Minneapolis: University of Minnesota Press.

Gordon-Reed, Annette. 2008. *The Hemingses of Monticello: An American Family*. New York: W. W. Norton.

Gotanda, Neil. 1998. "Tale of Two Judges: Joyce Karlin in People v. Soon Ja Du; Lance Ito n People v. O.J. Simpson." In *The House Race Built*, edited by Lubiano Waneema, 66–86. New York: Vintage Books.

Goździak, Elżbieta M. 2008. "On Challenges, Dilemmas, and Opportunities in Studying Trafficked Children." *Anthropological Quarterly* 81 (4): 903–24.

Gozdziak, Elzbieta M., and Elizabeth A. Collett. 2005. "Research on Human Trafficking in North America: A Review of Literature." *International Migration* 43 (1–2): 99–128.

Greenfield, Lawrence A., and Tracy T. Snell. 1999. "Women Offenders." Bureau of Justice Statistics Special Report; NCJ 175688. Washington, DC: U.S. Department of Justice, Office of Justice Programs.

Greer, Richard. 2000. "Dousing Honolulu's Red Lights." *Hawaiian Journal of History* 34: 185–202.

Grewal, Inderpal. 2005. *Transnational America: Feminisms, Diasporas, Neoliberalisms*. Durham, NC: Duke University Press.

Grewal, Inderpal, and Caren Kaplan. 2006. *Scattered Hegemonies: Postmodernity and Transnational Feminist Practices*. Minneapolis: University of Minnesota Press.

Grosfoguel, Ramon, Nelson Maldonado-Torres, and Jose David Saldivar. 2005. *Latin@s in the World-System: Decolonization Struggles in the 21st Century U.S. Empire*. Boulder, CO: Paradigm Publishers.

Grovogui, Siba N. 2010. "The Global South: A Metaphor, Not an Etymology." *Global Studies Review* 6 (3): http://www.globality-gmu.net/page/4?s.

Guerin, Frances, and Roger Hallas, eds. 2007. *The Image and the Witness: Trauma, Memory and Visual Culture*. London: Wallflower Press.

Guillaumin, Colette. 1995. *Racisms, Sexism, Power and Ideology*. New York: Routledge.

Guinn, David E. 2008. "Defining the Problem of Trafficking: The Interplay of U.S. Law, Donor, and the NGO Engagement and the Local Context in Latin America." *Human Rights Quarterly* 30 (1): 119–45.

Gurvitch, Georges. (1947) 1973. *Sociology of Law*. London: Routledge.

Gushulak, Brian D., and Douglas W. Macpherson. 2000. "Health Issues Associated with the Smuggling and Trafficking of Migrants." *Journal of Immigrant Health* 2 (2): 67–78.

Gutierrez, David G. 1996. *Between Two Worlds: Mexican Migrants in the United States*. Wilmington, DE: Scholarly Resources.

Haines, Staci. 2007. *Healing Sex: A Mind-Body Approach to Healing Sexual Trauma*. Edited by Felice Newman. New York: Cleis Press.

Hall, Stuart. 1980. "Cultural Studies: Two Paradigms." *Media, Culture and Society* 2: 57–72.

Hall, Stuart. 1996. "New Ethnicities." In *Stuart Hall: Critical Dialogues in Cultural Studies*, edited by David Morley and Kuan-Hsing Chen, 441–49. London: Routledge.

Hamilton, Margaret. 1978. "Opposition to the Contagious Diseases Acts, 1864–1886." *Albion: A Quarterly Journal Concerned with British Studies* 10 (1): 14–27.

Hannerz, Ulf. 1996. *Transnational Connections: Culture, People, Places*. London: Routledge.

Haq, Mahbubul. 1976. *The Poverty Curtain: Choices for the Third World*. New York: Columbia University Press.

Haraway, Donna. 1991. *Simians, Cyborgs and Women: The Reinvention of Nature*, New York: Routledge.

Harold, Marc M. 2006–7. "A New Kind of Traffic(king) Cop on the International 'Beat' of Human Trafficking." *Charleston Law Review* 97: 97–122.

Hartman, Saidiya, and Stephen Best. 2005. "Fugitive Justice." *Representations* 92 (1): 1–15.

Harvey, David. 1999. "The Body as Referent." *Hedgehog Review* 1 (1): 41–46.

Haynes, Dina Francesca. 2007. "(Not)Found Chained to a Bed in a Brothel: Conceptual, Legal, and Procedural Failures to Fulfill the Promise of the Trafficking Victims Protection Act." *Georgetown Immigration Law Journal* 21: 337–81.

Hekman, Susan. 2010. *The Material of Knowledge: Feminist Disclosures*. Bloomington: Indiana University Press.

Henson, Maria Rosa. 1996. *Comfort Woman: Slave of destiny*. Quezon City, Philippines: Philippine Center for Investigative Journalism.

Hesford, Wendy. 2011. *Spectacular Rhetorics: Human Rights Visions, Recognitions, Feminisms*. Durham, NC: Duke University Press.

Heyzer, Noeleen. 2002. "Combating Trafficking in Women and Children: A Gender and Human Rights Framework." *United Nations Entity for Gender Equality and the Empowerment of Women (UNIFEM)*. The Human Rights Challenge of Globalization: Asia-Pacific-US: The Trafficking in Persons, Especially Women and Children. Honolulu, HI. November 13–15, 2002. Accessed March 15, 2012. http://www.childtrafficking.org/pdf/user/unifem_gender_and_human_rights_framework.pdf.

Hicks, George. 1994. *The Comfort Women: Japan's Brutal Regime of Enforced Prostitution in the Second World War.* New York: W. W. Norton.

Hirata, Lucie Cheng. 1979. "Free, Indentured, Enslaved: Chinese Prostitutes in Nineteenth-Century America." *Signs* 5 (1): 3–29.

Hoang, Kimberly Kay, and Rhacel Salazar Parreñas, eds. 2014. *Human Trafficking Reconsidered: Rethinking the Problem, Envisioning New Solutions.* New York: International Debate Education Association.

Hochschild, Arlie Russell. 2000. "Global Care Chains and Emotional Surplus Value." In *On the Edge: Living with Global Capitalism,* edited by Will Hutton and Anthony Giddens, 130–46. London: Jonathon Cape.

Holland, Sharon Patricia. *Raising the Dead: Readings of Death and (Black) Subjectivity.* Durham, NC. Duke University Press, 2000.

Hondagneu-Sotelo, Pierrette. 2001. *Domestica: Immigrant Workers Cleaning and Caring in the Shadow of Affluence.* Berkeley: University of California Press.

Hondagneu-Sotelo, Pierrette, ed. 2003. *Gender and U.S. Immigration: Contemporary Trends.* Berkeley: University of California Press.

Hondagneu-Sotelo, Pierrette, and Ernestine Avila. 1997. "'I'm Here, But I'm There': The Meanings of Latina Transnational Motherhood." *Gender and Society* 11 (5): 548–71.

Hooks, Bell. 1989. *Talking Back: Thinking Feminist, Thinking Black.* Boston, MA: South End Press.

Hooks, Bell. 2000. *Feminist Theory: From Margin to Center.* Cambridge, MA: South End Press.

Hooks, Bell. 2009. *Belonging: A Culture of Place.* New York: Routledge.

Horlyck, Charlotte, and Michael J. Pettid, eds. 2014. *Death, Mourning, and the Afterlife in Korea: From Ancient to Contemporary Times.* Honolulu: University of Hawai'i Press.

Hornberger, Nancy H., and Serafin M. Coronel-Molina. 2004. "Quechua Language Shift, Maintenance, and Revitalization in the Andes: The Case for Language Planning." *International Journal of the Sociology of Language* 167: 9–67.

Horton, James Oliver, and Lois E. Horton. 2005. *Slavery and the Making of America.* New York: Oxford University Press.

Hsu, Ruth Y. 1996. "'Will the Model Minority Please Identify Itself?': American Ethnic Identity and Its Discontents." *Diaspora: A Journal of Transnational Studies* 5 (1): 37–63.

Hua, Julietta. 2011. *Trafficking Women's Human Rights.* Minneapolis: University of Minnesota Press.

Hua, Julietta, and Katsuri Ray. 2014. "Rights, Affect and Precarity: Post-Racial Formations in Carework." *Cultural Dynamics* 26 (1): 9–28.

Hu-Dehart, Evelyn. 2005. "On Coolies and Shopkeepers: The Chinese as *Huagong* (Laborers) and *Huashang* (Merchants) in Latin America / Caribbean." In *Displacements and Diasporas: Asians in the Americas,* edited by Wanni W. Anderson and Robert G. Lee, 78–111. New Brunswick, NJ: Rutgers University Press.

Huff, Cynthia. 1989. "'The Profoundly Female, and Feminist Genre': The Diary as Feminist Practice." *Women Studies Quarterly* 17 (3–4): 6–14.

Hughes, Donna M. 2004. "Best Practices to Address the Demand Side of Sex Trafficking." Department of State. August 2004. Accessed January 15, 2009. http://www.uri.edu/artsci/wms/hughes/demand_sex_trafficking.pdf.

Hughes, Donna, Katherine Chon, and Derek Ellerman. 2004. "Modern-Day Comfort Women: The U.S. Military, Transnational Crime, and the Trafficking of Women." Violence Against Women. Accessed December 15, 2011. http://www.uri.edu/artsci/wms/hughes/pubtrfrep.htm.

Huh, Kandice. 2003. "Discomforting Knowledge: Or, Korean 'Comfort Women' and Asian Americanist Critical Practice." *Journal of Asian American Studies* 6 (1): 5–23.

Human Rights Center. 2005. *Freedom Denied: Forced Labor in California.* Berkeley: University of California Press.

Human Rights Center and Free the Slaves. 2004. "Hidden Slaves: Forced Labor in the United States." Berkeley: University of California. Accessed March 29, 2012. https://escholarship.org/uc/item/4jn4joqg.

Hume, David. 1900. *An Enquiry Concerning Human Understanding.* Chicago: Open Court Publishing.

Hutton, Will, and Anthony Giddens, eds. 2000. *On the Edge: Living with Global Capitalism.* London: Jonathon Cape.

Ichioka, Yuji. 1980. "Amerika Nadeshiko: Japanese Immigrant Women in the United States, 1900–1924." *Pacific Historical Review* 49 (2): 339–57.

Inda, Jonathan. 2006. *Targeting Immigrants: Government, Technology, and Ethics.* Oxford, UK: Blackwell Press.

International Organization of Migration. 2006. "World Migration 2005: Costs and Benefits of International Migration." New Delhi: Academic Foundation.

Jenness, Valerie. 1990. "From Sex as Sin to Sex as Work: COYOTE and the Reorganization of Prostitution as a Social Problem." *Social Problems* 37 (3): 403–20.

Jew, Kimberly May. 2011. "Perspectives on Asian American Performance Art: Contexts, Memories, and the Making of Meaning on Stage. An Interview with Canyon Sam, Denise Uyehara, and Brenda Wong Aoki." *MELUS* 36 (4): 141–58.

Johnson, Brian D., and Sara Betsinger. 2009. "Punishing the 'Model Minority': Asian-American Criminal Sentencing Outcomes in Federal District Courts." *Criminology* 47 (4): 1045–90.

Johnston, Ellis M. 2000–2001. "Once a Criminal, Always a Criminal: Unconstitutional Presumptions for Mandatory Detention of Criminal Aliens." *Georgetown Law Journal* 89: 2593–635.

Jones, Laura. 2010. "'How Do the American People Know . . . ?': Embodying Post-9/11 Conspiracy Discourse." *GeoJournal* 75 (4): 359–71.

Jones, Steve. 2013. "Gender Monstrosity: Deadgirl and the Sexual Politics of Zombie-Rape." *Feminist Media Studies* 13 (3): 525–39.

Jordan, Ann D. 2010. "Human Rights or Wrongs? The Struggle for a Rights-Based Response to Trafficking in Human Beings." *Gender and Development* 10 (1): 28–37.

Jordan, Don, and Michael Walsh. 2008. *White Cargo: The Forgotten History of Britain's White Slaves in America.* New York: New York University Press.

Jung, Moon Ho. 2005. "Outlawing 'Coolies': Race, Nation, and Empire in the Age of Emancipation." *American Quarterly* 57 (3): 677–701.

Jung, Moon-Ho. 2006. *Coolies and Cane: Race, Labor, and Sugar in the Age of Emancipation.* Baltimore, MD: Johns Hopkins University Press.

Jyrkinen, Marjut. 2012. "McSexualization of Bodies, Sex and Sexualities: Mainstreaming the Commodification of Gendered Inequalities." In *Prostitution, Harm and Gender Inequality: Theory, Research and Policy,* edited by Maddy Coy, 13–32. New York: Routledge.

Kang, Laura Hyun Yi. 2002. *Compositional Subjects: Enfiguring Asian/American Women.* London: Duke University Press.

Kang, Millian. 2010. *The Managed Hand: Race, Gender, and the Body in Beauty Service Work.* Berkeley: University of California Press.

Kaplan, Caren, Norma Alarcon, and Minoo Moallem. 1999. *Between Woman and Nation: Nationalisms, Transnational Feminisms, and the State.* Durham, NC: Duke University Press.

Kaplan, Sara Clarke. 2007. "Love and Violence/Maternity and Death: Black Feminism and the Politics of Reading (Un)representability." *Black Women, Gender & Families* 1 (1): 94–124.

Kara, Siddharth. 2009. *Sex Trafficking: Inside the Business of Modern Slavery.* New York: Columbia University Press.

Karmen, Andrew. 2010. *Crime Victims: An Introduction to Victimology.* Seventh edition. Belmont, CA: Wadsworth Cengage Learning.

Keire, Mara L. 2001. "The Vice Trust: A Reinterpretation of the White Slavery Scare in the United States 1907–1917." *Journal of Social History* 35 (1): 5–41.

Keller, Nora Okja. 1998. *Comfort Woman.* New York: Penguin.

Kelly, Patty. 2008. *Lydia's Open Door: Inside Mexico's Most Modern Brothel.* Berkeley: University of California Press.

Kelly, Robin. 2002. *Freedom Dreams: The Black Radical Imagination.* Boston, MA: Beacon Press.

Kempadoo, Kamala. 2007. "The War on Human Trafficking in the Caribbean." *Race Class* 49: 79–85.

Kempadoo, Kamala, and Jo Doezema, eds. 1998. *Global Sex Workers: Rights, Resistance, and Redefinition.* New York: Routledge.

Kempadoo, Kamala, Jyoti Sanghera, and Bandana Pattanaik, eds. 2005. *Trafficking and Prostitution Reconsidered: New Perspectives on Migration, Sex Work, and Human Rights.* New York: Paradigm Publishers.

Kim, Kathleen. 2007. "Psychological Coercion in the Context of Modern-Day Involuntary Labor: Revisiting *United States v. Kozminski* and Understanding Human Trafficking." *University of Toledo Law Review* 38 (Spring): 941–72.

Kim, Kathleen. 2009. "The Trafficked Worker as Private Attorney General: A Model for Enforcing the Civil Rights of Undocumented Workers." *University of Chicago Legal Forum* 247: 247–316.

Kim-Gibson, Dai Sil. 1999. *Silence Broken: Korean Comfort Women.* Parkersburg, IA: Mid-Prairie Books.

Kinney, Edi C.M. 2006. "Appropriations for the Abolitionists: Undermining Effects of the U.S. Mandatory Anti-Prostitution Pledge in the Fight Against Human Trafficking and HIV/AIDS." *Berkeley Journal of Gender, Law & Justice* 21: 158–94.

Kirkby, Diane. 1991. "Writing the History of Women Working: Photographic Evidence and the 'Disreputable Occupation of Barmaid.'" *Labour History* 61 (Nov.): 3–16.

Kristof, Nicholas D., and Sheryl Wudunn. 2009. *Half the Sky: Turning Oppression into Opportunity for Women Worldwide.* New York: Alfred A. Knope.

Krumholz, Linda. 1992. "The Ghosts of Slavery: Historical Recovery in Toni Morrison's *Beloved.*" *African American Review* 26 (3): 395–408.

Kurahashi, Yuko. 1999. *Asian American Culture on Stage: The History of East West Players.* New York: Routledge.

Kyle, David, and Rey Koslowski. 2001. *Global Human Smuggling: Comparative Perspectives.* Baltimore, MD: Johns Hopkins University Press.

Laczko, Frank. 2005. "Data on Research on Human trafficking." *International Migration* 43 (1–2): 5–16.

Laczko, Frank, and Marco A. Gramegna. 2003. "Developing Better Indicators for Human Trafficking." *Brown Journal of World Affairs* 10 (1): 179–94.

Lather, Patti. 1986. "Research as Praxis." *Harvard Educational Review* 56 (3): 257–78.

Laub, Dori. 1992. "Bearing Witness or the Vicissitudes of Listening." In *Testimony: Crisis of Witnessing in Literature, Psychoanalysis and History,* edited by Shoshana Felman and Dori Laub, 57–92. New York: Routledge.

Laub, Dori. 1995. "Truth and the Testimony: Process & The Struggle." In *Trauma: Explorations in Memory,* edited by Cathy Caruth, 61–75. Baltimore, MD: Johns Hopkins University Press.

Lauren, Paul Gordon. 2011. *The Evolution of International Human Rights: Visions Seen.* Third edition. Philadelphia: University of Pennsylvania Press.

Lawrence, Ken. 1976. *Karl Marx on American Slavery.* Tougaloo, MS: Freedom of Information Service.

Lawston, Jodie Michelle, and Martha Escobar. 2009–10. "Policing, Detention, Deportation, and Resistance: Situating Immigrant Justice and Carcerality in the 21st Century." *Social Justice* 36 (2): 1–6.

Lee, Erika. 2002. 2002. "The Chinese Exclusion Example: Race, Immigration, and American Gatekeeping, 1882–1924." *Journal of American Ethnic History* 21 (3): 36–62.

Lee, Erika. 2003. *At America's Gates: Chinese Immigration During the Exclusion Era, 1882–1943.* Chapel Hill: University of North Carolina Press.

Lee, Erika. 2007. "The 'Yellow Peril' and Asian Exclusion in the Americas." *Pacific Historical Review* 76 (4): 537–62.

Lee, Erika, and Judy Yung. 2010. *Angel Island: Immigrant Gateway to America.* Oxford: Oxford University Press.

Lee, Ivy, and Mie Lewis. 2003–4. "Human Trafficking from a Legal Advocate's Perspective: History, Legal Framework and Current Anti-Trafficking Efforts." *University of California Davis Journal of International Law and Policy* 169: 169–95.

Lee, Stacey J. 1994. "Behind the Model-Minority Stereotype: Voices of High- and Low-Achieving Asian American Students." *Anthropology & Education Quarterly* 25 (4): 413–29.

Lefebvre, Henri. 2005. *The Production of Space.* Translated by Donald Nicholson-Smith. Malden, MA: Blackwell Publishing.

Lehti, Martti, and Kauko Aromaa. 2006. "Trafficking for Sexual Exploitation." *Crime and Justice* 34 (1): 133–227.

Leidholdt, Dorchen, and Janice G. Raymond. 1990. *The Sexual Liberals and the Attack on Feminism.* New York: Pergamon Press.

Lessard, Micheline. 2009. "'Cet ignoble trafic': The Kidnapping and Sale of Vietnamese Women and Children in French Colonial Indochina, 1873–1935." *French Colonial History* 10: 1–34.

Lever, Janet, David Kanouse, and Sandra H. Berry. 2005. "Racial and Ethnic Segmentation of Female Prostitution in Los Angeles County." *Journal of Psychology and Human Sexuality* 17 (1–2): 107–29.

Levitt, Peggy. 2001. *The Transnational Villagers.* Berkeley: University of California Press.

Liang, Zai, and Wenzhen Ye. 2001. "From Fujian to New York: Understanding the New Chinese Immigration." In *Global Human Smuggling: Comparative Perspectives,* edited by David Kyle and Rey Koslowski, 187–215. Baltimore, MD: Johns Hopkins University Press.

Lie, John. 1995. "The Transformation of Sexual Work in 20th-Century Korea." *Gender & Society* 9 (3): 310–27.

Limoncelli, Stephanie A. 2010. *The Politics of Trafficking: The First International Movement to Combat the Sexual Exploitation of Women.* Stanford, CA: Stanford University Press.

Lipsitz, George. 1998. *Possessive Investment in Whiteness.* Philadelphia, PA: Temple University Press.

Liss, Andrea. 1998. *Trespassing Through Shadows. Memory, Photography & the Holocaust* Minneapolis: University of Minnesota Press.

Livingston, Jessica. 2004. "Murder in Juarez: Gender, Sexual Violence, and the Global Assembly Line." *Frontiers: A Journal of Women Studies* 25 (1): 59–76.

Logan, Enid Lynette. 2011. *"At This Defining Moment": Barack Obama's Presidential Candidacy and the New Politics of Race.* New York: New York University Press.

López, Kathleen M. 2013. *Chinese Cubans: A Transnational History.* Chapel Hill: University of North Carolina Press.

Lopez, Kristina M., and Holly V. Miller. 2011. "Ethnicity, Acculturation, and Offending: Findings from a Sample of Hispanic Adolescents." *Open Family Studies Journal* 4: 27–37.

López-Garza, Marta, and David R. Diaz. 2001. *Asian and Latino Immigrants in a Restructuring Economy: The Metamorphosis of Southern California.* Stanford, CA: Stanford University Press.

Lorde, Audre. 1987. *Sister Outsider: Essays & Speeches by Audre Lorde.* Berkeley, CA: The Crossing Press.

Lowe, Lisa. 1996. *Immigrant Acts: on Asian American Cultural Politics.* Durham, NC: Duke University Press.

Lowe, Lisa. 2006. "The Intimacies of Four Continents." In *Haunted by Empire: Geographies of Intimacy in North American History,* edited by Ann Laura Stoler, 191–212. Durham, NC: Duke University Press.

Lowe, Lisa. 2015. *Intimacies of Four Continents.* Durham, NC: Duke University Press.

Lugones, María. 1987. "Playfulness, 'World'-Travelling, and Loving Perception." *Hypatia* 2 (2): 3–19.

Lugones, María. 2003. *Pilgrimages/Peregrinajes: Theorizing Coalition Against Multiple Oppressions.* Lanham, MD: Rowman & Littlefield.

Lugones, María. 2007. "Heterosexualism and the Colonial/Modern Gender System." *Hypatia: A Journal of Feminist Philosophy* 22 (1): 186–219.

Lugones, María. 2010. "Toward a Decolonial Feminism." *Hypatia* 25 (4): 742–59.

Lui, Mary Ting Yi. 2009. "Saving Young Girls from Chinatown: White Slavery and Woman Suffrage, 1910–1920." *Journal of the History of Sexuality* 18 (3): 393–417.

Luibhéid, Eithne. 2002. *Entry Denied: Controlling Sexuality at the Border.* Minneapolis: University of Minnesota Press.

Luibhéid, Eithne. 2008. "Sexuality, Migration, and the Shifting Line Between Legal and Illegal Status." *GLQ: A Journal of Lesbian and Gay Studies* 14 (2–3): 289–315.

Lustig, Deborah Freedman, and Kenzo K. Sung. 2013. "Dissolving Borders: Reframing Risk, Delinquent Peers, and Youth Violence." *Children and Youth Services Review* 35 (8): 1197–205.

Lutnick, Alexandra. 2016. *Domestic Minor Sex Trafficking: Beyond Victims and Villains.* New York: Columbia University Press.

Lynes, Krista Geneviève. 2011. "Visual Currencies: Documenting India's Red-Light Districts." *Signs* 37 (1): 1–24.

Lyotard, Jean-François. 1988. *The Differend: Phrases in Dispute.* Manchester: Manchester University Press.

MacKinnon, Catharine. 2006. *Are Women Human? And Other International Dialogues.* Cambridge, MA: The Belknap Press of Harvard University Press.

Mahdavi, Pardis. 2014. *From Trafficking to Terror: Constructing a Global Social Problem (Framing 21st Century Social Issues).* New York: Routledge.

Mahdavi, Pardis, and Christine Sargent. 2011. "Questioning the Discursive Construction of Trafficking and Forced Labor in the United Arab Emirates." *Journal of Middle East Women's Studies* 7 (3): 6–35.

Mahmood, Saba. 2005. *Politics of Piety: The Islamic Revival and the Feminist Subject.* Princeton, NJ: Princeton University Press.

Manzo, Kate. 2005. "Exploiting West Africa's Children: Trafficking, Slavery and Uneven Development." *Area* 37 (4): 393–401.

Martin, Diana. 1991. "Chinese Ghost Marriage." In *An Old State in New Settings*, JASO Occasional Papers, edited by Hugh D.R. Baker and Steven Feuchtwang, no. 8, 25–43. Oxford, UK: JASO.

Martinez, Daniel, and Jeremy Slack. 2013. "What Part of 'Illegal' Don't You Understand? The Social Consequences of Criminalizing Unauthorized Mexican Migrants in the United States." *Social & Legal Studies* 22 (4): 535–55.

Martinez, Ramiro, and Matthew T. Lee. 2000. "On Immigration and Crime." In *Criminal Justice 2000: The Changing Nature of Crime*, Vol. I, edited by Gary LaFree and Robert J. Bursik Jr., 485–524. Washington, DC: National Institute of Justice.

Marx, Karl. 1847. *The Poverty of Philosophy: A Reply to M. Proudhon's Philosophy of Poverty.* New York: International Publishers.

Marx, Karl, and Frederick Engels. 1998 *The Communist Manifesto.* Modern edition. London: Verso.

Masika, Rachel, ed. 2002. *Gender, Trafficking and Slavery.* Oxford, UK: Oxfam.

Massey, Douglas S., Joaquin Arango, Graeme Hugo, Ali Kouaouci, Adela Pellegrino, and J. Edward Taylor. 1994. "An Evaluation of International Migration Theory: The North American Case." *Population and Development Review* 20 (4): 699–751.

Massey, Douglas S., and Nancy A. Denton, eds. 1993. *American Apartheid: Segregation and the Making of the Underclass.* Cambridge, MA: Harvard University Press.

Massey, Douglas S., Jorge Durand, and Nolan J. Malone. 2003. *Beyond Smoke and Mirrors: Mexican Immigration in an Era of Economic Integration.* New York: Russell Sage Foundation.

Mbembe, Achille. 2003. "Necropolitics." Translated by Libby Meintjes. *Public Culture* 15 (1): 11–40.

McClain, Charles, ed. 1994. *Asian Americans and the Law: Historical and Contemporary Perspectives.* 4 vols. New York: Routledge.

McConnell, Joyce E. 1991–2. "Beyond the Metaphor: Battered Women, Involuntary Servitude and the Thirteenth Amendment." *Yale Journal of Law & Feminism* 4: 207–54.

Menjívar, C., and D. Kanstroom, eds. 2014. *Constructing Immigrant "Illegality": Critiques, Experiences, and Responses.* New York: Cambridge University Press.

Menjívar, Cecilia, and Leisy J. Abrego. 2012. "Legal Violence: Immigration Law and the Lives of Central American Immigrants." *American Journal of Sociology* 117 (5): 1380–421.

Merleau-Ponty, Maurice. 1968. *The Visible and the Invisible: Followed by Working Notes.* Edited by Claude Lefort. Translated by Alphonso Lingis. Evanston, IL: Northwestern University Press.

Merleau-Ponty, Maurice. 2002. *Phenomenology of Perception.* London: Routledge.

Merry, Sally Engle. 2000. *Colonizing Hawai'i: The Cultural Power of Law.* Princeton, NJ: Princeton University Press.

Meyers, Diana Tietjens. 2011. "Two Victim Paradigms and the Problem of 'Impure' Victims." *Humanity: An International Journal of Human Rights, Humanitarianism, and Development* 2 (2): 255–75.

Mignolo, Walter. 2000. *Local Histories/Global Designs: Coloniality, Subaltern Knowledges, and Border Thinking.* Princeton, NJ: Princeton University Press.

Minh-ha, Trinh T. 1993. "The Totalizing Quest of Meaning." In *Theorizing Documentary,* edited by Michael Renov, 92–107. London: Routledge.

Mirzoeff, Nicholas. 2006. "On Visuality." *Journal of Visual Culture* 5 (1): 53–79.

Mitchell, Ronald K., Bradley R. Agle, and Donna J. Wood. 1997. "Toward a Theory of Stakeholder Identification and Salience: Defining the Principle of Who and What Really Counts." *Academy of Management Review* 22 (4): 853–86.

Mohanty, Chandra Talpade. 2003 "'Under Western Eyes' Revisited: Feminist Solidarity Through Anticapitalist Struggles." *Signs* 28 (2): 499–535.

Mohanty, Chandra Tapalde, and M. Jacqui Alexander, eds. 1997. *Feminist Genealogies, Colonial Legacies, Democratic Futures.* New York: Routledge.

Mohanty, Chandra Tapalde, Ann Russo, and Lourdes Torres, eds. 1991. *Third World Women and the Politics of Feminism.* Bloomington: Indiana University Press.

Moises, Arce. 2006. "The Societal Consequences of Market Reform in Peru." *Latin American Politics & Society* 48 (1): 27–54.

Molland, Sverre. 2011. "'I Am Helping Them': 'Traffickers', 'Anti-Traffickers' and the Economies of Bad Faith." *Australian Journal of Anthropology* 22: 236–254.

Moon, Katharine H.S. 1997. *Sex Among Allies: Military Prostitution in U.S.-Korea Relations.* New York: Columbia University Press.

Morgan, Edmund S. 2003. *American Slavery, American Freedom: The Ordeal of Colonial Virginia.* New York: W. W. Norton.

Morris, Madeline. 2000. "In War and Peace: Rape, War, and Military Culture." In *War's Dirty Secret: Rape, Prostitution, and Other Crimes Against Women*, edited by Barstow, Anne Llewellyn, 167–203. Cleveland, OH: Pilgrim Press.

Morrison, Toni. 1987. *Beloved: A Novel.* New York: A. A. Knopf.

Mountz, Alison. 2010. *Seeking Asylum: Human Smuggling and Bureaucracy at the Border.* Minneapolis: University of Minnesota Press.

Mountz, Alison, and Jennifer Hyndman. 2006. "Feminist Approaches to the Global Intimate." *Women's Studies Quarterly* 34 (1–2): 446–63.

Mullin, Katherine. 2004. "'The Essence of Vulgarity': The Barmaid Controversy in 'Sirens' Episode of James Joyce's *Ulysses*." *Textual Practice* 18 (4): 475–95.

Muñoz, José Esteban. 1999. *Disidentifications: Queers of Color and the Performance of Politics.* Minneapolis: University of Minnesota Press.

Musto, Jennifer. 2013. "Domestic Minor Sex Trafficking and the Detention-to-Protection Pipeline." *Dialect Anthropology* 37: 257–76.

Narayan, Uma. 1997. *Dislocating Cultures: Identities, Traditions, and Third World Feminism.* New York: Routledge.

Nevins, Joseph. 2002. *Operation Gatekeeper: The Rise of the Illegal Alien and the Making of the US-Mexico Boundary.* New York: Routledge.

Ngai, Mae. 2004. *Impossible Subjects: Illegal Aliens and the Making of Modern America.* Princeton, NJ: Princeton University Press.

Ngai, Mae M. 2007. "Birthright Citizenship and the Alien Citizen." *Fordham Law Review* 75 (5): 2521–30.

Nicola, Andrea Di, Andrea Cauduro, Marco Lombardi, and Paolo Ruspini, eds. 2009. *Prostitution and Human Trafficking: Focus on Clients.* New York: Springer Science+Business Media.

Nimako, Kwame, and Stephen Small. 2012. "Collective Memory of Slavery in Great Britain and the Netherlands." In *New Perspectives on Slavery and Colonialism in the Caribbean*, edited by Marten Schalkwijk and Stephen Small, 92–115. The Hague, Netherlands: Amrit and NiNsee.

Oakley, Ann. 1976. *Woman's Work: The Housewife, Past and Present.* New York: Random House.

Obokata, Tom. 2005. "Trafficking of Human Beings as a Crime Against Humanity: Some Implications for the International Legal System." *International and Comparative Law Quarterly* 54 (2): 445–57.

Ogoshi, Aiko, and Kiyoko Shimizu. 2000. "Japanese Women Who Stand with Comfort Women." In *War's Dirty Secret: Rape, Prostitution, and Other Crimes Against Women*, edited by Anne Llewellyn Barstow, 26–37. Cleveland, OH: Pilgrim Press.

Oh, Bonnie B.C., and Margaret D. Stetz. 2001. *Legacies of the Comfort Women of World War II*. Armonk, NY: M. E. Sharpe.

Omi, Michael, and Howard Winant. 1994. *Racial Formation in the United States: From the 1960s to the 1990s*. Second edition. New York: Routledge.

Ong, Aihwa, and Stephen J. Collier. 2005. *Global Assemblages: Technology, Politics, and Ethics as Anthropological Problems*. Malden, MA: Blackwell Publishers.

Ono, Kent A., and Vincent N. Pham. 2009. *Asian Americans and the Media*. Cambridge, UK: Polity Press.

Oriola, Bukola. 2016. *Imprisoned: The Travails of a Trafficked Victim*. Spring Lake Park, MN: Bukola Publishing.

Ott, Brian L., and Eric Aoki. 2002. "The Politics of Negotiating Public Tragedy: Media Framing of the Matthew Shepard Murder." *Rhetoric & Public Affairs* 5 (3): 483–505.

Outshoorn, Joyce. 2004. *The Politics of Prostitution: Women's Movements, Democratic States, and the Globalisation of Sex Commerce*. New York: Cambridge University Press.

Park, Edward J.W., and John S.W. Park. 1999. "A New American Dilemma?: Asian Americans and Latinos in Race Theorizing." *Journal of Asian American Studies* 2 (3): 289–309.

Parreñas, Rhacel Salazar. 2001a. "Mothering from a Distance: Emotions, Gender, and Intergenerational Relations in Filipino Transnational Families." *Feminist Studies* 27 (2): 361–90.

Parreñas, Rhacel Salazar. 2001b. *Servants of Globalization: Women, Migration, and Domestic Work*. Stanford, CA: Stanford University Press.

Parreñas, Rhacel Salazar. 2008. *The Force of Domesticity: Filipina Migrants and Globalization*. New York: New York University Press.

Parreñas, Rhacel Salazar. 2011. *Illicit Flirtations: Labor, Migration, and Sex Trafficking in Tokyo*. Stanford, CA: Stanford University Press.

Parreñas, Rhacel Salazar, Maria Cecilia Hwang, and Heather Ruth Lee. 2012. "What Is Human Trafficking? A Review Essay." *Signs* 37 (4): 1015–29.

Parreñas, Rhacel Salazar, and Lok C. D. Siu. 2007. *Asian Diasporas: New Formations, New Conceptions*. Stanford, CA: Stanford University Press.

Parson, Nia. 2010. "'I Am Not (Just) a Rabbit Who Has a Bunch of Children!': Agency in the Midst of Suffering at the Intersections of Global Inequalities, Gendered Violence, and Migration." *Violence Against Women* 16 (8): 881–901.

Pascoe, Peggy. 1996. "Miscegenation Law, Court Cases, and Ideologies of 'Race' in Twentieth-Century America." *Journal of American History* 83 (1): 44–69.

Pascoe, Peggy. 2009. *What Comes Naturally: Miscegenation Law and the Making of Race in America*, Oxford: Oxford University Press.

Pastor, Robert A. 2011. *The North American Idea: A Vision of a Continental Future*. New York: Oxford University Press.

Pateman, Carole. 1988. *The Sexual Contract*. Cambridge, UK: Polity Press.

Patterson, Orlando. 1982. *Slavery and Social Death: A Comparative Study*. Cambridge, MA: Harvard University Press.

Peffer, George Anthony. 1986. "Forbidden Families: Emigration Experiences of Chinese Women Under the Page Law, 1875–1882." *Journal of American Ethnic History* 6 (1): 28–46.

Perez, Emma. 1999. *The Decolonial Imaginary: Writing Chicanas into History*. Bloomington: Indiana University Press.

Perez, Laura E. 2007. *Chicana Art: The Politics of Spiritual and Aesthetics Alterities*. Durham, NC: Duke University Press.

Peterson, V. Spike. 1999. "Sexing Political Identities/Nationalism as Heterosexism." *International Feminist Journal of Politics* 1: 34–65.

Portes, Alejandro. 2007. "Migration, Development, and Segmented Assimilation: A Conceptual Review of the Evidence." *Annals of the American Academy of Political and Social Science* 610 (1): 73–97.

Potocky, Miriam. 2010. "Effectiveness of Services for Victims of International Human Trafficking: An Exploratory Evaluation." *Journal of Immigrant and Refugee Studies* 8 (4): 359–85.

Povinelli, Elizabeth A. 2011. *Economies of Abandonment: Social Belonging and Endurance in Late Liberalism*. Durham, NC: Duke University Press.

Preston-White, Eleanor, Christine Varga, Herman Oosthuizen, Rachel Roberts, and Frederick Blose. 2000. "Survival Sex and HIV/AIDS in an African City." In *Framing the Sexual Subject: The Politics of Gender, Sexuality, and Power*, edited by Richard Parker, Regina Maria Barbosa, and Peter Aggleton, 165–90. Berkeley: University of California Press.

Priest, Myisha. 2010. "'The Nightmare Is Not Cured': Emmett Till and American Healing." *American Quarterly* 62 (1): 1–24.

Quijano, Aníbal. 2007."Coloniality and Modernity/Rationality." *Cultural Studies* 21 (2–3): 168–78.

Quijano, Aníbal, and Immanuel Wallerstein. 1992. "Americanity as a Concept, or the Americas in the Modern-World System." *International Social Sciences Journal* 134 (4): 549–57.

Quirk, Joel. 2006. "The Anti-slavery Project: Linking the Historical and Contemporary." *Human Rights Quarterly* 28 (3): 565–98.

Quirk, Joel. 2011. *The Anti-slavery Project: From the Slave Trade to Human Trafficking.* Philadelphia: University of Pennsylvania Press.

Raheja, Michelle. 2010. *Reservation Reelism: Redfacing, Visual Sovereignty, and Representations of Native Americans in Film.* Lincoln: University of Nebraska Press.

Ray, Raka, and Seemin Qayum. 2009. *Cultures of Servitude: Modernity, Domesticity, and Class in India.* Stanford, CA: Stanford University Press.

Raymond, Janice M. 2002. "The New UN Trafficking Protocol." *Women's Studies International Forum* 25 (5): 491–502.

Reddy, Chandan. 2011. *Freedom with Violence: Race, Sexuality, and the US State.* Durham, NC: Duke University Press.

Regis, Ethel. 2013. "Mediating Global Filipinos: The Filipino Channel and the Filipino Diaspora." PhD diss., University of California, Berkeley.

Reilly, Niamh. 2009. *Women's Human Rights: Seeking Gender Justice in a Globalizing Age.* Cambridge, UK: Polity Press.

Rentschler, Carrie A. 2004. "Witnessing: US Citizenship and the Vicarious Experience of Suffering." *Media, Culture & Society* 26: 296–304.

Richie, Beth. 2012. *Arrested Justice: Black Women, Violence and America's Prison Nation.* New York: New York University Press.

Ringdal, Nils. 2004. *Love for Sale: Global History of Prostitution.* London: Atlantic Books.

Roberts, Kenneth M. 1996. "Neoliberalism and the Transformation of Populism in Latin America: The Peruvian Case." *World Politics* 48 (1): 82–116.

Rodriguez, Juana Maria. 2003. *Queer Latinidad: Identity Practices, Discursive Spaces.* New York: New York University Press.

Rodriguez, Robyn M. 2010. "Migrant Heroes: Nationalism, Citizenship and the Politics of Filipino Migrant Labor." *Citizenship Studies* 6 (3): 341–56.

Roe, Clifford. 1911. *The Great War on White Slavery.* New York: Garland Publishing.

Rollins, Judith. 1987. *Between Women: Domestics and their Employers.* Philadelphia, PA: Temple University Press.

Román, Ediberto. 2013. *Those Damned Immigrants: America's Hysteria over Undocumented Immigration.* New York: New York University Press.

Román-Odio, C. 2013. *Sacred Iconographies in Chicana Cultural Productions.* New York: Palgrave MacMillan.

Romero, Mary. 1992. *Maid in the U.S.A.* New York: Routledge.

Rosaldo, Renato. 1993. *Culture & Truth: The Remaking of Social Analysis.* Boston: Beacon Press.

Roth, Wendy D. 2012. *Race Migrations: Latinos and the Cultural Transformation of Race.* Stanford, CA: Stanford University Press.

Ruiz, Vicki L. 1998. *From Out of the Shadows: Mexican Women in Twentieth-Century America.* New York: Oxford University Press.

Rumgay, Judith. 2005. *When Victims Become Offenders: In Search of Coherence in Policy and Practice.* London: Fawcett Society. Accessed December 4, 2014. http://www.fawcettsociety.org.uk/documents/When%20Victims%20Become%20Offenders%20Report%2014.12.04.pdf.

Sadowski-Smith, Claudia. 2008. "Unskilled Labor Migration and the Illegality Spiral: Chinese, European, and Mexican Indocumentados in the United States, 1882–2007." *American Quarterly* 60 (2008): 779–801.

Sadruddin, Hussein, Natalia Walter, and Jose Hidalgo. 2005. "Human Trafficking in the United States: Expanding Victim Protection Beyond Prosecution Witnesses." *Stanford Law & Policy Review* 16 (2): 379–415.

Said, Edward. 1978. *Orientalism.* New York: Vintage Books.

Salari, Sonia. 2015. *Family Violence Across the Life Course: Research, Policy and Prevention.* Dubuque, IA: Kendall Hunt Publishing.

Saldaña-Portillo, Josefina. 2001. "Who's the Indian in Aztlán? Re-Writing Mestizaje, Indianism, and Chicanoismo from the Lacandón." In *The Latin American Subaltern Studies Reader,* edited by Lleana Rodríguez, 402–23. Durham, NC: Duke University Press.

San Juan Jr., E. 2009. "Overseas Filipino Workers: The Making of an Asian-Pacific Diaspora." *Global South* 3 (2): 99–129.

Sandoval, Chela. 2000. *Methodology of the Oppressed.* Minneapolis: University of Minnesota Press.

Sassen, Saskia. 1998. *Globalization and Its Discontents: Essays on the New Mobility of People and Money.* New York: The New Press.

Sassen, Saskia. 2001. *The Global City: New York, London, Tokyo.* Second edition. Princeton, NJ: Princeton University Press.

Sassen, Saskia. 2002. *Global Networks, Linked Cities.* New York: Routledge.

Saunders, Daniel G. 1986. "When Battered Women Use Violence: Husband-Abuse or Self-Defense?" *Victims and Violence* 1 (1): 47–60.

Scarpa, Sylvia. 2008. *Trafficking in Human Beings: Modern Slavery.* Oxford: Oxford University Press.

Schaefer-Gabriel, Felicity. 2011. "Transnational Media Wars over Sex Trafficking: Abolishing the 'New Slave Trade' or the New Nativism?" In *Circuits of Visibility: Gender and Transnational Media Cultures,* edited by Radha Sarma Hegde, 103–23. New York: New York University Press.

Schaeffer, Felicity Amaya. 2012. *Love and Empire: Cybermarriage and Citizenship Across the Americas (Nation of Newcomers: Immigrant History as American History).* New York: New York University Press.

Schellstede, Sangmie Choi. 2000. *Comfort Women Speak: Testimony by Sex Slaves of the Japanese Military.* New York: Holmes & Meier.

"The Scope of the White Slave Traffic Act." 1917. *Virginia Law Review* 4 (8): 653–60.

Scott, James C. 1990. *Hidden Transcripts: Domination and the Arts of Resistance*. New Haven, CT: Yale University Press.

Seagraves, Anne. 1994. *Soiled Doves; Prostitution in the Early West*. Hayden, ID: Wesanne Publications.

Seale, Clive, Giampietro Gobo, Jaber F. Gubrium, and David Silverman, eds. 2004. *Qualitative Research Practice*. London: Sage.

Segrave, Marie, Sanja Milivojevic, and Sharon Pickering. 2000. *Sex Trafficking: International Context and Response*. Portland, OR: Willan Publishing.

Shah, Nayan. 2001. *Contagious Divides: Epidemics and Race in San Francisco's Chinatown*. Berkeley: University of California Press.

Shah, Nayan. 2011. *Stranger Intimacy: Contesting Race, Sexuality, and the Law in the North American West*. Berkeley: University of California Press.

Shah, Sonia, ed. 1999. *Dragon Ladies: Asian American Feminists Breathe Fire*. Cambridge, MA: South End Press.

Shefer, Elaine. 1991. "The 'Bird in the Cage' in the History of Sexuality: Sir John Everett Millais and William Holman Hunt." *Journal of the History of Sexuality* 1 (3): 446–80.

Shelley, Louise. 2010. *Human Trafficking: A Global Perspective*. New York: Cambridge University Press.

Sherman, Susan G., Katherine Footer, Samantha Illangasekare, Erin Clark, Erin Pearson, and Michele R. Decker. 2015. "'What Makes You Think You Have Special Privileges Because You Are a Police Officer?' A Qualitative Exploration of Police's Role in the Risk Environment of Female Sex Workers." *AIDS Care* 27 (4): 473–80.

Shim, Doobo. 1998. "From Yellow Peril Through Model Minority to Renewed Yellow Peril." *Journal of Communication Inquiry* 22: 385–409.

Shohat, Ella. 2001. "Area Studies, Transnationalism, and the Feminist Production of Knowledge." *Signs* 26 (4): 1269–72.

Shudson, Michael. 1978. *Discovering the News: A Social History of American Newspapers*. New York: Basic Books.

Silliman, Jael, and Anannya Bhattacharjee, eds. 2002. *Policing the National Body: Sex, Race, and Criminalization*. Cambridge, MA: South End Press.

Sirmans, M. Eugene. 1963. "The Legal Status of the Slave in South Carolina, 1670–1740." *Journal of Southern History* 28 (4): 462–73.

Siu, Lok C.D. 2005. *Memories of a Future Home: Diasporic Citizenship of Chinese in Panama*. Stanford, CA: Stanford University Press.

Slack, Edward R. Jr. 2009. "The *Chinos* in New Spain: A Corrective Lens for a Distorted Image." *Journal of World History* 20 (1): 35–67.

Smith, Linda A., Samantha Heally Vardaman, and Melissa A. Snow. 2009. *Domestic Minor Sex Trafficking: America's Prostituted Children*. Arlington, VA: Shared Hope International.

Smith, Linda Tuhiwai. 1999. *Decolonizing Methodologies: Research and Indigenous Peoples.* London: Zed Books.

Smith, Margo L. 1975. "The Female Domestic Servant and Social Change: Lima, Peru." In *Women Cross-Culturally,* edited by Ruby Rohrlich-Leavitt, 163–80. Berlin: Walter de Gruyter Mouton.

Smith, Neil. 1993. "Homeless/Global: Scaling Places." In *Mapping the Futures: Local Cultures, Global Change,* edited by Jon Bird, Barry Curtis, Tim Putnam, George Robertson, and Lisa Tickner, 87–120. London: Routledge.

Smolej, Mirka. 2010. "Constructing Ideal Victims? Violence Narratives in Finnish Crime-Appeal Programming." *Crime, Media, Culture* 6 (1): 69–85.

Soderlund, Gretchen. 2005. "Running from the Rescuers: New U.S. Crusades Against Sex Trafficking and the Rhetoric of Abolition." *NWSA Journal* 13 (3): 64–87.

Soderlund, Gretchen. 2011. "The Rhetoric of Revelation: Sex Trafficking and the Journalistic Exposé." *Humanity: An International Journal of Human Rights, Humanitarianism, and Development* 2 (2): 193–211.

Soh, Sarah C. 2008. *The Comfort Women: Sexual Violence and Postcolonial Memory in Korea and Japan.* Chicago: Chicago University Press.

Sohoni, Deenesh, and Tracy W.P. Sohoni. 2014. "Perceptions of Immigrant Criminality: Crime and Social Boundaries." *Sociological Quarterly* 55 (1): 49–71.

Sookkasikon, Pahole Yotin. 2010. "Human Trafficking." In *Encyclopedia of Asian American Issues Today,* vol. 1, edited by Edith Wen-Chu Chen and Grace J. Yoo. California: ABC-CLIO.

Spivak, Gayatri Chakrovarty. 1988. "Can the Subaltern Speak?" In *Marxism and the Interpretation of Culture,* edited by C. Nelson and L. Grossberg, 271–313. Basingstoke, UK: Macmillan Education.

Spivak, Gayatri Chakrovarty. 1993. *Outside in the Teaching Machine.* New York: Routledge.

Srikantiah, Jayashri. 2007. "Perfect Victims and Real Survivors: The Iconic Victim in Domestic Human Trafficking Law." *Immigration and Nationality Law Review* 87: 157–211.

Stark, Christine, and Rebecca Whisnant. 2004. *Not for Sale: Feminists Resisting Prostitution and Pornography.* Victoria, Australia: Spinifex.

Steinberg, Richard H., and Jonathan M. Zasloff. 2006. "Power and International Law." *American Journal of International Law* 100 (1): 64–87.

Sterling-Fausto, Anne. 2000. *Sexing the Body.* New York: Basic Books.

Stetson, Dorothy McBride. 2004. "The Invisible Issue: Prostitution and Trafficking of Women and Girls in the United States." In *The Politics of Prostitution: Women's Movements, Democratic States and the Globalization of Sex Commerce,* edited by Joyce Outshoorn, 245–64. Cambridge, UK: Cambridge University Press.

Stoecker, Sally, and Louise Shelley, eds. 2004. *Human Traffic and Transnational Crime: Eurasian and American Perspectives.* Lanham, MD: Rowman & Littlefield.

Stryker, Robin. 2003. "Mind the Gap: Law, Institutional Analysis and Socio-Economics." *Socio-Economic Review* 1: 335–367.

Sturdevant, Saundra Pollack, and Brenda Stoltzfus, eds. 1992. *Let the Good Times Roll: Prostitution and the U.S. Military in Asia.* New York: The New Press.

Su, Julie A. 1997–8. "Making the Invisible Visible: The Garment Industry's Dirty Laundry." *Gender, Race, & Justice* 1: 405–417.

Su, Julie A., and Chanchanit Martorrell. 2001. "Exploitation and Abuse in the Garment Industry: The Case of the Thai Slave-Labor Compound in El Monte." In *Asian and Latino Immigrants in a Restructuring Economy: The Metamorphosis of Southern California,* edited by Marta Lopez-Garza and David R. Diaz, 21–45. Stanford, CA: Stanford University Press.

Sudbury, Julia. 2005. *Global Lockdown: Race, Gender, and the Prison-Industrial Complex.* Edited by Julia Sudbury. New York: Routledge.

Swan, Suzanne C., and David L. Snow. 2002. "A Typology of Women's Use of Violence in Intimate Relationships." *Violence Against Women* 8 (3): 286–319.

Tadiar, Neferti Xina M. 1998. "Prostituted Filipinas and the Crisis of Philippine Culture." *Millennium: Journal of International Studies* 27 (4): 927–54.

Tadiar, Neferti Xina M. 2004. *Fantasy-Production: Sexual Economies and Other Philippine Consequences for the New World Order.* Hong Kong: Hong Kong University Press.

Takaki, Ronald T. 1989. *Strangers from a Different Shore: A History of Asian Americans.* Boston, MA: Little, Brown.

Tan, Michael L. 2000. "AIDS, Medicine, and Moral Panic in the Philippines." In *Framing the Sexual Subject: The Politics of Gender, Sexuality, and Power,* edited by Richard Parker, Regina Maria Barbosa, and Peter Aggleton, 143–64. Berkeley: University of California Press.

Therien, Jean-Philippe. 1999. "Beyond the North-South Divide: The Two Tales of World Poverty." *Third World Quarterly* 20 (4): 723–42.

Todres, Jonathan. 2009. "Law, Otherness, and Human Trafficking." *Santa Clara Law Review* 49: 605–72.

Trask, Haunani-Kay. (1993) 1999. *From a Native Daughter: Colonialism and Sovereignty in Hawai'i.* Monroe, ME: Common Courage Press, 1999.

Trodd, Zoe. 2013. "Am I Still Not a Man and a Brother? Protest Memory in Contemporary Antislavery Visual Culture." *Slavery & Abolition: A Journal of Slave and Post-Slave Studies* 34 (2): 338–52.

Trouillot, Michel-Rolph. 1995. *Silencing the Past: Power and the Production of History.* Boston, MA: Beacon Press.

Truong, Thanh-Dam. 2001. "Human Trafficking and Organised Crime." Working Paper 339, Institute of Social Studies, The Hague, Netherlands.

Tuck, Eve, and C. Ree. 2013. "A Glossary of Haunting." In *Handbook of Autoethnography,* edited by Stacey Homan Jones, Tony E. Adams, and Carolyn Ellis, 639–58. New York: Routledge.

Turner, Stuart. 2007. "Memory for Trauma." In *Resilience, Suffering, and Creativity: The Work of the Refugee Therapy Center*, edited by Aida Alayarian, 29–44. London: Karnac Books.

Tyldum, Guri, and Anette Brunovskis. 2005. "Describing the Unobserved: Methodological Challenges in Empirical Studies on Human Trafficking." *International Office for Migration* 43 (1–2): 17–34.

Vance, Carole S. 2011. "Thinking Trafficking, Thinking Sex." *GLQ: A Journal of Lesbian and Gay Studies* 17 (1): 135–43.

Van den Anker, Christien. 2004. *The Political Economy of New Slavery*. Basingstoke, UK: Palgrave Macmillan.

Van der Kolk, Bessel A. 1998. "Trauma and Memory." *Psychiatry and Clinical Neurosciences* 52 (S1): 52–64.

Van Dijck, Jose. 2004. "Composing the Self: Of Diaries and Lifelogs." *Fibre Culture: Internet Theory, Criticism, Research* 3. Accessed February 1, 2011. http://www.fibreculture.org/journal/issue3/issue3_vandijck.html.

Wadhia, Shoba Sivaprasad. 2015. *Beyond Deportation: The Role of Prosecutorial Discretion in Immigration Cases*. New York: New York University Press.

Walklate, Sandra. 2006. "Changing Boundaries of the 'Victim' in Restorative Justice: So Who Is the Victim Now?" In *Handbook of Restorative Justice: A Global Perspective*, edited by Dennis Sullivan and Larry Tifft, 273–85. New York: Routledge.

Walklate, Sandra. 2007. *Imagining the Victim of Crime*. New York: Open University Press.

Walkowitz, Judith R. 1980. *Prostitution and Victorian Society: Women, Class, and the State*. Cambridge, UK: Cambridge University Press.

Wallerstein, Immanuel. 1999. *The End of the World As We Know It: Social Science for the Twenty-first Century*. Minneapolis: University of Minnesota Press.

Warren, Kay. 2007. "The 2000 UN Human Trafficking Protocol: Rights, Enforcement, Vulnerabilities." In *The Practice of Human Rights: Tracking Law Between the Global and the Local*, edited by Mark Goodale and Sally Engle Merry, 242–70. Cambridge, UK: Cambridge University Press.

Weber, Max. 1978. *Basic Concepts in Sociology*. London: Peter Owen.

Wechsler, Robert. 1998. *Performing Without a Stage: The Art of Literary Translation*. New Haven, CT: Catbird Press.

Weitzer, Ronald. 2007. "The Social Construction of Sex Trafficking: Ideology and Institutionalization of a Moral Crusade." *Politics & Society* 35 (3): 447–75.

Welch, Claude E. Jr. 2009. "Defining Contemporary Forms of Slavery: Updating a Venerable NGO." *Human Rights Quarterly* 31 (1): 70–128.

West, Cornell. 2001. *Race Matters*. New York: Vintage Books.

Whisnant, Rebecca, and Christine Stark, eds. 2004. *Not for Sale: Feminists Resisting Prostitution and Pornography*. North Melbourne, Victoria: Spinifex Press.

Widdows, Heather. 2009. "Border Disputes Across Bodies: Exploitation in Trafficking for Prostitution and Egg Sale for Stem Research." *International Journal of Feminist Approaches to Bioethics* 2 (1): 5–24.

Williams, Raymond. (1976) 1983. *Keywords: A Vocabulary of Culture and Society.* New York: Oxford University Press.

Wilson, William Julius. 2009. *More Than Just Race: Being Black and Poor in the Inner City.* New York: W. W. Norton.

Wong, Edlie. 2015. *America and the Long 19th Century: Racial Reconstruction: Black Inclusion, Chinese Exclusion, and the Fictions of Citizenship.* New York: New York University Press.

Wong, Tom K. 2015. *Rights, Deportation, and Detention in the Age of Immigration Control.* Stanford, CA: Stanford University Press.

Woods, Tryon P. 2013. "Surrogate Selves: Notes on Anti-trafficking and Anti-blackness." *Social Identities* 19 (1): 120–34.

Wright, Melissa W. 2006. *Disposable Women and Other Myths of Global Capitalism.* New edition. New York: Routledge.

Wynter, Sylvia. 1994. "Beyond Miranda's Meanings: Un/Silencing the 'Demonic Ground' of Caliban's 'Woman'." In *Out of the Kumbia: Caribbean Women and Literature,* edited by Carole Boyce Davies and Elaine Savory Fido, 355–72. Trenton, NJ: Africa World Press.

Yoshiaki, Yoshimi. 2000. *Comfort Women: Sexual Slavery in the Japanese Military During World War II.* New York: Columbia University Press.

Young, James E. 2003. "Between History and Memory: The Voice of the Eyewitness." In *Witness and Memory: The Discourse of Trauma,* edited by Ana Douglass and Thomas A. Vogler, 275–283. New York: Routledge.

Youngberg, Quentin. 2005. "Morphology of Manifest Destiny: The Justified Violence of John O'Sullivan, Hank Morgan, and George W. Bush." *Canadian Review of American Studies* 35 (3): 315–33.

Yuh, Ji-Yeon. 2002. *Beyond the Shadow of Camptown: Korean Military Brides in America.* New York: New York University Press.

Yun, Lisa. 2008. *The Coolie Speaks: Chinese Indentured Laborers and African Slaves in Cuba.* Philadelphia, PA: Temple University Press.

Zhao, Heping. 2012. "Rhetorical Implications of the Chinese Detainees' Ghostly Poems at Angel Island: Lonely Voices, Alien Discourse, and Collective Identity." In *Book of Proceedings: 2nd International Conference on Human and Social Sciences, ICHSS 2012* 3, edited by Antonello Biagini, Giovanna Motta, Andrea Carteny, and Alessandro Vagnini, 27–34. Rome: MCSEER.

Zia, Helen. 2000. *Asian American Dreams: The Emergence of an American People.* New York: Farrar, Straus and Giroux.

Human Trafficking in the Media

Films

Documentaries

Anonymously Yours. 2002. Dir. Gayle Ferraro. Aerial Productions and University of California Extension Center for Media and Independent Learning.

Born into Brothels: Calcutta's Redlight Kids. 2004. Dir. Zana Briski and Ross Kauffman. Per. Kochi, Avijit Halder, and Shaanti Das. Redlight Films, HBO/Cinemax Documentary, Sundance Institute Documentary Fund, Thinkfilm.

Call + Response. 2008. Dir. Justin Dillon. Featuring Madeleine Albright, Kevin Bales, and David Batstone. Fair Trade Pictures.

Cargo Innocence Lost. 2008. Dir. Michael Cory Davis. Per. Elen Koleva and George Zlatarev. Journey Film Group.

The Corporation. 2003. Dir. Mark Achbar and Jennifer Abbott. Big Media Corporation.

Cracked, Not Broken. 2007. Dir. Paul Perrier. Open Door Films.

Dirty Money: Business of High End Prostitution. 2008. CNBC.

Dying to Leave. 2003. Dir. Chris Hilton and Aaron Woolf. Per. Rachael Blake. Hilton Cordell & Associates.

Eden. 2013. Dir. Megan Griffiths. Per. Jamie Chung, Beau Bridges, Matt O'Leary. Eden Productions, Centripetal Films, Clatter & Dinn.

The End of Poverty? 2009. Dir. Philippe Diaz. Per. Martin Sheen, John Christensen, and William Easterly. Cinema Libre Studio.

Food Inc. 2008. Dir. Robert Kenner. Per. Michael Pollan, Eric Schlosser, and Richard Lobb. Magnolia Pictures, Participant Media, and River Road Entertainment.

Hummingbird. 2004. Dir. Holly Mosher. Hollywoodnt Productions.

Lives for Sale: A Documentary on Human Trafficking. 2010. Dir. Gayla Jamison. Maryknoll and Lightfoot Films and Odyssey Networks.

Living Along the Fenceline. 2011. Dir. Lina Hoshino and Gwyn Kirk. Women for Genuine Security.

Not for Sale. 2006. Dir. Marie Vermeiren. Coalition Against Trafficking in Women and the European Women's Lobby.

Not for Sale: The Documentary. 2007. Dir. Robert Marcarelli. The Not for Sale Campaign.

Not My Life. 2011. Dir. Robert Bilheimer. Narrator, Glenn Close. Worldwide Documentaries.

The Price of Sex. 2011. Dir. Mimi Chakarova.

Red Leaves Falling. 2009. Dir. Monica D. Ray. Stairway Foundation, Neko Animation Studio Manila, Wild Fire and Hit Sounds Studio.

Responding to Victims of Human Trafficking: A Training for Victim Service Providers. 2003. Dir. United States Department of Justice Office of Justice Programs and Office of Victims of Crime. SafeHorizon.

Sacrifice: The Story of Prostitutes from Burma. 1998. Dir. Ellen Bruno. BrunoFilms.

Say I Do: Unveiling the Stories of Mail Order Brides. 2012. Dir. Arlene Ami. CTV, Telefilm Canada, British Columbia Film, and the National Film Board.

Sexual Assault Response Teams: Partnering for Success. 2005. Office of Justice Programs and Safe Neighborhoods.

Silence Broken: Korean Comfort Women. 1999. Dir. Dai Sil Kim-Gibson. Dai-Sil Productions.

Sold in America. 2009. Dir. Chelo Alvarez-Stehl. Chelo Alvarez Stehl and Cari Lutz.

Streetwise Kids. 1996. Journeyman Pictures.

Sugar Babies. 2007. Dir. Amy Serrano. Siren Studios.

Tin Girls. 2003. Dir. Miguel Bardem. Produce+/Canal+, New Atlantis.

Trading Women. 2003. David A. Feingold. Per. Autumn Dornfeld, Angelina Jolie, Michael Nathanson. Ophidian.

Trafficked: Slavery in America. 2011. Dir. MSNBC. Per. Meridith Vieira.

Very Young Girls. 2007. Dir. David Schisgall and Nina Alvarez. Swinging T. Productions.

Women for Sale. 2009. Dir. Nili Tal. Create Space.

Dramas

Amazing Grace. 2006. Dir. Michael Apted. Per. Ioan Gruffudd, Albert Finney, and Michael Gambon. Fourboys Films, Walden Media, Bristol Bay Productions, Ingenious Film Partners, and Roadside Attractions.

Amistad. 1997. Dir. Steven Spielberg. Per. Djimon Hounsou, Matthew McConaughey, and Anthony Hopkins. Dreamworks SKG and Home Box Office.

Beloved. 1998. Dir. Jonathan Demme. Per. Oprah Winfrey, Danny Glover, and Thandie Newton. Clinica Estetico, Harpo Films, and Touchstone Pictures.

Blood Diamond. 2006. Dir. Edward Zwick. Per. Leonardo DiCaprio, Djimon Hounsou, and Jennifer Connelly. Warner Bros. Pictures, Virtual Studios, Spring Creek Productions, Bedford Falls, Initial Entertainment Group, and Lonely Film Productions GmBH & Co. KG.

Criminal Minds. 2011. "Supply & Demand." Molly McNaughton, David Naylor, and Karolyne Oak, Producers. CBS.

Dollhouse. 2009–10. Creator Joss Whedon. Per. Eliza Dushku, Harry Lennix, and Fran Kranz. 20th Century Fox Television and Boston Diva Productions.

Ghosts. 2006. Dir. Nick Broomfield. Channel 4 Television Corporation, Film4, Head Gear Films.

The Guardian. 2001. Dir. David Hollander. Per. Simon Baker, Alan Rosenberg, and Raphael Sbarge. David Hollander Productions, Gran Via, CBS Productions, Sony Pictures Television, Columbia TriStar television, Rosecrans Productions Inc., and Sony Pictures Entertainment.

Holly. 2006. Dir. Guy Moshe. Per. Ron Livingston and Chris Penn. City Light Pictures.

Human Cargo. 2004. Dir. Brad Turner. Per. Kate Nelligan, Nicholas Campbell, and Bayo Akinfemi. Force Four Entertainment and Howe Sound Films.

Human Trafficking. 2005. Dir. Christian Duguay. Per. Mira Sorvino, Donald Sutherland, and Robert Carlyle. For Sale Productions (Muse), Muse Entertainment Enterprises, RHI Entertainment.

Hustle and Flow. 2005. Dir. Craig Brewer. Per. Terrence Howard, Ludacris, and Anthony Anderson. Parmount Pictures.

The Jammed. 2007. Dir. Dee McLachlan. Per. Emma Lung, Veronica Sywak, and Saskia Burmeister. Film Victoria, Jammed Films, and The Picture Tank.

Kiss of the Dragon. 2001. Dir. Chris Nahon. Per. Jet Li, Bridget Fonda and Tcheky Karyo. Europa Co., Twentieth Century Fox Film Corporation, Quality Growth International Ltd., Current Entertainment, Immortal Entertainment and Canal+.

Lilya 4-Ever. 2002. Dir. Lukas Moodysson. Per. Oksana Akinshina, Artyom Bogucharskiy, and Pavel Ponomaryov. Memfis Film, Det Danske Filminstitut, Film I Vast, Nordisk Film-TV-Fond, Svenska Filminstitutet, Sveriges Television, and Zentropa Entertainments.

Machine Gun Preacher. 2011. Dir. Marc Forster. Per. Gerard Butler, Michelle Monaghan, and Michael Shannon. Presented by Relativity Media; in association with Virgin Produced, 1984 Private Defense Contractors, Mpower Pictures, ITS Capital, and Merlina Entertainment; and produced by GG Filmz, MGP Productions, Moonlighting Films, Safady Entertainment; and as apparatus by Apparatus Productions.

Maria Full of Grace. 2004. Dir. Joshua Marston. Per. Catalina Sandino Moreno, Guilied Lopez, and Orlando Tobon. HBO Films, Fine Line Features, and Journeyman Pictures.

Miss Bala. 2011. Dir. Gerardo Naranjo. Per. Stephanie Sigman, Noe Hernandez, and Irene Azuela. Canana Films, Consejo Nacional Para La Cultura y Las Artes, Eficine 226, Fondo de Inversion y Estimulos, Fox International Productions, Instituto Mexicano de Cinematografia, Nuevo Negocios DM San Luis, Promecap.

Nikita. 2010. Creator Craig Silverstein. Per. Maggie Q., Shane West, and Lyndsy Fonseca. Sesfonstein Productions, Wonderland Sound and Vision, Warner Bros. Television, and Nikita Films.

Slumdog Millionaire. 2008. Dir. Danny Boyle and Loveleen Tandan. Per. Dev Patel, Freida Pinto, and Saurabh Shukla. Celador Films, Film4, and Pathe Pictures International.

Svetlana's Journey. 2004. Dir. Michael Cory Davis. Per. Gergana Djikelova, Maxim Gentchev, and Elvira Ivanova. Topform Studio Inc..

Taken. 2008. Dir. Pierre Morel. Per. Liam Neeson, Maggie Grace, and Famke Janssen. Europa Corp., M6 Films, Grive Productions, Canal+, TPS Star, All Pictures Media, and Wintergreen Productions.

Trade. 2007. Dir. Marco Kreuzpaintner. Per. Kevin Kline, Kathleen Gati, and Paulina Gaitan. Lionsgate, Roadside Attractions, Centropolis Entertainment, VIP 4 Medienfonds, Brass Hat Films, Reelmachine.

Traffic. 2000. Dir. Steven Soderbergh. Per. Michael Douglas, Benicio del Toro, and Catherine Zeta-Jones. Bedford Falls Productions, Compulsion Inc., Initial Entertainment Group, Splendid Medien, and USA Films.

The Whistleblower. 2011. Dir. Larysa Kondracki. Per. Rachel Weisz, Monica Belluci, and Vanessa Redgrave. Samuel Goldwyn Films.

News Articles (also see Notes)

"An Ohio River City Comes Back to Its Shoreline." Keith Schneider. *New York Times.* June 6, 2012, B-8.

"Bay Area Woman Found Guilty of Trafficking Nanny from Peru: Conviction Is First in Human Trafficking Trial in Northern District of California." U.S. Immigration and Customs Enforcement. October 9, 2009. ice.gov/pi/nr/0910/0910090oakland .htm.

"Coco Real Estate Agent Convicted of Forced Labor." CBS 5 Crime watch. October 5, 2009.

"Comfort Women—South Korea—1000th Rally for Justice." Craig Johnson. CNN (Xinhua). December 14, 2011. Accessed December 17, 2011. http://news.blogs.cnn.com /2011/12/14/south-korean-comfort-women-mark-1000th-rally-for-japan-apology.

"Couple Sentenced for Slavery of Pinay." Cynthia De Castro. *The Asian Journal Blog.* January 29, 2008. Asianjournal.com.

"Couple Sentenced in Maid Abuse Case." *USA Today.* January 29, 2008. Accessed September 28, 2011. http://www.usatoday.com/news/nation/2008-01-29-2013858599_x .htm.

"Diary of a Sex Slave the Story: How We Reported the Series." Meredith May. *San Francisco Chronicle.* October 9, 2006, A-5. Accessed October 9, 2006. http://www .sfgate.com/news/article/DIARY-OF-A-SEX-SLAVE-THE-STORY-How-we -2468544.php.

"'Diary' Series Is a Misleading Portrait of Korean Americans." Helene Kim and Jeong Shin. *San Francisco Chronicle.* October 24, 2006, B-7.

"Filipina Who Says She Was a Slave Wants Family Here." K. Connie Kang. *Los Angeles Times.* September 6, 2004.

"Former IMF Chief Dominique Strauss-Kahn *is* Counter-Suing a Hotel Maid Who Accused Him of Sexual Harassment, Seeking $1 Million in Damages." BBC. May 15, 2012. Accessed May 15, 2012. http://www.bbc.co.uk/news/world-us-canada -18072141.

"Free, But Trapped: In San Francisco, You Mi Begins to Put Her Life Back Together— But the Cost Is High." Meredith May. *San Francisco Chronicle.* October 9, 2006.

Accessed October 9, 2006. http://www.sfgate.com/news/article/DIARY-OF-A-SEX-SLAVE-THIRD-OF-A-FOUR-PART-2468512.php.

"Freedom Center Fights to Survive; Battered by Tough Economy, Slavery Museum Tries to Widen Appeal with a Broader Scope." Mark Curnutte. *USA Today.* February 3, 2012, News, 3A.

"Hollywood Executive Treated His Filipina Maid Like a Slave." Andrew Gumbel. *Independent on Sunday.* September 12, 2004, First Edition, Foreign News, 21.

"Hollywood Lawyer, Pinay Wife in Slavery Conviction File Bankruptcy." Janet Napales. GMA News. February 6, 2008. Accessed February 6, 2008. http://www.gmanetwork.com/news/story/79553/pinoyabroad/hollywood-lawyer-pinay-wife-in-slavery-conviction-file-bankruptcy.

"How an infamous Berkeley Trafficking Case Fueled Reform." S.F. Public Press. February 16, 2012. Accessed March 19, 2012. http://sfpublicpress.org/news/2012-02/how-an-infamous-berkeley-human-trafficking-case-fueled-reform.

"How Lakireddy Case Spurred California Sex Trafficking Laws." New America Media: Law & Justice. Accessed February 17, 2012. http://newamericamedia.org/2012/02/how-lakireddy-case-spurred-california-sex-trafficking-laws.php.

"Kobe's Sitting Pretty: Five Years After Rape Charges, Bryant Again Becomes an Appealing Endorser." Tim Lemke. *Washington Times.* May 13, 2008, C01.

"Madam's Fall Offers Look at Lucrative Sex Trade." Tim Wyatt. *Dallas Morning News.* May 10, 2006. Accessed May 10, 2006. http://www.dallasnews.com/sharedcontent/dws/news/localnews/ stories/DN-sexdallas_08 met.State.Edition l.ceod677.htm.

"The Maid's Tale." Christopher Dickey. *Newsweek.* July 25, 2011. Accessed September 28, 2011. http://www.thedailybeast.com/newsweek/2011/07/24/dsk-maid-tells-of-her-alleged-rape-by-strauss-kahn-exclusive.html.

"Maid Who Won Suit Against Sony Executive Decries Slavery." Laura Wides. *Sacramento Bee.* September 3, 2004. http://www.genderberg.com/phpNuke/modules.php?name=News&file=article&sid=9.

"Mildred Baena, Arnold Schwarzenegger's Mistress Breaks Silence." CBS/Associated Press. June 14, 2011. Accessed September 28, 2011. http://www.cbsnews.com/8301-31749_162-20071135-10391698.html.

"Peruvian Nanny Exploited in Shocking ICE Case." KTVU. November 18, 2008. http://www.ktvu.com/news/18012707/detail.html.

"Pinay's Former Bosses Plead Guilty to Human Trafficking." Yong B. Chavez. *Filipino Online.* August 22, 2007. http://filipinonline.blogspot.com/2007/08/pinays-former-bosses-pleads-guilty-to.html.

"PVE Attorney to Be Honored for Pro Bono Work." Amy Artino. *Palos Verdes Peninsula News* (California). May 20, 2010, State and Regional News.

"Sex Slaves or Capitalists? Arrest of 42 S. Korean Women in Dallas Brothel Raids Stirs Debate on How Trafficking Laws Used." Paul Meyer. *Dallas Morning News.* May 8,

2006. http://www.dalasnews.com/sharedcontent/dws/dn/latestnews/stories/DN
-sexslaves_07met.State.Bulldog.7eae7bb.html.

"Sex Trafficking: San Francisco Is a Major Center for International Crime Networks
That Smuggle and Enslave." Meredith May. *San Francisco Chronicle.* October 6, 2006.
Accessed October 6, 2006. http://www.sfgate.com/news/article/SEX-TRAFFICKING
-San-Francisco-Is-A-Major-Center-2468554.php.

"Sex-Trafficking Video Goes Viral." Fairfax Media (Australia). Accessed April 27, 2012.
http://www.theage.com.au/world/sextrafficking-video-goes-viral-20120426
-1xmzo.html.

"'Slave' Case Rests in the Hands of Jury." Geneva Whitmarsh. *Santa Monica Daily Press.*
Vol. 3, issue 24. August 25, 2004.

"Success Story, Japanese-American Style." *New York Times Magazine.* January 9, 1966.

"Sweatshops Under the American Flag." *New York Times.* May 10, 2002. http://www
.nytimes.com/2002/05/10/opinion/sweatshops-under-the-american-flag.html.

"2 Held in Jeffco in Human Smuggling Case." Myung Oak Kim. *Rocky Mountain News*
(Denver, CO). September 26, 2007. Accessed September 15, 2012. http://m.rocky
mountainnews.com/news/2007/Sep/26/2-held-in-jeffco-in-human-smuggling
-case/.

"Two Swedes Jailed for Life for Running a Philippine Cybersex Den." BBC News: Asia-
Pacific. May 11, 2011. http://www.bbc.co.uk/news/world-asia-pacific-13356721.

"U.S. Agents Crack West Coast Human Smuggling, Trafficking Ring: Forced Prostitution Alleged in San Francisco, Los Angeles Arrests." Bureau of International
Information Programs, U.S. Department of State. July 1, 2005. Accessed August 1,
2005. http://www.america.gov/st/washfile-english/2005/July/20050701182254cmre
tropo.2110865.html.

"Walnut Creek Woman Charged with Holding Peruvian Nanny as Indentured Servant." Robert Salonga. *San Jose Mercury News.* November 19, 2008.

"A Woman. A Prostitute. A Slave." *New York Times.* November 27, 2010. Opinion
pages. Accessed November 27, 2010. http://www.nytimes.com/2010/11/28/opinion
/28kristof.html.

"Woman Indicted for Allegedly Exploiting Nanny." Henry K. Lee. *San Francisco Chronicle.* November 20, 2008. Accessed April 31, 2009. http://www.sfgate.com/bayarea
/article/Woman-indicted-for-allegedly-exploiting-nanny-3184255.php.

"The World's Largest Employment Category for Children Under 16 Is Domestic Work
in the Homes of Others." Transcripts. *Anderson Cooper 360.* CNN. January 24,
2007.

"A Youthful Mistake: You Mi Was a Typical College Student, Until Her First Credit Card
Got Her into Trouble." Meredith May. *San Francisco Chronicle.* October 8, 2006.
Accessed October 8, 2006. http://www.sfgate.com/news/article/A-YOUTHFUL-MIS
TAKE-You-Mi-was-a-typical-college-2487822.php.

Press Releases (also see Notes)

Air Force Airman Sentenced to 10 Years in Federal Prison for Attempted Online Enticement of a Minor. Middle District of Florida U.S. Attorney's Office press release (Florida, July 24, 2012).

Announcing Awardees from OVC's Services for Domestic Minor Victims of Human Trafficking Grant Program. Office for Victims of Crime press release (Washington, DC, December 1, 2009).

Assistance for Victims of Human Trafficking from Office of Minister of Citizenship and Immigration. Stop the Trafficking Coalition press release (Canada, May 11, 2006).

Attorney General Announces Legislative Initiative to Combat Child Pornography and Obscenity on the Internet. Attorney General, U.S. Department of Justice, 06-232 press release (Washington, DC, April 21, 2006).

Author Takes Novel Approach. Joe Hilley press release (Fairhope, Alabama, April 28, 2006).

Bay Area Man Charged with Engaging in Sex with Minors in Cambodia: Case Highlights International Cooperation to Target Child Sex Tourists. Immigration Customs Enforcement press release (San Francisco, April 26, 2005).

Brothel Owner Sentenced to 10 Years for Coercing Korean Aliens into Prostitution. Department of Justice press release (Washington, DC, July 18, 2006).

Californians Against Sexual Exploitation Act ("CASE Act") to Strengthen California Laws to Fight Human Trafficking and Sexual Abuse. California Against Slavery (Fremont, CA, October 13, 2012).

Dozens Charged in International, Internet-Based Child Pornography Investigation: "Chat Room" Allegedly Used to Trade Images of Child Sexual Molestation. Office of Public Affairs U.S. Department of Homeland Security, U.S. Immigration and Customs Enforcement press release (Washington, DC, March 15, 2006).

Dyncorp International Statement on "The Whistleblower." Dyncorp International Statement (Falls Church, VA, 2011).

EEOC Resolves Slavery and Human Trafficking Suit Against Transbay Steel for an Estimated $1 Million: Federal Agency Says 48 Thai Welders Forced to Work Without Pay in Squalid Conditions. United States Equal Employment Opportunity Commission press release (Washington, DC, December 8, 2006).

Flower Mound Police Department Receives Forfeited Proceeds. Internal Revenue Service: Criminal Investigation, Dallas Field Officer press release (Dallas, TX, August 9, 2007).

For Family's Sake, Stop the Street Prostitution! Family First Lobby press release (New Zealand, April 6, 2006).

Germany Rolls Out Welcome Mat for Sex Traffickers and Pimps: Thousands of Women Trafficked for Prostitution During World Cup Games. Buying Sex is Not a Sport Campaign (Washington, DC, May 1, 2006).

Germany's Sex Shacks Tarnish the World Cup. Statement at Press Conference by Janice Shaw Crouse, Ph.D., Concerned Women for America (Washington, DC, May 1, 2006).

HHS Awards Contract to Support Human Trafficking Victims: Catholic Bishops Will Partner to Help Restore Victims' Lives. U.S. Department of Health and Human Services press release (Washington, DC, April 18, 2006).

Human Rights Disaster in Germany. Statement at Press Conference on Germany, Sex Trafficking & World Cup Games. By Donna M. Hughes, Professor & Carlson Endowed Chair in Women's Studies, University of Rhode Island (Washington, DC, May 1, 2006).

Human Trafficking Task Force Formed in Los Angeles: Justice Department Awards $450,000 Grant to L.A.P.D. to Fund Training of Entire Force to Help Officers Recognize and Help Victims of Human Trafficking. Debra W. Yang, United States Attorney, Department of Justice (Central District of California, January 24, 2005).

Immigrant African Communities in U.S. Struggle over Human Trafficking and Ritual Killings: Micro Study of Major Global Problems. Africans in America press release (New York, May 15, 2012).

Internet & Free Speech Leaders Blast Village Voice Media over Child Sex Trafficking Controversy on Backpage.com. Human Rights Project for Girls press release (Seattle, WA, July 20, 2012).

Michigan Couple Charged with Obscenity and Child Pornography Violations. U.S. Department of the Justice press release (Washington, DC, April 24, 2006).

Minister Solberg Keeps Promise to Victims of Human Trafficking. The Future Group press release (Calgary, Canada, May 11, 2006).

New Process Benefits Victims of Human Trafficking Seeking College Aid. U.S. Department of Education press release (Washington, DC, May 9, 2006).

Newly Formed SA [South Asian] Community Group Expresses Solidarity with Victims of Labor and Sexual Exploitation in Case. Alliance of South Asians Taking Action press release (San Francisco Bay Area, April 11, 2000).

Obama on National Slavery and Human Trafficking Prevention Month: President Urges Global Community to Protect Victims, Prosecute Traffickers. The White House Office of the Press Secretary (Washington, DC, January 4, 2010). America Archive .gov. Accessed March 15, 2012. http://www.america.gov/st/texttrans-english/2010 /January/20100105105309xjsnommiso.6237757.html#ixzz1jZ2nnXQi.

Pimp Sentenced to 10 Years in Prison on Pandering. Kenneth L. Wainstein, United States Attorney for the District of Colombia, Judiciary Center press release (Washington, DC, May 5, 2006).

Press Conference: Groups Condemn Germany's World Cup Sexcapades. Concerned Women for America press release (Washington, DC, May 1, 2006).

San Francisco Brothel Owner Sentenced to One Year in Prison for Money Laundering: Owner Forfeits $1,000,000. United States Department of Justice, United States
Attorney Scott N. Schools press release (Northern District of California, March 7,
2007).

Secretary Napolitano Launches First-of-Its-Kind Campaign to Combat Human Trafficking. Department of Homeland Security, Office of the Press Secretary press release (Washington, DC, July 22, 2010). Accessed July 23 2010. http://www.aila.org
/content/default.aspx?docid=32690.

Smith: German World Cup Scores for Pimps and Johns Thousands Trafficked for Prostitution During Soccer Games—Groups to Join Smith in Cal for Action at Capitol
Hill Press Conference. Representative Christopher Smith, R-NJ, Vice Chairman,
House International Relations Committee press release (Washington, DC, April 28,
2006).

Statement on Germany's World Cup Prostitution Plans. Barrett Duke, Ph.D., Vice President for Public Policy and Research, Southern Baptist Ethics & Religious Liberty
Commission (Nashville, TN, and Washington, DC, May 1, 2006).

Students, Community Organizations Will Walk Against Human Trafficking to Raise
Awareness and Advocate for Anti-Human Trafficking Policies. Vietnamese Alliance to Combat Human Trafficking press release (Westminster, CA, April 19, 2006).

Three Persons Plead Guilty in Child Sexual Exploitation and Interstate Prostitution Case.
Northern District of Iowa, U.S. Attorney's Office press release (Iowa, July 25, 2012).

Two Egyptian Nationals Plead Guilty to Holding Domestic Worker in Involuntary
Servitude. United States Department of Justice, Debra Wong Yang, United States
Attorney, press release No. 06-089 (Central District of California, June 29, 2006).

We Are Proud to Announce the Official Establishment of Survivor Services Education
and Empowerment Network (SSEEN). Veronica's Voice press release (Kansas City,
KS, May 7, 2006).

Culture (Art/Literature)

Art

Cartoons

Archer, Dan. *Borderland: Seven Stories as Told by Victims of Human Trafficking.* 2010.
http://www.archcomix.com/trafficking/.

Traffick, Inc. Graphic Novels. http://www.kickstarter.com/projects/meetjustice/art-and
-advocacy-human-trafficking-in-the-usa.

Floral

Christie, Gayle. *Rosa's Story.* Pressed Floral Collage. http://www.florage.com/articles
/Rosas-story.html.

Museum Exhibits

Between a Rock and a Hard Place: A History of American Sweatshops, 1820—Present. Peter Liebhold and Harry Rubenstein, Curators. Smithsonian Institution's National Museum of American History (NMAH) and Office of Exhibits Central (OEC), American History Museum. April 22, 1998–December 10, 1998. Accessed March 1, 2012. http://americanhistory.si.edu/sweatshops/index.htm.

National Underground Railroad Freedom Center. *Invisible,* Permanent Exhibit. Cincinnati, Ohio. http://www.freedomcenter.org/.

Painters

Bloom, Beth. *Diary of a Sex Slave.* http://www.bethbloomdesigns.com/paintings.

Ibbitson, Glenn. *Consignment.* http://www.smokingbrushfineart.com/consignment.html.

Stark, Christine. Christinestark.com.

Photography

Kids with Cameras. Calcutta, India. http://www.kids-with-cameras.org/kidsgallery/.

Matsui, Tim. 20080311_PNH_001.jpg. Tim Matsui Multimedia Storytelling. 5120X3143 Pixels. Cambodia Human Trafficking, Labor Migration.

Silverstein, Judy. "Alone." Crossing the Bridge. Judy Silverstein Photography. alone1.jpg. 384×576 Pixels. Accessed April 20, 2006. www.judysilverstein.com.

Silverstein, Judy. "Body Language." Crossing the Bridge. Judy Silverstein Photography. Body language1.jpg. 384×556 pixels. Accessed April 20, 2006. www.judysilverstein.com.

Silverstein, Judy. "Boys Too." Crossing the Bridge. Judy Silverstein Photography. Boys too1.jpg. 576×427 pixels. Accessed April 20, 2006. www.judysilverstein.com.

Silverstein, Judy. "Girls for Sale." Crossing the Bridge. Judy Silverstein Photography. Girls for sale1.jpg. 384×576 pixels. April 20, 2006. Accessed April 20, 2006. www.judysilverstein.com.

Silverstein, Judy. "On the Corner." Crossing the Bridge. Judy Silverstein Photography. On the corner1.jpg. 475×576 pixels. Accessed April 20, 2016. www.judysilverstein.com.

Silverstein, Judy. "Potential Customer." Crossing the Bridge. Judy Silverstein Photography. Potential customer1.jpg. 576×379 pixels. Accessed April 20, 2006. www.judysilverstein.com.

Silverstein, Judy. "So Young." Crossing the Bridge. Judy Silverstein Photography. So young1.jpg. 537×351 pixels. Accessed April 20, 2006. www.judysilverstein.com.

Silverstein, Judy. "Take Your Pick." Crossing the Bridge. Judy Silverstein Photography. Take your pick1.jpg. 576×384 pixels. Accessed April 20, 2006. www.judysilverstein.com.

Performances

Computers Are a Girl's Best Friend. Praba Pilar. February 20, 2009. http://www.change
.org/petitions/attend-global-disconnects-the-internet-human-trafficking.

The Escape and Rescued Memories: New York Stories. Lenora Lee. May 8 and 9, 2014.
Asia Society, New York.

Fabric: The Story of El Monte. Henry Ong, Playwright. 2010. http://www.trafficking
project.org/2010/07/fabric-story-of-el-monte-ca-72.html.

My Real Name. Carol Chehade, Playwright. November 16, 2007. University of California, Berkeley.

Public Exhibits

Bought & Sold: The Exhibit. Artworks for Freedom. http://artworksforfreedom.org
/index.php#/bought-sold—the-exhibit/LockedInTrickedOut.

Gift Box: Things Are Not Always What They Seem. UN.GIFT, Stop the Traffik, http://
ungiftbox.org/, 2012.

The Journey Against Sex Trafficking. Emma Thompson, UNODC. 2008. http://www
.unodc.org/unodc/en/press/releases/2008-02-06-2.html.

National Anti-Trafficking Art Exhibit in Hanoi. Vietnam, 2012, http://mtvexit.org/blog
/mtv-exit-launches-the-first-ever-national-anti-trafficking-art-exhibition-in
-hanoi-2/.

Slavery in the Everyday. Students & Artists Fighting to End Human Slavery. Worth Ryder Gallery.

We, Asian Sex Workers. SF Sex Worker Film and Arts Festival, July 14, 2007–July 22,
2007. http://www.sfstation.com/we-asian-sex-workers-art-exhibit-e70161.

Literature

Keller, Nora Okja. 1998. *Comfort Woman.* New York: Penguin.

Keller, Nora Okja. 2003. *Fox Girl.* New York: Penguin.

Lee, Chang-Rae. 2000. *A Gesture Life: A Novel.* New York: Riverhead Trade.

Morrison, Toni. 1987. *Beloved: A Novel.* New York: A. A. Knopf.

Memoirs

Amaya, Barbara. 2015. *Nobody's Girl: A Memoir of Lost Innocence, Modern Day Slavery & Transformation.* Pittsburgh, PA: Animal Media Group.

Bissell, Anne. 2004. *Memoirs of a Sex Industry Survivor.* Ventura, CA: Cleopatra
International Publications.

Dahl, Luke G. 2017. *Daddy's Curse: A Sex Trafficking True Story of a 8-Year Old Girl.*
Stockholm: Cedenheim Publishing.

Flores, Theresa. 2007. *The Sacred Bath: An American Teen's Story of Modern Day Slavery.* Lincoln, NE: iUniverse.

Flores, Theresa. 2010. *The Slave Across the Street.* Boise, ID: Ampelon Publishing.

Hall, Shyma. 2014. *Hidden Girl: The True Story of a Modern-Day Child Slave*. New York: Simon & Schuster.

Jessen, Jenni. 2016. *The Lucky One: A Chilling True Account of Child Sex Trafficking and One Survivor's Journey from Brutal Captivity to a Life of Freedom*. Colorado Springs, CO: Compass 31.

Lloyd, Rachel. 2012. *Girls Like Us: Fighting or a World Where Girls Are Not for Sale: A Memoir*. New York: Harper Perennial.

Oriola, Bukola. 2016. *Imprisoned: The Travails of a Trafficked Victim*. Spring Lake Park, MN: Bukola Publishing.

Oriola, Bukola. 2016. *A Living Label: An Inspirational Memoir and Guide*. Edited by Nora Flom, Ann Brown, Shereen Rubenstein, and Florrie Burke. Spring Lake Park, MN: Bukola Publishing.

Phelps, Carissa, and Lorkin Warren. 2013. *Runaway Girl: Escaping Life on the Streets*. New York: Penguin.

Rosenblatt, Katarina. 2014. *Stolen: The True Story of a Sex Trafficking Survivor*. Grand Rapids, MI: Revell.

Smith, Holly Austin. 2014. *Walking Prey: How America's Youth Are Vulnerable to Sex Slavery*. New York: Palgrave Macmillan.

Smith, Jabali. 2017. *Slave*. Green Bay, WI: Titletown Publishing.

Journalist Publications

Cacho, Lydia. 2014. *Slavery Inc.: The Untold Story of International Trafficking*. Berkeley, CA: Soft Skull Press.

Hepburn, Stephanie, and Rita Simon. 2013. *Human Trafficking Around the World: Hidden in Plain Sight*. New York: Columbia University Press.

Skinner, E. Benjamin. 2009. *A Crime So Monstrous: Face-to-Face with Modern Day Slavery*. New York: Free Press.

INDEX

Page numbers in italics refer to figures.

245

communities of color, as more likely to be criminalized for trafficking, 16
conspiracies, criminal: as more dangerous than crimes by individuals, 145; terrorism and, 145–46; as threat to U.S., 145
Constable, Nicole, 76, 99
coolie laborers: and legacy of slavery in agricultural work, 60; and legacy of slavery in territories, 29; and racialization of migrant labor, 60
Coolie Trade Prohibition Act of 1862, 23, 29
Coughenour, John C., 142
COYOTE. *See* Call Off Your Old Tired Ethics
coyotes, trafficking of youths by, 137–38
criminal activity of migrants: and negation of victimhood frame, 5–7, 45; public perception vs. reality of, 10
criminality frame for trafficking: as creation of anti-trafficking movement, 8; racialized logic of, 76
criminalization of migrants: as critical term, 9–12; factors contributing to, 10–11; impact on migrant workers, 10; militarization of U.S. borders and, 11, 30, 145–47; role of victimhood, citizenship, and legality dualities in, 40; U.S. history of, 10; U.S. legislation and policies on, 10
Customs and Border Patrol (CBP), efforts to curtail trafficking, 138

DACA (Deferred Action for Childhood Arrivals), 4
dark web, government monitoring of, 143, 144
DARPA. *See* Defense Advanced Research Projects Agency
Davis, Angela, 11, 54
Deadgirls (2008 film), 134
death, physical, social, and civil forms of, 121
death, social: and human/nonhuman status of Korean women migrants, 134; of undocumented immigrants, racialized poor, and criminalized people of color, 123, 135; of victims of trafficking, 127, 135
de Baca, Luis C., 43
decolonial form of witnessing, 9, 13–16, 16–18, 19, 101, 115, 116, 148
Defense Advanced Research Projects Agency (DARPA), 143, 144
Deferred Action for Childhood Arrivals. *See* DACA

de Genova, Nicholas, 30
Deleuze, Gilles, 100
Department of Health and Human Services (HHS): and image of trafficked people as people of color or immigrants, 51–52; Look Beneath the Surface campaign, 51–53; Rescue and Restore campaign, 51; support for trafficking survivors, 51
Department of Homeland Security (DHS), rubric for assessing trafficking, 8
Department of Social Welfare and Development (DSWD), 92
Department of State, U.S., on trafficking as modern-day slavery, 43
deportability: and appeals to victimhood, 8; of defendants in ghost case, 29, 30; genealogy of legal events underlying, 28–29; militarization of nation-state borders and, 30; of prostitutes, 29, 91, 129; state regulation of, 25
Derrida, Jacques, 72
diasporas: and migrant laborers, as interchangeable terms, 10; shaping by systems requiring exploitation of each other, 143
differential consciousness: in approach to trafficking, 13–14; definition of, 13
Ding, Fang Ping, 34–35
Doezema, Jo, 64, 68
domestic work: as challenge to sisterhood, 99; changing race and ethnicity in history of, 61–63; as exempt from Fair Labor Standard Act, 63, 191n79; as gendered, 63; as invisible, 63; legacy of slavery in, 59–60, 61–62; racialization of, 62–63; as reproductive labor, 99; as site where labor and sex trafficking co-occur, 71; types of, 71
domestic workers: assumptions about sexual availability of, 78; in China, perceived lack of protections for, 34, 35; exploitation of, as common, 78; invisibility of abuses of, 71, 72, 73, 87, 90–91, 105, 110–12; and legacy of slavery, 59–60, 61–62; as mostly female, 71; number in U.S., 71; organizing of, 93; types of, 71. *See also* trafficking of domestic workers
double vision, in reading trafficking narratives, 8
drug dealing, and reduced sympathy for immigrants, 5–7

U.S. influence on international law on, 49. *See also* sex trafficking; sex workers
prostitution ring on West Coast: law enforcement surveillance of, 140–43, 147–48; recruitment of Asian women by, 140–41
Public Law 78 (1951), 60
PWC. *See* Pilipino Workers Center

Qayum, Seemin, 99
quasi-event of human trafficking: characteristics of, 28; ghost case as, 28

racial categories, divers meanings in homosocial relations, 103
racialized sexualities: and Asian women as both dragon lady and lotus blossom, 124, 130–32; in Chinese immigrant sex workers, 65–66; definition of, 64; and laws on trafficking, 50, 64–68; and suffrage movement, 66; in *United States v. Lundbergs* (2017), 91
racial profiling of migrants, state laws allowing for, 10
racisms, historical, and access to freedom, 55–56
Raheja, Michelle, 196n63
Ray, Katsuri, 24
Ray, Raka, 99
Raymond, Janice, 48
reconciliation, resurrection of comfort women and, 121, 135
Ree, C., 27
refugees, number of, in 2005, 177n107
reproductive labor, as traditional purview of women and minority groups, 99
rescue narratives: anti-trafficking activists and, 7, 54, 131–32; comfort women and, 123; human rights appeals and, 3; in perfect victim cases, 85; and victimhood narrative, 144
Richie, Beth, 11
Roberts, Kyong "Jackie," 127–28
Roe, Clifford, 66
Rollins, Judith, 99
Román-Odio, Ediberto, 169n29, 177n92
Romero, Mary, 63, 99
Roosevelt, Franklin D., 62
Rosa, Lola. *See* Henson, Maria Rosa Luna (Lola Rosa)
Rosaldo, Renato, 8

SAGE. *See* Standing Against Global Exploitation
St. James, Margo, 67
San Diego, as corridor of migration, 58
Sandoval, Chela, 13
Sanghera, Jyoti, 45, 68
San Juan, E., Jr., 79
Sarmiento, Marcel, 134
Saul (trafficked child), 1–3, 4, 15
Schaeffer, Felicity Amaya, 24, 40, 68, 142
Schwarzenegger, Arnold, 78
security: alternative human rights approach to, 148; balancing with privacy and human rights, 139; as central ideology in twenty-first century, 139; climate of fear created by focus on, 145–46, 147–48; current dependence on carceral and militarized responses, 143, 144; and furtherance of invisibilities, 148; humanitarian approaches to, 143–44; and increased government surveillance, 140–43; and people as quantifiable numbers, 143, 144; as risk management, 144; and tethered subjectivity, 142, 145–47
Sederholm, Bo Stefan, 92
Senate Bill 1070, 79
servitude: cultures of, 99, 187n22; industries of, 99; involuntary, 99, 187n17; migrants' transfer of cultural perceptions about, 99; U.S. attitudes toward, 187n23
settler colonialism: and citizenship as tool of exclusion, 29; legacies of, and concepts of victimhood, 93–94; liberal democratic, and necropolitics, 135; normalization of, in U.S. immigration policy, 15; reassertion of, in ghost case, 28. *See also* colonial modernities
sex traffickers: films on, 130–32, 133; registration as sex offenders, California proposition proposing, 39–40
sex trafficking: in Asia, annual number of women trafficked, 91–92; debate on activities included in, 7, 8, 26, 67–68; growing movement to address, 92; intersection with labor trafficking, 92; in Japan, annual number of women trafficked, 91; legal efforts to stop, 39–40, 46, 48–49; vs. trafficking, 7, 49, 64, 92; of white women, linking of slavery with, in anti-trafficking discourse, 64–65, 66–67. *See also* prostitution; sex workers

trafficking cases: complexity of, 91; and complexity of U.S. legal system, 50–51; types of courts and charges for, 168n8. See also specific cases under *United States*

Trafficking in Persons (TIP) report: on number of trafficked persons, 92; on number of trafficking convictions, 11, 165–66n42; on prevention of trafficking, 80; ranking of nations in, 80

trafficking of domestic workers: and acceptable vs. unacceptable levels of exploitation, 83–84; cases crossing into visibility, 72, 73, 110–12; from China, 34–35; invisibility of, 71, 87, 105; and perfect victim status, criteria for, 73, 85; from Philippines, 73, 76; and racialized structures of class and legal status, 73, 82; and reification of "good" vs. "bad" immigrant distinction, 73; states with large volume of, 72; victims, as predominantly women of color, 72, 73. *See also* Cindy (trafficked domestic worker); Tess (trafficked domestic worker); *United States v. Dann* (2010)

Trafficking Victims Protection Act (TVPA), 7, 47, 49–51; and complexity of U.S. legal system, 50–51; and criteria for trafficking determination, 24; definition of "severe" trafficking, 49; force, fraud, or coercion as criteria in, 49, 50, 186n4; and legal relief for trafficking victims, 11; and organ trafficking, 50; psychological coercion as criterion in, 49–50; reasons for enacting, 49–50; on severe forms of human trafficking, 186n4; and U.S. ranking of countries by human trafficking response, 182n44; and victim identification, 50, 53

transnational crime groups, in U.S. security threat, 139

transnational feminist framework: as critical term of analysis, 3, 9, 11–12; definition of, 12; disruption of regulatory practices of nation-state by, 25; in ghost case, 22–23; methodology, 17, 22–23; need for, 16; on patriarchal oppression, 68; scholarship on, 12; and tethered subjectivity, 12; and unsettled witnessing, 22–27

transnational processes, gendered dynamics of, 12

transpacific neoliberal partnerships, and Asian women as both dragon lady and lotus blossom, 124

Treaty of Guadalupe (1848), 57

Trodd, Zoe, 169n30

Trump administration: and immigrants as perceived threat, 137; increased immigration restrictions under, 4, 139, 164n12, 196n3; rescinding of DACA, 4; and separation of migrant children from parents, 86

Tuck, Eve, 27

T-Visas, 2; eligibility for, vs. legal liability of abusers, 88, 89, 91; legal recognition of victimhood and, 41, 50, 51; moral criteria for receiving, 129; number issued, 11, 189–90n65; obtaining through trickery, 106, 189–90n65; and pliable citizenship, 24; as relief for trafficking victims, 11, 106, 138

TVPA. *See* Trafficking Victims Protection Act

Tydings McDuffie Act of 1934, 56, 77

undocumented immigrants: criminalization of, consequences for migrants, 76; debate on, focus on moral character rather than human rights in, 76; required cooperation in investigations, 130; social death of, 123

United Nations: Beijing Platform for Action, 55; on coercion as criteria for trafficking, 88; Convention Against Transnational Organized Crime, 7, 24, 47; Fourth World Conference on Women, 55; laws and policies on trafficking, 46–49; Protocol to Prevent, Suppress and Punish Trafficking in Persons, Especially Women and Children, 7, 24, 46–47; Suppression of the Traffic in Women and Children policy (1921), 46; Suppression of the Traffic in Women of Full Age policy (1933), 46

United Nations Development Fund for Women (UNIFEM), 59

United Nations High Commissioner for Refugees, 1

United Nations Office on Drugs and Crime (UNODC), 18

United States (U.S.): anti-trafficking laws in, 47, 49–51; and assumed hiddenness of

worth, neoliberal ideologies of, 134

Wyatts, Tim, 129

yellow-face: and anti-immigration policies, 133; Asian women's participation in, 132; and film portrayals of Asians, 133; as survival strategy, 132, 133

Yellow Peril discourse, and portrayals of Asian immigrants as threat, 129, 130, 133

Yoon Geum-ee. *See* Yun Guem-i

Yun Guem-i, 117–18, 119, 134

Zasloff, Jonathan M., 173n29, 173n32

Zhu, Kesheng, 142

zombies: *Deadgirl* film on, 134; Korean sex workers as, 117; millennial zombies, 117, 122; theory of, 121; zombie imperialism, 135. *See also* living(dead) subjects